PHILOSOPHICAL EXPLORATIONS

A Series Edited by George Kimball Plochmann

Dewey, Russell, Whitehead

Philosophers as Educators

by
BRIAN PATRICK HENDLEY

Foreword by
GEORGE KIMBALL PLOCHMAN

Introduction by
ROBERT S. BRUMBAUGH

SOUTHERN ILLINOIS UNIVERSITY PRESS

CARBONDALE AND EDWARDSVILLE

LA
126
.H42
1986

89 88 87 86   4 3 2 1

Library of Congress Cataloging in Publication Data

Hendley, Brian Patrick, 1939-
    Dewey, Russell, Whitehead : philosophers as educators.

    (Philosophical explorations)
    Bibliography: p.
    Includes index.
    1. Education—Philosophy—History.   2. Dewey, John,
1859-1952.   3. Russell, Bertrand, 1872-1970.
4. Whitehead, Alfread North, 1861-1947.   I. Title.
II. Series.
LA126.H42   1986   370'.1   85-2148
ISBN 0-8093-1229-8
ISBN 0-8093-1243-3 (pbk.)

To Margaret, my wife and friend

Contents

Illustrations

Foreword
George Kimball Plochmann

T HE NUMBER OF PHILOSOPHERS who closely consider education is far smaller than the number of men and women who could legitimately be called philosophers in a more general sense. Even so, the list is respectably large, and in certain cases, as with Rousseau and Herbart, some of their principal writings—and major sources of fame—have been devoted to education. Others have published or left behind sometimes lesser but still important works dealing almost entirely with educational matters: Augustine, Locke, Kant, Spencer, and two of the three men whom Professor Hendley treats in the present book, Bertrand Russell and Alfred North Whitehead. One has the feeling that in times to come the books and essays by Russell on education will be looked upon as interesting examples of a movement to liberalize the upbringing of the young, while his *Principles of Mathematics*, together with the even more forbidding work on which he collaborated with Whitehead and whose very Latinized title chills the hearts of graduate students, will be read with admiration and indeed a feeling of awe. Whitehead's own contribution to *Principia Mathematica* was equally impressive, though it may also be that his intricate, frequently tortuous but always rewarding *Process and Reality: An Essay in Cosmology* is the legacy for which he will be most honored, rather than his *The Aims of Education and Other Essays*. John Dewey, on the other hand, will always be remembered as a great thinker in the educational field not only because *Democracy and Education*, along with his other writings on the subject, can be appreciated and put into practice but also because of the internal dialectical structure of his entire philosophy. His educational theory is both a segment and the pervading summation of his system of metaphysics, logic, biologico-psychology, political science, and theory of art as experience.

The three men chosen for this study of the practical in relation to the theoretical were very nearly contemporaries, and they had many other points of resemblance as well, including the fact that they were natives of prosperous English-speaking countries in which freedom of speech fared appreciably better than elsewhere; and, although Russell was a titled man, they all lived what were essentially lives of a middle-class and highly educated sort. Two of the three men became nonagenarians, and Whitehead lived into his late eighties; all three were prolific, much-read, much-studied authors; all had exceptionally broad backgrounds extending from interests in the older classics of the humanities to the very latest in modern science; all three were to some extent what might be called freethinkers—not exactly radicals, certainly not cultists and flag-wavers—in their time. It was to be supposed, therefore, when they chose to contribute seriously to the educational life of their epoch that they would be relatively unbound by crusty traditions and dust-covered formulas. On the other hand, if as philosophers they were not fools, they would avoid rushing into educational arenas without first examining and reexamining all their principles bearing upon the experiences they were likely to encounter as administrators and teachers. The principles involved in the transmission of knowledge would normally be drawn chiefly, I think, from five disciplines: logic, rhetoric, psychology, ethics, and politics, each adding essentials to the study of sound educational practices.

The last page of Plato's *Laws* sets forth in simple terms but with his usual subtle overtones the question of transition from theoretical discourse to thoughtful action: It is time to establish the state that has been planned in such detail, says the Lacedemonian, and we need the continued advice of our unnamed Athenian companion, who has already given us such good counsel. The successful institution, Plato is hinting, will benefit greatly from advice given by the man having the best plans, though he may well not be the sole founder to do the actual building of the state as a living institution. In the administering of the Laboratory School and the Beacon Hill School, a dilemma was evident. Such an organization will have the advantage of a highly gifted and far-seeing guide who has a grasp of general principles and many of the most ingenious ways they may be applied in the thousand contingencies likely to arise in the operations of a school. Yet a person of this sort, if dominating the leadership of the institution, will tend to obscure—I do not say consciously stifle—the suggestions of those less favored, and this will reduce the very freedom men such as Dewey and Russell were bent upon promoting. If, however, two or more independent minds jointly administer, then it is likely that divided counsels will damage the unity of purpose both Dewey and Russell also wished wholeheartedly to establish and maintain. The former difficulty nearly spoiled the experiment dominated by John Dewey, while Beacon Hill came to an end because of the domestic difficulties of the two equally strong-minded Russells, warring over each other's peristent and vigorous infidelities. Whitehead's participation in the administration of educational facilities was, as Hendley makes clear, of such a different sort that neither horn of this dilemma could puncture the results of his labors.

The assumption of responsible educators, from Plato and Aristotle onward, has been that in order to develop whole human beings it is necessary somehow to introduce into them knowledge as a whole. One cannot breed a *kalokagathon*, the paragon of bodily, moral, and mental excellence, the gentleman or gentlewoman in the primary and proper sense, simply by drilling them with a few unpleasant pushups, some choice sermons and admonitions, and isolated snatches of history, mathematics, biology, politics, and a couple of sonnets. That is no doubt better than nothing, but it falls a long distance short of the desired unity for which education should strive, a unity which is not reachable except by the help of others. Those others must have encompassed this unity through their native gifts and uncounted hours of discipline which enabled them to live easily the habits they so often arduously acquired. This integration at a high level of excellence was obviously the aim, and in some respects the accomplishment, of all three of the thinkers taken up in this volume. Whether, on the other hand, a goal so demanding could possibly be reached in the few short years when the Laboratory School enjoyed the headship of Dewey or when the Beacon Hill project was guided by Russell and his wife together, or when Whitehead took an active role in school and university affairs, is another question. It may have sufficed for some, more impressionable and docile with solid memories as well. On the other hand, it is unlikely that any of the three philosophers thought that their administrative work would be of such brief duration, and two of them doubtless were at a loss to explain why their principles, so self-evident to them, together with personal records so unimpeachable, would be insufficient to ensure a far longer-lasting and better-accepted system of education.

All these are vital considerations with which every educator must deal if he can think for himself and be stimulated rather than trammeled by old traditions and modern fads. The creative men, the originators, in educational theory—and Hendley has very wisely chosen to discuss men of this stamp together—are rare, and perhaps rarer than creative mathematicians or embryologists or musicological experts, for many kinds of intellectual strength must first be inherited and cultivated, then blended, in order to be a great teacher and leader in education, who must in addition be a person of outstanding good will. Professor Brian Hendley has spared no pains to assemble the accounts, which he documents with precision, of three efforts, very different on the outside but surprisingly similar if one looks at their inner content, and points a moral not only sensible but timely from their partial successes and partial failures for the benefit of philosophers of education of our day and of every persuasion.

Acknowledgments

I WANT TO THANK THE following for permission to quote from their materials: the Joseph Regenstein Library of the University of Chicago, the Bertrand Russell Archives at McMaster University, the Public Record Office, Chancery Lane, London, the State Historical Society of Wisconsin in Madison, Dora Russell, and Victor Lowe. I also would like to thank the following for allowing me to consult their materials: the Surrey Record Office, Kingston upon Thames, the British Academy, the library of Teachers College/Columbia University, the Harvard College Library, Yale University Library, the Boston Public Library, the Center for Process Studies in Claremont, California, the Morris Library and the Center for Dewey Studies at Southern Illinois University in Carbondale, and the archives of the Imperial College of Science and Technology in London.

The following individuals were of great help to me: my colleagues, Jim Horne and Larry Haworth, for continuing advice on how to write a book; my secretary, Esther Kennel, for typing the final draft; the Interlibrary Loan Office of the University of Waterloo Library for filling my most esoteric requests; Bob Brumbaugh, who is my mentor in the truest sense of the term; David Harley for sharing his knowledge of Beacon Hill School and introducing me to Katherine Tait; Carl Spadoni for assistance at the Russell Archives above and beyond the call of duty; Jo Ann Boydston, who can answer any question on Dewey; Victor Lowe for his patient responses to my queries; John Cobb; Paul Weiss; Richard Peters; Mrs. J. Pingree for finding me the photograph of Whitehead; the late A. H. Johnson for a memorable afternoon of tea and reminiscence about Whitehead; Maetel Grant and the volleyball group, who help me keep body and soul together; my parents, who still are my biggest fans; my family, who tolerated my fluctuating moods during the writing of the book; and my wife, who was always there when I needed her.

I gratefully acknowledge the financial assistance of the UW/SSHRC Research Grant Subcommittee which enabled me to travel and consult primary sources and to hire Jim Gough to develop the bibliography. My dean, Robin

Banks, and my chairman, Rolf George, were strong supporters of the project. I especially want to thank my editor, George Kimball Plochmann. He has taught me more about writing style and grammar than I managed to learn through all too many years of schooling. His unfailing humor and steady encouragement made the dreary task of revision one that was pleasant and stimulating. If I am the father of this book, he is the godfather.

Having acknowledged all the help I have received, I must hold myself responsible for any shortcomings that remain in the book. It must now stand on its own and I wish it well.

A final note: Throughout this work I have tried to avoid male-oriented language, but have not been able to do so in all instances. Part of this problem derives from the English language itself, part from the orientation of the philosophers discussed here. I must ask the reader tacitly to correct any remaining defects wherever he or she may find them.

Introduction
Robert S. Brumbaugh

T HE EXPLORATION OF THEORY in relation to practice is no recent invention. To Socrates and Plato in their encounters with politicians and Sophists, it seemed that inquiry must take the form of a search for precise definitions. In the *Euthyphro*, for example, Socrates is convinced that if only Euthyphro, an Athenian priest and thus a public official, will give him an accurate definition of piety, Socrates can then defend himself from the charge of impiety brought against him. Through Plato's early and middle dialogues, the search for definition goes hand in hand with the conviction that when one has reached an adequate formula, there will be no difficulty in recognizing its application. Even in the middle books of the *Republic*, where Plato recognizes the need for practical experience to supplement theoretical studies, he seems to think that just about any sort of practice will do. In contrast to the detailed account of objectives and curriculum of his ideal Academy, the "application" is prescribed and abruptly dismissed.

In his later dialogues, however, Plato recognizes that the application of theory to practice is by no means the simple matter he had earlier thought. This is especially true in the *Laws*. Abstract definitions of terms need to be accompanied by examples, appeals to experience, and occasionally by special models to make their applications clear.

Much Twentieth-century work in educational philosophy has carried on the project of Socrates, in his search for definitions. Where common sense and traditional techniques are lacking in precision, as they have often been in educational theory, definitions are both badly needed and hard to come by. Yet we must agree with Plato's later insight. A successful analysis of meaning and definition of such terms as "learning" or "educating" are only lexicographical exercises until their connections with practice are specified. We need models, examples, demonstrations, and sometimes even new institutions to show the relevant meaning of abstract statements of goals and definitions. Such is the task that was set for the three philosophers whose work has been detailed by Professor Hendley.

Bertrand Russell's ideal for education is a double one. Where logical and scientific precision is possible, we must be devoted to its pursuit. Where it is not, we must not allow the social pressures put upon children by family, school, and community to produce credulous, superstitious, and sadistic adults. Those pressures may stem from religion, from an appeal to patriotism, from traditional customs of child training; in any case, they are most undesirable. This means that education must practice a separation of the search for what is true from an acceptance of what is generally believed. It did not mean in Russell's case that he would impose a different set of dogmatic rules in place of the others, but that he would protect the freedom of the child to form independent judgments about moral questions, judgments based on first-hand experience. Russell did not propose to demonstrate or test his ideas in any standard British "public" school. Any school is, after all, a social institution; there is no way to modify it so it will embody a new idea of freedom that is antisocial or at least asocial. But given a country estate for its setting, a modest tutorial staff, some servants, and a small group of students whose parents approve the project, a demonstration of the application of his theory could be carried on. Russell did this for seven years.

John Dewey defines the ideal goal of education as social effectiveness in a modern democracy, in some ways the very opposite of Russell's account. In place of formal logic Dewey puts an experimental method of inquiry. His own theoretical objection is to customs and definitions that set up sharp dualisms where in fact there is real continuity. School versus society, self versus others, theory versus practice, future paradise versus present vale of tears—all those are unrealistic and erroneous in their defined, sharp exclusiveness. What Dewey's ideas require is continuity: of kindergarten and university, school and society, science and industry, experimental methods and generally approved teaching practices. The institutional aim translates into a pilot model for public schools (taking this expression in the American sense) which will advance democracy. Notice that in addition to continuity, the theory requires unremitting evaluation, with feedback used for revision. The Laboratory School of the University of Chicago, Dewey's project, was a practical application approximating these implications of the theory. This was a more selective sample than a large public school would have been. I think this was theoretically consistent because the first tests of materials and ideas were to be run under optimum circumstances, if possible; further extensions could come later if early indications were favorable.

Professor Hendley holds that Dewey's theoretical writings subsequent to his leaving the school show little influence of the school's actual practices. This may be correct, but as late as the mid-1920s and through the 1930s, the Laboratory School, as it was called, instituted various courses and projects inspired by Dewey's own theories, and the contrast with Russell's Beacon Hill school stands out clearly when we consider some of these projects. Incidentally, the dates, just now chosen, are those when my wife and I were pupils in the Laboratory School. Our group seems not to have written as much autobiographical material about their school years as did the students of Russell. There may be some underlying reason: Our creative writing program lent very little encouragement to autobiography!

To begin at the entrance, an inscription to the east of the Blaine Hall doors read, KNOWLEDGE IS POWER. Where Russell's students strolled through a countryside estate, Dewey's (I was among them) marched through the U.S. Steel rolling mills in South Chicago, through the University of Chicago heating plant (I believe that was a field trip in chemistry, no less), and through the Back of the Yards neighborhood on the city's West Side. Oddly enough, however, it was Dewey's students, not Russell's, who each had a small personal garden. There was a constant flurry of testing and measuring, and a less constant but still firm implementation of theoretical rejections of so-called dualism. It seems less odd today than it did in 1924 to have boys study cooking and girls carpentry, or to have a complete small machine shop and printshop as part of a college preparatory secondary school. It may well be that reflexive modifications in the light of tested experience were slow, but still, a good deal *was* going on. Ironically enough, one of the best examples of overcoming "false dualisms" was the introduction of a course in classics for high school juniors, taught by Robert Maynard Hutchins and Mortimer J. Adler, both of them strongly committed Aristotelians.

Whitehead's position and contribution is harder to state simply. Perhaps one way to look at it is to look upon it as revaluating an accepted Nineteenth-century hierarchy of educational values. There were three parts to school: disciplines, activities, and enrichments. Disciplines were what counted most; activities, such as glee clubs and athletics, "let off steam"; enrichments, including piano playing, drawing, and so forth, were "nice" but educationally peripheral.

We can use this simple hierarchy to locate all three of our three educators. Russell's insight was right: Discipline of a true sort goes badly—in fact not at all—with institutional and social superstition and intimidation, though such true discipline must remain integral with education. Dewey's addendum was right, as well. Activities may be as important as, or even more important than, abstract exercises in making ideas meaningful and in developing character. Not until 1934, however, did John Dewey in *Art as Experience* admit that "enrichment" might have a significance roughly comparable to "activities." Russell evidently assumed that aesthetic activities and opportunities were always on hand, just as they were in his model, but they were sadly lacking in the other school systems. Whitehead's new idea, one finally defined in its full generality in 1925, was that "concrete seeing," the old enrichment component, was at least as important as the disciplines and activities. He had a second idea, also new, which like that of Dewey's proposed to do away with a dualism: The best research minds in the academic world should be concerned with *teaching*: of mathematics (1911), arts and crafts (1919), natural science (1920), the classics (1922), of virtually everything (1925), including business (1933).

There was something about Whitehead's ideas which implied that the innovations they suggested were conceptual rather than institutional. To take his own examples employed at various times, one might try to encourage appreciative sensitivity by looking at French Impressionist paintings or the docks of London or some ornamental bookbinding or a sunset. *Which* of these did not much matter, so long as one recognized that this added the dimension of a perception that what was being looked at was actually there. What was *not* implied was a reshaping of institutions, using a planetarium, say, to simulate a vivid sunset; rather, it was a forty-five-degree adjustment of institutional aims, together with any random supply of illustrative material. While appreciation was being furthered in the curricular scene, moreover, discovery of the best ways of teaching mathematics, science, classics, and history was to enlist, at the other pole, the skills of the most advanced research institutes and scholars in the world. The conceptual clarity of the new, sophisticated analysis of number, continuity, and functions would find its way, in suitable form, into the texts and teacher's manuals of the elementary school. Again, the need for new precision seemed not to imply a need for a new institutional design but instead a revision of objectives and ways of thinking within already existing schemes. (Several of Whitehead's early addresses to groups of advanced mathematicians on the teaching of their subject must have come as a real surprise for them!) Thus Whitehead's applications of his ideas, as he tried to make them practical and clear, were not by way of new institutional design, as had been those of Russell and Dewey, but by conceptual redirection, which he encouraged both by reading technical papers to societies and by cooperation with all sorts of planning committees. As a result, except for papers to austere academies on the mundane theme of teaching, or casual addresses to technical schools on the arcane theme of learning, Whitehead's activity was largely anonymous and thus difficult to document. He intended it to remain that way, and it has so remained to this day. But his reconstruction of concepts by addresses to learned societies, and policy changes by participation in committees was his selected way of giving ideas meaning in concrete application.

It seems clear that, ideally, the aims of education should include individual authenticity, aesthetic sensitivity, social effectiveness, and intellectual discipline. Whether these aims are mutually compatible or whether all or any of them are practically attainable are separate questions. Plato, in the *Republic*, argued that there is no logical conflict, but as recently as 1954 the National Education Association *Yearbook* expressed strong doubts regarding whether these various objectives could simultaneously be realized practically. Hendley's book is a study of educational philosophy carrying its discussion one phase beyond the clarifying conceptual analysis needed to make sense of routines at best muddled. After giving the refined definitions of key notions, it turns to the next question, that of the way relevant applications and examples will look in practice. His concluding chapter offers a challenge to the reader to do again, and one hopes, to do even better, what Plato envisaged in his day and what Russell, Dewey, and Whitehead undertook so many centuries later.

CHAPTER ONE

The Reconstruction of the Philosophy of Education

IN A RECENT STUDY of developmental trends in the philosophy of education, Sven Erik Nordenbo claims that "The line of development in the past 25 years in the Anglo-Saxon countries could roughly be described as 'the rise and decline of analytic educational philosophy.' Analytic educational philosophy emerged out of nothing at the end of the fifties . . . bloomed through the sixties and has in the seventies been exposed to pressure."[1] Those of us who study, teach, and write about contemporary philosophy of education will recognize this as an accurate description of its recent past. It has undergone a rebirth, followed by rapid growth, and has gradually tapered off into the present state of stagnation and increasing self-doubt.

After the death of John Dewey in 1952, educational philosophy was relegated to a relatively minor position, and philosophers tended to pay less and less attention to educational issues. One of the first stirrings of new life was a symposium on "Philosophy and Education" held at the American Philosophical Association Eastern Division meetings in 1955. Two papers were presented: one by Harry Broudy on "How Philosophical Can Philosophy of Education Be?", the other by Kingsley Price, "Is a Philosophy of Education Necessary?"[2] Broudy distinguished between theory-building and theory-evaluation as two phases of philosophical activity and argued that both were needed to make the philosophy of education philosophically genuine and educationally helpful. Price maintained that the philosophy of education is necessary to the discipline of education because "it provides an analysis of its obscure terms, a metaphysical supplement to its statements of fact, and a clarification, justification, and correction of its moral recommendations."[3]

This symposium inspired the publication of a special issue of the *Harvard Education Review* in the Spring of 1956 in which twenty-five contributors responded to the question, "What should be the aims and methods of a philosophy of education?"[4] The answers given were by no means uniform, some authors stressing the importance of analysis, others the need for the synthesis of educational ideas; but there were clear indications that interest was reviving in the field. The National Society for the Study of Education produced its Fifty-fourth Yearbook in 1955 on the theme "Modern Philosophies and Education,"[5] and not long after, Israel Scheffler edited a useful collection of modern readings on *Philosophy and Education*.[6] A further impetus came from the student unrest in the sixties which forced many academics to think through their goals and methods of teaching. Those of us in philosophy departments became vividly aware of the fact that students expected us to *teach* as well as to *do* philosophy. Practical pedagogical problems could no longer be dismissed by vague allusions to the value of learning for its own sake. Roused from their dogmatic slumbers, philosophers began in earnest to consider theories of education and proposals for radical change. In the United States, thinkers of the first rank such as William Frankena at the University of Michigan and Israel Scheffler at Harvard led the way in approaching education as a domain of thought and experience worthy of philosophical scrutiny.[7] Books and new journals began to proliferate and philosophy of education societies flourished. The dispute over the nature, methods, and aims of the philosophy of education continued, but most authors agreed that what they were doing was new, exciting, and worthwhile.

In England there was a similar pattern of development. There had been a few attempts to philosophize about education, most notably the books by C. D. Hardie, *Truth and Fallacy in Educational Theory* (1942), and D. J. O'Connor, *An Introduction to the Philosophy of Education* (1957);[8] but the real revival of interest took place in the sixties. This was largely owing to the work of Richard Peters and his colleagues at the University of London Institute of Education. Indeed, if there is one individual who in his role as teacher, administrator, author, and editor can be singled out as the leading exponent of the "new" philosophy of education, it is Peters. He more than anyone else is responsible for the fact that, as Nordenbo points out, "the educational philosophy of the past 25 years has changed from being a subject pursued by educationists interested in philosophy to a subject mainly studied by philosophers interested in education."[9] Even those who disagree with Peters must take his ideas into account, for he has initiated or been directly involved in most of the current discussions and debates now taking place in the literature.[10]

It was in his Inaugural Lecture (for the Chair of the Philosophy of Education at London, delivered in December 1963)[11] that Peters set the tone for much of what was to follow. There he argued that for all the public debate and theoretical speculation about the aims, content, and proper methodology of education, there is an urgent necessity to get clearer about the concept of "education" itself. We need to explicate its essence or indicate central uses of the term before we can meaningfully discuss what, how, or why we are educating the young. "Education" is not the sort of concept that marks out any particular type of process or activity, says Peters; rather, it suggests criteria to which processes or activities must conform if they are to be correctly termed "educational."[12] Such conceptual clarification is preeminently the task of the philosopher of education.

In his influential book, *Ethics and Education*,[13] Peters spells out this task in greater detail. He depicts the philosopher as a kind of spectator who sets out to "detachedly ponder upon and probe into activities and forms of discourse in which he and others engage." Like any other reflective thinker, the philosopher tries to disengage himself and step back from the hurly-burly of everyday life in order to try to make some sense out of what is being said and done. In seeking such understanding, the philosopher's special stock in trade is "the disciplined demarcation of concepts, the patient explication of the grounds of knowledge and of the presuppositions of different forms of discourse"[14] He reflects upon what Peters calls "first-order" activities, such as doing science, painting pictures, worshipping, or educating the young, and asks "second-order" questions about them. Thus, we have philosophies *of* science, art, religion, and education. According to Peters, the questions a philosopher raises about first-order activities are "basically the same questions asked by Socrates at the beginning— the questions 'What do you mean?' and 'How do you know?' "[15] The philosopher of education, then, looks for the meaning of the concept "education" and evaluates arguments which seek to justify certain educational procedures and goals. He sets forth criteria for the proper use of the term "education"; that is, "it implies that something worth while is being or has been intentionally transmitted in a morally acceptable manner."[16]

Although Peters sees his questions as basically the same as those asked by Socrates, he does not claim to have achieved the same result. When Socrates asked his questions, he, at least in Plato's version, seemed to think they had a final answer. Truth was to be sought through a dialectical advance toward the grasping of unchanging Forms. When one knew the Form of "justice" or "piety" or "virtue," one knew what they were once and for all. Peters does not claim to have explicated the essence of education, that is, to have found a set of characteristics that can be regarded as essential irrespective of the context. He is well aware of the dangers of setting one's foot "on the primrose path that leads to essentialism." He favors the questioning attitude displayed by Socrates when confronted with complex theoretical and practical problems, without the Platonic claim that the ultimate outcome of such questioning will be an answer that can stand forevermore.

An example might make Peters's point clearer. Consider the line of questioning followed by Socrates in the *Meno*. Meno has pressed him to say whether virtue can be taught, or if it is the result of practice, or whether men possess it by nature or in some other way.[17] Modern-day values-education programs often seem to be based on Meno's premise that we all know what virtue is, and the problem is simply how we are to go about inculcating it in the young through schooling. The controversies about such programs may have more to do with the ends than the proposed means. More discussion and argument about the *nature* of virtue would seem to be required before we can develop *methods* of teaching it in our schools.[18] This would be in the spirit of Socrates himself, who does not answer Meno's question but poses a number of his own to the effect that we cannot talk about the teachability of "virtue" until we get clear as to what virtue is. Discovering a satisfactory definition proves to be an elusive goal, and the dialogue ends with the two men agreeing that although virtue may ideally be based on knowledge, it seems to come to man only as a gift of the gods. My students soon become impatient with the course of the argument and share Meno's growing annoyance with Socrates's questions. They see the whole enterprise as logical nit-picking and as a failure to confront the real issue. Although it is true that Meno still cannot offer an acceptable definition of "virtue," it can be said that by the end of the dialogue he has become less impetuous about finding the most efficient way of teaching it.[19] The reader as well has benefited from the attempt to clarify the concept and now has a better idea of the complexity of the problem.

Peters is advocating a return to this sort of philosophical questioning of educational concepts. He sees conceptual analysis as a necessary preliminary to taking effective action, participating in meaningful discussion, or even engaging in further reflective thinking. In his *The Logic of Education* (1970), written in collaboration with Paul Hirst, Peters admonishes the philosopher of education to make explicit the principles which underlie the use of words in order to become clearer "both about how things are and about the sorts of decisions that have to be made in dealing with them." The reason so much care must be devoted to clarifying key concepts is that we will then be able to "look through the words at the problems of explanation, justification or practical action that occasion such a reflective interest."[20] Clarity aids the man of thought and the man of action. It serves to make both theoretical and practical issues more manageable. Puzzling about the meaning of "virtue" in the *Meno,* for example, sets the stage for Plato's theory of the just man in a just society in the *Republic,* which, in turn, forms the basis for his specific educational proposals. While we may not be able to achieve wisdom by grasping the essential nature of "education," we can get a better sense of what we are talking about and what we hope to accomplish.

Having established this link with past philosophizing, Hirst and Peters encounter difficulties in their own efforts to define "education." They rule out finding a definition in the strong sense of the word: listing the logically necessary and sufficient conditions for the correct use of a term. Such definitions are either trivial (as when we define a "bachelor" as "an unmarried male") or are part of an artificially constructed symbolic system (as in Euclidean geometry where a "triangle" is defined as having "three angles equal to two right angles"). They neglect to mention that this sense of definition also applies to the "What is X?" sorts of questions asked by Socrates.[21] Whatever characteristics we may list for a process or activity to be properly called "educational," we cannot claim that this and only this set of characteristics exhausts the meaning of the term. There seem to be counterexamples to every definition we can provide.

Nor do Hirst and Peters feel that "education" can be defined in the weak sense of listing the logically necessary conditions without claiming that they are sufficient. For example, we might say that "punishment" entails that "something unpleasant is done to someone"—a logically necessary condition—although the fact that something unpleasant is being done to someone is no guarantee that this is a case of "punishment" since something else may have occurred, such as an accident—not a sufficient condition. We cannot say, "If X is an educational process, then criteria a, b, and c have to be met." Even Peters's very general definition of "education" in *Ethics and Education* does not cover all the cases where it still makes perfectly good sense to call a process or activity "educational" despite the fact that it may fail to satisfy one or the other of his criteria.

Rather than continue to look for some single essence or nature or clear set of conditions, Hirst and Peters would have us consider the family resemblances among different processes and activities which enable us to distinguish central cases of "education" from peripheral ones. This leads them to the claim that when we defend the ideal of an "educated person" we are really speaking of the nineteenth-century notion of someone with an all-round development: morally, intellectually, spiritually. This ideal has very much taken root in educational circles, and, as Peters puts it elsewhere, "it is natural, therefore, for those working in educational institutions to conceive of what they are doing as being connected with the development of such a person."[22]

It is not my intention to take the reader through all the ins and outs of Peters's analysis, but merely to describe it in enough detail to convey a sense of its ultimate futility. Starting with bold logical objectives and ending with a questionable empirical claim about word usage among educators (which, even if true, is surely not a strong basis for a statement of the way the term *should* be understood), Hirst and Peters manage to provide little clarity and even less impetus to further thought and action. The circuitous path by which they have arrived at their definition has been criticized for not reflecting common usage,[23] for ignoring the human context in which words change and develop,[24] and for reflecting the bias of a male cognitive perspective.[25]

My own quarrel with this way of proceeding is that it seems unnecessarily cut off from any sense of continuity in the history of ideas. For all their talk of following in Socrates's footsteps, Hirst and Peters concentrate on how words are used by their associates or by those engaged in educational pursuits. They almost stumble upon a definition from the nineteenth century that they like, with no explanation of who propounded such a view then, or what arguments were used to justify this ideal, or how such an ideal applies in our high-technology societies today. All of this is done under the aegis of simply analyzing the way terms are being used at present. I submit that this makes for a sterile analysis, cut off from the vital context of words, ideas, and actions in which the terms are used and developed, and that it weakens their own argument since they want to say that a certain definition is the correct one, that is, not only that this is the way the term or concept is being used but that it should be so understood.

The problem of narrowness of focus is even more acute in those philosophers of education who see themselves as following the approach of Hirst and Peters. They delight in posing counterexamples to proposed definitions, which leads to further refinements and distinctions, more counterexamples, higher abstraction, and less relevance to educational thought and action. Following Peters's suggestion, contemporary philosophers of education have analyzed a large number of concepts such as "teaching," "discipline," "interest," "creativity," "learning by discovery," "student rights," and "open education." Some of these analyses have helped to bring out exactly what is at issue. In many cases, however, conceptual analysis has become an end in itself, and little concern is felt for the usefulness of its results.

Some concepts, such as "indoctrination," have proved to be so fertile a ground for analysis that a whole subliterature has been built up around them, and opposing positions have been staked out according to which of four criteria (intention, consequences, method, content) one wants to defend as being necessary conditions for calling an educational process or activity indoctrination.[26] Some authors have become so closely indentified with a specific argument or point of view that their names have become a kind of shorthand for discussing different positions in an ongoing controversy.[27] Frequently, one article is taken as pivotal for the analysis, and all subsequent writing on the topic begins with a brief appraisal (usually negative) of this article.[28] Much of the writing in the field has now taken on the flavor of an in-house dispute or the proceedings of a private, rather boring debating society.

What has happened to the philosophy of education in the last twenty-five years is that it has become more and more "professionalized" and further and further removed from the very real problems that initiated such reflective thinking in the first place. This is a phenomenon that has been attributed to analytic philosophy as a whole by Richard Rorty, who describes it as being left "without a genealogy, a sense of mission, or a metaphilosophy."[29] Rorty's remarks on the way such philosophers are trained nicely fits many of the new philosophers of education and deserves to be quoted in full:

> Training in philosophy turned into a sort of "casebook" procedure, of the sort found in law schools. Student's wits were sharpened by reading preprints of articles by currently fashionable figures, and finding objections to them. The students so trained began to think of themselves neither as continuing a tradition nor as participating in the solution of the "outstanding problems" at the frontiers of a science. Rather, they took their self-image from a style and quality of argumentation. They became quasi-lawyers rather than quasi-scientists—hoping that an interesting new case would turn up.[30]

It strikes me that Rorty's characterization of the "quasi-lawyer" is particularly apt for budding philosophers of education. Hirst and Peters themselves have become the center of attention, and newcomers to the field cut their teeth on their articles in order to establish an academic identity. Little attention is paid to actual educational problems or to the history of educational philosophy. This is not to argue that we should all revert to being "quasi-scientists" who provide world views based on supposedly timeless truths. I do not think that the answer to being too narrow in one's conceptual analysis is to be so broad as to be virtually incomprehensible. Unfortunately, many advocates of the present way of doing things in philosophy see our alternatives in just such a stark either/or fashion.

For instance, when some years ago I suggested that philosophers of education had more to offer than the analysis of concepts and that they should return to their traditional role of general theory building, I was sharply taken to task for misrepresenting what philosophers can and should do by arguing that they once again propound such large-scale views or working hypotheses (as Dewey called them) about man and society. According to John Wilson, "Obviously they are *not* 'working hypotheses,' as if philosophers were scientists. If they are 'theories,' how in the world are they to be proved or disproved? What *special* expertise does the philosopher have that justifies our paying him a salary to spin these high-flown webs, to produce 'philosophies' whose *truth* or *value* is—for all we have been told—not open to assessment?"[31] Since the philosopher is clearly not a scientist, he should not try to act as one. For Wilson, " 'General theory-building' has been practised by philosophers wanting to off-load their own fantasies on other men for ages."[32]

My own view has been that philosophers are eminently well suited for the important task of general theory building in education since they are educated persons, in Peters's sense of having an all-round development, who come from a distinguished tradition of general theory building and who often have to face educational problems first-hand as teachers in the classroom.[33] I do not think this requires superhuman abilities, nor do I see it as an exercise in fantasy. The truth of an educational theory, like those put forth by Plato, Rousseau, and Dewey, can indeed be questioned; but that is not to say that we cannot evaluate it at all in terms of reasonableness, adherence to the facts as we understand them, and value as a guiding ideal. Such theories can help us put a number of details into perspective as well as give us a sense of direction and inspiration. Educators need to have their sights raised above the insistent demands of budgets, enrollment projections, salary disputes, and the latest report of the buildings and grounds committee.

We all need to be challenged to think about more fundamental issues such as the rights of the individual and his responsibilities to the state, the role of the school as conveyor of a cultural heritage and agent for social change, the content of knowledge, and the means to disciplined thinking as well as its proper application. Philosophers have had valuable things to say about such topics in the past, and it is fatuous to ignore them on the grounds that their theories have not been proved or disproved. It is downright foolhardy to dissuade philosophers from even making the attempt to deal with such issues because they are not scientists. Can we scientifically resolve such problems? Should the modern-day Meno turn to the social psychologist to learn whether virtue can be taught? Are we now able to resolve long-standing disputes on the aims, content, and methods of education by pointing to some definitive experiment or adhering to a special scientific formula? Although there have been a few notable exceptions,[34] philosophers of education in this period of rebirth have shied away from theory building and concentrated on the analysis of terms.

Not only are such philosophical analyses disconnected from any attempt at theory building, they also usually take place in isolation from current work being done on education in other disciplines. Psychologists, sociologists, historians, literary critics, anthropologists, and many others have interesting things to say about how or why or even whether we should educate the young. Education is a human phenomenon that can be studied in vastly different cultural, political, religious, and economic settings. By directing their attention solely to the definition of terms, philosophers of education cut themselves off from data that might well have a bearing on the issues behind the words. Peters himself has come to realize that isolated analysis is not the best appraoch and has called for a broader, more synthetic method in which philosophers integrate the findings of various educational specialists around concrete problems.[35] Unfortunately, his call has gone largely unheeded.

Lack of a genealogy, in the sense of seeing itself as continuing a tradition of general theory building and isolation of approach from the findings of other types of educational research, has made for a high degree of abstraction in much of contemporary philosophy of education. The philosophy *of* education is no longer merely a second-order activity where we reflectively consider what is being done and said in education; it has become a kind of "third-order" activity in which we scrutinize what others say and think about what is said and done in the classroom. By concentrating on the clarification of concepts, we engage in thinking about thinking and we talk about talk and lose sight of the actual processes and activities that intitally occasioned our reflective interest. This high level of abstractness has been aptly summed up by T. W. Moore, an avowed disciple of Peters, in terms of a three-tiered model.[36] Moore would have us look on educational thought and practice as something on the order of a house with different floors. Each can be taken to represent a logically distinct level with each higher stage arising out of and depending upon the stage or stages below.

On the first or ground level are educational activities: "teaching, learning, training, demonstrating, punishing—the sort of activities to be found in class-rooms everywhere."[37] All of us have been there, for better or for worse, as students; some of us, as teachers, have never left. This common educational experience should ideally form the basis for meaningful discussion and com-munication, productive criticism, thoughtful change. In Moore's model, the foundation for educational thought and practice is what takes place at an interpersonal level on a day-to-day basis in the schools. This fairly commonplace observation is often lost sight of when one begins to enter the more esoteric realms of conceptual analysis. Our thinking should start with what is actually happening.

For Moore, in order to explain what is going on in the classroom and make normative judgments about it, we must ascend to a second level. This is the stage of educational theorizing, where theory is taken to mean "a body of connected principles, counsels, and recommendations aimed at influencing what goes on at the ground level." Such theory is practical, in that it aims at influencing educational activities through its prescriptions and recommenda-tions, and general, in that its recommendations are not meant to cover specific pedagogical situations so much as to spell out an overall view of the purposes and objectives of the educational process as a whole. Such a theory can in principle be put to the test and be accepted or rejected. "A valid educational theory," he says, "would be one that made morally acceptable assumptions about aims, correct and checkable assumptions about children, philosophically respectable assumptions about knowledge and verified assumptions about the effectiveness of methods."[38]

Although Moore recognizes the important contributions that philosophers such as Plato, Rousseau, and Dewey have made to educational theory, he feels that various factors, including the tremendous increase in psychological and sociological data together with what he calls the present uncertainty about values, make it very difficult to continue philosophizing about education in the traditional manner. Nowadays the practicing teacher must be his or her own general theorist of education. Philosophy can help by making clear the formal assumptions for any such theory, the conceptual framework within which one would attempt to develop a more general point of view; for example, by defining, as Peters does, what we mean by an "educated person" or delineating, as Hirst does, the logical structure of the different forms of knowledge into which such a person is to be initiated; but it is no longer to be seen as a direct source of such theories.

The proper place for the philosophy of education in Moore's model is on the third or most abstract level. The philosopher clarifies the concepts used by others, polices their arguments, and critically appraises their theories. Rather than the Scorates of the marketplace who engages all comers in philosophical discussion, we seem to get the Socrates lampooned in Aristophanes's *The Clouds,* floating high up in his basket and issuing obscure pronouncements about what is going on down below. Being aloof from more mundane concerns and freed from any practical considerations, the philosopher occupies his lofty position and apparently just waits for something to be said or thought so that he can proceed to analyze, criticize, and clarify. To me this is a good description, though unintentionally so, of the "professionalization" that now bedevils our discipline and of the irrelevance to other thinkers or educators of much of what we have to say in the philosophy of education.

It also strikes me as a blueprint for the production of what Whitehead has called "inert ideas," ideas that are "merely received into the mind without being utilised, or tested, or thrown into fresh combinations."[39] Such ideas lack vitality and relevance because they have not had to meet the test of practical experience. Whitehead decried the large number of inert or recondite ideas that he found in mathematics; I would extend his criticism to much of what is currently being done by analytic philosophers of education. They seem to have fallen into the trap that Dewey warned us against: taking philosophy as "so much nimble or severe intellectual exercise—as something said by philosophers and concerning them alone."[40] Dewey stressed the fact that "Unless a philosophy is to remain symbolic—or verbal—or a sentimental indulgence for a few, or else mere arbitrary dogma, its auditing of past experience and its program of values must take effect in conduct." This was especially true of the philosophy of education because "the educational point of view enables one to envisage the philosophic problems where they arise and thrive, where they are at home, and where acceptance or rejection makes a difference in practice."[41]

The isolation and abstraction so vividly depicted by Moore's three-tiered model can be contrasted to the interaction and practical concerns prompted by Dewey's view. I agree with Scheffler when he supports the conception of philosophy exemplified by the work of Dewey and the other pragmatists: "philosophy ought to connect detail with principle, analysis with vision[;] it should employ the resources of its tradition and its uncompromising logical criticism in illuminating the main realms of life and the problems of current thought and action."[42] I feel it is counterproductive for philosophers of education to analyze concepts in abstraction from the concrete reality to which they refer and in isolation from the traditions of educational philosophy and the recent findings of other disciplines. Moore is really describing the direction that contemporary philosophy of education has taken in adhering to the admonitions of Peters and his colleagues to concentrate on conceptual analysis. I think it is time to take stock of where we are and to appreciate the value of general theory building and the attention to what was actually happening in the classroom that was displayed by philosophers of education in the past.

This has been my motivation in writing this book. In it I look at the educational theories of three philosophers who were deeply involved in the practical concerns of education. Each man could be said to have attempted to practice what he preached about education. Dewey is the most obvious choice, for he was a pragmatist who thought that theory and practice should interact to their mutual benefit. It seemed a natural outgrowth of his attitude toward philosophy that he became head of the Department of Philosophy, Psychology, and Pedagogy at the University of Chicago and soon after afterward set up a University Elementary School in order to test some of his educational theories. Russell's interest in education was heightened with the birth of his two children, and he and his wife Dora decided they would set up their own school at Beacon Hill in which to educate them. Once committed to this project, they both devoted much thought, time, energy, and money to the Beacon Hill School. Although Russell later asserted that he had failed in his educational experiment, there is no doubt that the experience served to vitalize his ideas on education.

Whitehead is the unlikeliest candidate for such a study, since he never ran a school as did Dewey and Russell. Nonetheless, he maintained a continuing, prolonged contact with practical educational problems by serving as a university administrator, sitting on national and local education committees, acting as president of mathematical and scientific associations, and freely giving of his time to speak at teachers' meetings, Founders' Day ceremonies, and the like. Clearly, I am not arguing that only those philosophers who have run schools deserve to have their educational ideas taken seriously. What I favor is the concern for the practical ramifications of one's educational ideas that can be found in Dewey, Russell, and Whitehead. What they said and did about education helped these three philosophers to overcome the abstractness and isolation so prevalent in the philosophy of education today. If the field is to continue to grow and be effective, we must wean ourselves from the single-minded attachment to conceptual analysis and begin once again to develop general theories of education and pay attention to what is happening in the classroom. I am not advocating a nostalgic return to the past but a redirection for the future. Not all that Dewey, Russell, and Whitehead said and did about education is worthwhile; much of it does not hold up under critical scrutiny. Yet many of their ideas and practices can be seen as still having value and should stimulate further reflective thinking.

Richard Rorty has proposed that as an antidote to the professionalization of philosophy, philosophers should engage in an edifying discourse or conversation in which we educate one another regarding the alternative approaches that might be taken in attempting to make sense of the mulitdimensional aspects of human experience. For Rorty, there is no single correct way of catching the meaning of our experience, and we should all be open to the possibility of finding "new, better, more interesting, more fruitful ways of speaking."[43] John Smith has called for "the new need for a recovery of philosophy" in which philosphers see themselves "not as practitioners of a speciality with a technical language, but as reflective thinkers seeking to describe, interpret, and illuminate lived experience by making more precise the vague expression of ordinary communication."[44] Smith advises that we not abandon the attempt to clarify concepts and evaluate arguments; but neither should we ignore the value of formulating theories and testing one's ideas.

This book is meant to further the kind of conversation among philosophers that Rorty has in mind. In it I call for the recovery of the traditional tasks of the philosophy of education: synthesis, as well as analysis, general theory building, as well as conceptual clarification. Education has always needed a sense of direction, a view of the whole educational process that can encompass the mass of empirical data and subsume it under general principles. We need to reflect upon the kind of society we seek to promote, the nature of the human beings we are trying to educate, and the practical consequences of implementing certain hypotheses about aims, methods, and content. Philosophers such as Dewey,

Russell, and Whitehead took seriously the demands of educational theory and practice. We can learn from what they said and did and then move on to the current issues in education that require critical thought and informed action.

By recovering what was of value in past philosophizing about education and trying to think our way through some of the present problems facing educators, we will have begun what Dewey liked to call the reconstruction of the philosophy of education.[45] This will not only benefit those educators who need our critical guidance; it should also help us overcome the professionalization of our own discipline. I hope that my study of Dewey, Russell, and Whitehead as educators will contribute to this task of developing a fuller, more productive role for philosophers who share a concern for education.

CHAPTER TWO

John Dewey and the Laboratory School

I went to the Dewey School one day,
And saw the children all at play.
But when the tardy bell had rung,
All the classes had begun.
Some to Science, some to French,
Some to shop to work at the bench.

L.o.t.D.o.E., Dewey, Dewey, Dew-ee-ee.

When Thursday afternoon is here
There are excursions if it's clear
To Stony Island in Highland Park,
And they often stay till nearly dark.
Mister Gillett points here and there,
Showing things both strange and fair.

L.o.t.D.o.E., Dewey, Dewey, Dew-ee-ee.[1]

T HUS THE STUDENTS IMMORTALIZED in song the experimental school run by the Department of Pedagogy of the University of Chicago and headed from 1896 to 1904 by John Dewey. The refrain of the song is shorthand for "Laboratory of the Department of Education." Although the school was officially called the University Elementary School, it became popularly known as the "Dewey School" or, on the suggestion of Ella Flagg Young, the "Laboratory School."[2] Dewey himself often compared the function of this school in his department to that of laboratories in biology, physics, or chemistry. "Like any such laboratory," he said, "it has two main purposes: (1) to exhibit, test, verify, and criticize theoretical statements and principles; (2) to add to the sum of facts and principles in its special line."[3]

Having a school to test educational theories and ideas suited Dewey's pragmatic temper nicely. He thought that "the mere profession of principles without their practical exhibition and testing will not engage the respect of the educational profession" and that without such exhibition and testing, "the theoretical work partakes of the nature of a farce and imposture—it is like professing to give

Spring planting for the younger students at Dewey's Laboratory School. Photograph courtesy of the Lander MacClintock Collection, Special Collections, Morris Library, Southern Illinois University at Carbondale.

"thorough training in a science and then neglecting to provide a laboratory for faculty and students to work in."[4] Rather than separate the theory from the practice, we should bring the two together. This will result in a more viable, realistic set of ideas and principles of education as well as give direction and guidance to our day-to-day educational activities.

Dewey felt strongly that in education as in other areas of thought and action a well-ordered experiment requires that "There must be a continual union of theory and practice; of reaction of one into the other. The leading idea must direct and clarify the work; the work must serve to criticize, to modify, to build up the theory,"[5] In pedagogy especially, Dewey felt that we must escape the dualism between general principles and empirical routine or rule of thumb and instead promote a "vital interaction of theoretical principle and practical detail."[6] How he saw this taking place he spelled out in greater detail in an essay entitled "The Relations of Theory to Practice in Education."[7]

Dewey distinguishes two ways to approach practice in education: from the point of view of the apprentice and that of the laboratory. The apprentice approach would have us seek to give teachers a working command of the tools of their trade, a skill and proficiency in teaching methods, a control of the techniques of class instruction and management. With the laboratory approach, we "use practice work as an instrument in making real and vital theoretical instructions; the knowledge of subject-matter and of principles of education."[8] Here the immediate aim is not to produce efficient workmen but to supply the intellectual methods and materials of good workmanship, just as in other professional schools (architecture, engineering, medicine, law, etc.) where the aim is *"control of the intellectual methods* required for personal and independent mastery of practical skill, rather than at turning out at once masters of the craft."[9]

Dewey always insisted that teaching is a profession, and the training of teachers should follow scientific lines. Too often it had been thought that "anybody—almost everybody—could teach. Everybody was innocent at least until proved guilty."[10] The time had come to pay greater heed to the theory and practice of teaching. Although he favored the establishment of practice schools for teachers, he recognized that most practice schools only approximate ordinary conditions of teaching and learning, usually safeguarding the children's interest and supervising their activities to such an extent that "the situation approaches learning to swim without going too near the water."[11] He criticized normal practice work in education for depriving the practice teacher of responsibility for discipline in the classroom, and for its unrealistic aspects such as the continued presence of an expert teacher, the reduction of class size, and the use of predetermined lesson plans. The very context of such training for teachers militates against an immediate practical application because it fails to connect the theory with experience, even with the very practical experience of life that the apprentice-teacher has had before coming to learn how to teach in the first place.

Another factor often missing in such schemes is a lack of instruction in subject matter. Since there are obviously good teachers who have never had any training in practical pedagogy but show only a mastery of and enthusiasm for their subject matter (one wonders if Dewey had himself in mind here since he reputedly followed very few of the accepted methods for effective teaching[12]), "scholarship per se may itself be a most effective tool for training and turning out good teachers."[13] There is, Dewey points out, method in subject matter, scientific method, the method of the mind itself. True scholars are "so full of the spirit of inquiry, so sensitive to every sign of its presence and absence, that no matter what they do, nor how they do it, they succeed in awakening and inspiring like alert and intense mental activity in those with whom they come in contact."[14]

For Dewey, this applies to teachers at an elementary level of education as well as to those engaged in higher education. What is needed in the training of teachers is more of a continuity of classroom experience with actual conditions of teaching and learning as well as with real life experiences, more emphasis on the subject matter to be taught, more freedom and responsibility for the practice teacher. In a later formulation, Dewey said that the method of teaching is the method of an art. It involves the study of past operations and results that have been successful, thorough acquaintance with current materials and tools, and careful scrutinizing of one's own attempts to see what succeeds and fails.[15] This is what Dewey sought to provide in his Laboratory School.

The school was not meant to be a practice school in the ordinary sense; nor did Dewey see the training of teachers to be the main goal of the Department of Pedagogy. Rather, he saw the school as taking "teachers who have already considerable experience, and who now wish to acquaint themselves more thoroughly with the rational principles of their subject, and with the more recent of educational movements."[16] What he had in mind were former superintendents and normal school teachers. The Laboratory School would serve as a focus to keep the theoretical work in touch with the demands of practice and experimentally to test and develop methods of teaching. Dewey believed there was nothing the primary schools needed more than "the presentation of methods which are the offspring of a sound psychology, and have also been worked out in detail under the crucial tests of experience."[17]

He did not intend his school to "turn out methods and materials which can be slavishly copied elsewhere."[18] It sought to demonstrate certain principles as fundamental in education. It could be seen as having an indirect influence on public education by serving as an example of new experimental lines of thought and thereby preparing the public for the acceptance of similar changes in the system, by training specialists in theory and practice who could begin to make such changes, and by publishing the results of the experiment to make them available to teachers elsewhere.

Dewey undoubtedly saw this as an opportunity to break down the isolation he so often decried in education. Here at Chicago the beginning phases of the educational system (kindergarten and the elementary grades) were to be in vital contact with the highest (university and graduate school), and the more concrete and practical problems were to interact with the more abstract, theoretical speculations to the benefit of both. The traditional dualism between thought and action was thus to be overcome, and working hypotheses in education were to be exhibited and tested to prove their worth. In all this we could say that Dewey himself was attempting to practice what he preached about knowledge in general and about teaching and learning in particular. Students in the Department of Pedagogy were to be instructed in the history and theory of school systems, "the theory of the best attainable organization and administration in our own country under existing conditions," the historical development of ideas concerning education, and the bearings of psychology and sociology upon the curriculum and on teaching methods.[19] "The nerve of the whole scheme," said Dewey in an early statement to President William Rainey Harper of the University of Chicago, is "the conduct of a school of demonstration, observation, and experiment in connection with the theoretical instruction."[20]

Harper evidentally agreed that such a school would be a valuable component in the training of teachers, and Dewey's proposals were approved by the Board of Trustees and an appropriation of $1,000 made to help get the school started. The rest of its income was expected to come from tuition and gifts from parents and friends.[21] The tale of this initial appropriation sheds some light on Dewey's subsequent falling out with Harper over the school. According to his wife, Alice Dewey, "The trustees of the University had felt the need of a laboratory of Psychology, but they were suspicious of a laboratory of Education. It so happened that in October of 1895 a sum of one thousand dollars had been appropriated for a Psychological laboratory. As no room or other facility for utilizing that fund could be provided, it was likely to revert. Influence upon the president at that moment brought him to consent to its use for Education, thus officially sanctioning the Educational phase of the new department."[22] Although it is certainly not unusual for a University administrator to reallocate funds already provided for in his budget, this does not seem to me to indicate the kind of enthusiastic support of the school that some have attributed to Harper.[23]

Even the thousand dollars had strings attached to it, for it was "not in cash, but in tuitions of graduate students who were to teach in the school."[24] As his daughter, Jane Dewey, put it, "The University allowed one thousand dollars in free tuition to teachers in the school, but gave no further financial aid. For the seven and a half years of its existence friends and patrons contributed more to the support of this school than did the University."[25] On top of this, Dewey was required to submit an annual budget to Harper for consideration and approval by the university trustees. Small wonder that Dewey reportedly found the financial relationship between his school and the university "trying and, at times, even vexing."[26] Some of the financial difficulties faced by the school can be gleaned from Dewey's Report to the President for the year July 1898–July 1899. Total expenses were listed as $12,870.26, of which tuition covered $4,916.00. "The University gave seven free scholarship tuitions, aggregating $840.00 in return for service in the school," according to the report, and the rest of the money had to be made up by personal gifts. About $350.00 was realized from a series of lectures given by Dewey to parents, students, and friends of the school and subsequently published as the book *The School and Society*.[27]

The school opened in January 1896, with sixteen pupils, aged six to nine, and with Miss Clara I. Mitchell, formerly of the Cook County Normal School, in charge and Mr. F. W. Smedley, a graduate student of pedagogy, directing the manual training work.[28] In October 1896, the school changed locations and added Miss Katherine Camp, formerly of the Pratt Institute, to teach science and the domestic arts. She later became Mrs. Katherine Camp Mayhew and with her sister, Anna Camp Edwards, a history teacher and special tutor for older children, wrote a thorough and detailed history of the school. After several changes of location and the addition of more staff, the school's enrollment eventually grew to 140 students of from four to fifteen years of age with a teaching staff of twenty-three and ten part-time assistants.[29] Dewey served as director, Mrs. Dewey as principal, and Ella Flagg Young, who was later to become Chicago's first superintendent of schools, as supervisor of instruction.[30]

Each of these women exerted a strong influence on Dewey. Jane Dewey claimed that her father "regards Mrs. Young as the wisest person in school matters with whom he has come in contact in any way, . . . Contact with her supplemented Dewey's educational ideas where his own experience was lacking in matters of practical administration, crystallizing his ideas of democracy in the school and, by extension, in life."[31] His wife was said to be a moving force behind the school. According to Max Eastman, Dewey would never have started a Dewey school had it not been for his wife Alice. "Dewey never did anything, except think . . . unless he got kicked into it . . . Mrs. Dewey would grab Dewey's ideas—and grab him—and insist that something be done. . . . Dewey's view of his wife's influence is that she put 'guts and stuffing' into what had been with him mere intellectual conclusions."[32]

The Deweys had more than an academic interest in the school since by 1902 four of their own children were enrolled.[33] Even before they came to Chicago, Alice was said to be keen on trying out some of John's theories on their children at home. While Dewey was at the University of Michigan, this was said to have led to "many unconventional and unexpected situations which, when created in the presence of outsiders, caused considerable merriment and comment, 'Old Ann Arborites,' according to one report, 'still regale themselves with tales of how the Dewey methods worked.' "[34] However amusing these early attempts might have been to some outside observers, the experimental approach of the Laboratory School was no laughing matter among professional educators. In 1900, A. B. Hinsdale, professor of the Science and the Art of Teaching and a colleague of Dewey's at the University of Michigan, claimed, "More eyes are now fixed upon The University Elementary School at Chicago than upon any other elementary school in the country and probably in the world—eyes watching to see the outcome of the interesting experiment."[35]

Mayhew and Edwards state that the students in the Laboratory School came mainly from professional families.[36] McCaul estimates that most were faculty children from middle- or upper-class backgrounds.[37] The vast majority of parents were strong supporters of the school. At the beginning of the second year a Parents' Association was formed "to assure financial support for the school and to provide information about its radical departures in method and content." For three years "a parents' class was formed, open to all members, in which Mr. Dewey set forth his theories, discussed them, and answered questions regarding the activities of the school.[38] Although Dewey counted on the parents for moral and financial support for his endeavors, not all of them were totally enamoured with what was going on in the school. One father made this caustic comment about his son's experiences there: "One year at the University Preparatory Laboratory, otherwise known as the D—School (supply the proper word, not on Sunday, please!) nearly ruined him. We have to teach him how to study. He learned to 'observe' last year."[39]

Ella Flagg Young maintained that people who came to the school with preconceived notions on how teaching and learning were to be carried out often went home disappointed with what they had seen. Traditional ideas of order and discipline, of the role of the teacher and the place of the student, of how it should be manifest that something had been learned, even of the posture of the child in his or her seat, all these tended to obscure what was actually being accomplished.[40] Laura Runyon has described her first visit to the school as a curious parent who found that her initial scepticism gave way to an enthusiastic endorsement of what was happening.[41] She liked what she saw so much that she became a teacher of history at the school and wrote an M.A. thesis at the University of Chicago on *The Teaching of Elementary History in the Dewey School* (1906, unpublished).

Unfortunately, most of our information about the school and its achievements is of just that sort of personal and impressionistic writing. Harold Rugg bemoans the fact that no systematic and critical appraisal of Dewey's educational experiment was ever made. He points out, "Mayhew and Edwards assembled scattered comments on the success of the School made by visiting educators, parents, and former pupils—'thirty years after.' But these are all pro-Dewey and so far as I can see contribute nothing to the needed critical appraisal of the educational product. Students of educational reconstruction will regret . . . that the Dewey group did not conduct a *systematic and objective inquiry* into the traceable effects of the school's work in the later lives of its graduates."[42]

It is not entirely fair of Rugg to chide the Dewey group for failing to employ methods of social scientific investigation and evaluation which it happened were themselves in a very embryonic stage at the turn of the century. The teachers did manage to write a number of accounts of the ongoing activities of the school and the rationale behind them which were published in the *University* [of Chicago] *Record* from 1896 to 1899. During 1900, Dewey edited nine issues of *The Elementary School Record*, "which dealt exclusively with the practices, content, and rationale of the University School."[43] Typed reports and summaries of 1901 and 1902 were collected and edited by Laura L. Runyon. Alice Dewey had collected a great deal of material pertinent to the school, intending to write its history; but she died in 1927, and the task fell to Katherine Mayhew and her sister Anna Edwards. Dewey collaborated with them and contributed parts of the book, some from previous writings and some new. The most important of the latter eventually became "The Theory of the Chicago Experiment," an appendix to their book. In addition, some of Dewey's writings and talks at the time (for example, those collected in the book, *The School and Society*) make specific reference to the school and its operations.

I would like to consider this material in order to explain the operations of the Laboratory School and, so far as can be gathered, why things were done as they were. My aim is not to pass judgment on the educational products of the school, nor is it primarily to make comparisons with what Dewey tried to do and what is being done in elementary education today. What I hope to find is some link between the practice and the theory, some indication of whether the theoretical principles and the practical details did indeed interact, some indication of the way the leading ideas affected the day-to-day practice and whether or not the ensuing practical results had any impact on the theory. It should be especially interesting to see if a case could be made for Dewey's having changed any of his important educational theories because of what happened when he tried to put them into practice in the Laboratory School. The remainder of this chapter is a summary of the educational practices of the Laboratory School together with an evaluation of how these relate to its underlying theories. A final section considers some recent criticisms of Dewey's educational views in light of what we have seen of their practical exhibition and testing.

DEWEY'S SCHOOL: THE THEORY BEHIND IT

The social and intellectual milieu in which Dewey set up his school was a vibrant one. Chicago was growing rapidly, with a large influx of immigrants and with diametrically opposed levels of great wealth and abject poverty. Dewey was to become directly acquainted with people on both levels. The mood of the city fathers was for progress, which many thought could be purchased, given the right amount of cash. Marshall Field, Cyrus McCormick, Philip Armour,

Gustavus Swift, and George Pullman typified the powerful businessmen of the day who amassed great fortunes and began to think of leaving behind a legacy, something that would carry on their names after they had fought their last financial battle. Many turned to educational projects for this purpose. Thus, Philip Armour founded the Armour Institute of Technology of 1892, giving it a million dollars a year for five years. George Pullman willed a million dollars in 1897 to found a manual-training school for boys. Not to be outdone, Mrs. Emmons Blaine, daughter of Cyrus McCormick, donated a million dollars to support the educational endeavors of Colonel Francis Parker.[44]

Parker was the principal of the Cook County Normal School (later the Chicago Normal School) from 1883 to 1899. He was forced to contend with the educational authorities on behalf of his extremely child-centered approach to elementary education. In 1899, Mrs. Blaine decided to free him from such harassment and offered him a million dollars so he could train teachers and instruct children in full accordance with his theories and ideals.[45] President Harper at the University of Chicago became quite interested in this bequest and persuaded Mrs. Blaine to turn the money over to the university board of trustees for the purpose of erecting a new building on campus and assimilating Parker and his staff into the university's faculty.[46] As we shall see, this would eventually have bad effects upon the status of Dewey's school.

This renewed interest in education in Chicago came at an opportune moment. J. M. Rice had spent five months in 1892 visiting schools across America. Having personally observed more than 1,200 teachers at their work in the schools of thirty-six cities and some twenty institutions for the training of teachers, he deplored the lack of public interest in the education of the young, saying that it smacked of "criminal negligence."[47] Rice was highly critical of the meager training required of public school teachers. Only a small percentage were normal school graduates. Some had attended a normal school or high school for one or more terms, while a very large number were licensed to teach based on their having been educated at a grammar school and perhaps having received a "little extra coaching."[48] Obviously, this did not make for much of a grasp of the subject matter to be taught or for much formal training in the methods of teaching or the principles of pedagogy—the very things Dewey deemed necessary for a properly trained teacher.

Rice was especially critical of the public schools of Chicago, which, he charged, used unscientific, antiquated, and often absurd methods of teaching. They concentrated on "busy work," the students mechanically copying words from the book or on the board. One class had been supplied with only one reading book, which was dutifully read and reread until the end of the term. Some schools ran for only a half day, but with no break for recess. In a typical geography lesson, students read a question from their books and then searched for the answer on the map. Heavy emphasis was placed on learning by rote, usually to no apparent purpose. The only exception he saw was the school run by Parker which stressed the freedom and growth of the child and attempted to "bring the child into close contact with nature in the beautiful park of twenty acres in which the school is situated."[49]

Dewey was familiar with such shortcomings in the schools and frequently argued against resorting to heavy-handed discipline, memorization, or even sugar-coating the material in order to arouse the child's interest. He explained that interest (from *inter-esse*: to be between) involves breaking down the distance between the pupil and the subjects to be studied in order to develop their organic union. Genuine interest implies that one is wholeheartedly involved with what one is doing.[50] Dewey thought that the curriculum was too often thought of as fixed and final, something to be handed down in a ready-made fashion to the student. But the subject matter, which represents the accomplished results of adult experience, cannot be made a substitute for the child's own experience, nor can it be simply imposed or grafted upon it. We must recognize the connection between the reflectively formulated, logical, and more objective human experience of the curriculum and the relatively disjointed, emotional, subjective experiences of the child. A key point of Dewey's is that there is no difference in kind between the child's experience and the forms of study that make up the curriculum.[51] The child and the curriculum are two limits defining a single process. Education is a process of continuous reconstruction of the child's present experience by means of the adult experience represented by "the organized bodies of truth that we call studies."[52] We show proper concern for the child by using the subject matter as the means to develop his or her individual abilities. The subject matter is the working capital which enables the teacher to determine the environment of the child so that he or she may grow to full potential. "It says to the teacher: Such and such are the capacities, the fulfillments in truth and beauty and behavior, open to these children. Now see to it that day by day the conditions are such that *their own activities* move inevitably in this direction, toward such culmination of themselves."[53]

Dewey is not, as is often charged, advocating a strictly child-centered approach to education. He does not downplay the importance of the materials to be studied. They represent our intellectual and cultural heritage, the best that man has accomplished thus far. What he objects to is forgetting that this subject matter stems from human experience of the same kind as that of the child in the classroom. Instead of trying to impose it upon the child or clothe it "with factitious attraction, so that the mind may swallow the repulsive dose unaware,"[54] we should treat it as a means to reconstruct the child's experience and promote his or her growth. Dewey would have us appreciate that the curriculum has a logical and a psychological side to it. It is a more reflective, abstract, logical rendering of experience. It needs to be psychologized, reinstated or restored to the experience from which it has been abstracted, "turned over, translated into the immediate and individual experiencing within which it has its origin and significance."[55] The function of this subject matter for Dewey is "strictly interpretative or mediatory"—it enables the child to reconstruct his or her experience and grow.[56] Education, for Dewey, is growth in and of experience.

In addition, Dewey believes that "all education proceeds by the participation of the individual in the social consciousness of the race."[57] This involves not only coming to understand the reflectively formulated experience conveyed by the subjects of study in school, it also entails living and working and thinking with other human beings at all stages of the individual's development. He wanted his school to be neither child-centered, nor curriculum-centered; it was to be "community centered."[58] This meant that the school should be a living community in which the child was an active participant. As he put it, "Education being a social process, the school is simply that form of community life in which all those agencies are concentrated that will be most effective in bringing the child to share in the inherited resources of the race, and to use his own powers for social ends."[59]

Since the child lives and grows in communities such as the family, the neighborhood, the school, and the state, Dewey stressed continuity of community activity as much as possible. School activities were to connect with home activities so that the child would be interested in pursuing them. They were then to lead, by means of the curriculum, toward habits of doing, thinking, and feeling that would be part of the productive social life of an adult. Our social inheritance was the means to personal growth and to the progress of society for Dewey. One way to pursue such individual and social growth was by introducing the child to the kind of occupations that he or she would be familiar with (and, it is hoped, interested in) from the home. In Dewey's school, therefore, students engaged in cooking, sewing, manual training, pottery making, weaving, and so on. Dewey thought that these activities "represent, as types, fundamental forms of social activities; and that it is possible and desirable that the child's introduction into the more formal subjects of the curriculum be through the medium of these activities."[60] He saw activities such as cooking, carpentry, and sewing as being constructive in themselves "while socially they represent the fundamental activities of the race."[61]

Thus, the visitor to the Laboratory School would not see children sitting in neat rows, quietly reading or reciting according to some set format. Instead, he would find them engaged in activities Dewey felt recapitulated man's past and provided a good introduction to the more formal studies of the traditional curriculum. In weaving, for example, the child can learn of the different types of material and where they came from and how important this was for early mankind geographically as well as economically. Some elementary mathematics and science might also be included while putting the finishing touches on the end product. In describing how this occurred at his school, Dewey somewhat rhapsodically proclaimed that "you can concentrate the history of all mankind into the evolution of the flax, cotton, and wool fibres into clothing."[62] Ordinary household occupations served both a retrospective and a prospective purpose for Dewey. They showed students where man had come from and how he had reached his present level of knowledge skills, while preparing for their own future thinking and activity as adults, which was to be achieved by the more formalized studies of mathematics, history, geography, and science.

At no time did Dewey have in mind a kind of primitive job training for the students. As he himself pointed out, "Coming as the children did mainly from professional families, there was little prospect of any utility of this sort."[63] Nor did he have in mind the kind of "culture-epoch" theory popular at the time. This was a notion, derived from Herbart, that there was a direct parallelism between the development of the child and the historical development of the human race. This parallelism was supposed to guide our selection and arrangement of the materials to be studied in the curriculum so that "the appropriate basis of the content of study at each period of child growth is the culture products (literature especially) of the corresponding period of race development." Dewey said the theory could best be summed up by a line from Goethe: "The youth must always begin anew in the beginning, and as an individual traverse the epochs of the world's culture."[64] Although he admitted that one could trace a general correspondence between the cultural products of each epoch and the stages of development of the child, Dewey himself denied that there was an exact parallel and argued that we should focus our primary attention on the personal growth of the child. He also objected to the emphasis placed by the theory on the products of a given age without much consideration of the "physical conditions which originated those products."[65]

The main thing, in Dewey's eyes, was to have children in school engage in social occupations providing a link with their home lives, have an active participation in the social life of the school, and enjoy a good introduction to the more formal, disciplined, abstract modes of adult thought and activity that would prepare them to be productive workers and responsible citizens when they left school. The underlying factor was experience: the experience the child had before coming to school, the experience in school itself, and the development of dispositions and habits which make up a large part of adult experience. In this way Dewey saw no major problem of creating interest in the subjects to be studied because they were not foreign to the experience of the students. Nor would it be difficult to relate one subject to another or show their relevance to life. As he put it, "Experience has its geographical aspect, its artistic and its literary, its scientific and its historical sides. All studies arise from aspects of the one earth and the one life upon it. . . . Relate the school to life, and all studies are of necessity correlated."[66]

Dewey was insistent that it was the process of learning, rather than the products that were learned, that was most important. He thought that the scientific attitude of mind was particularly worth promoting. This did not come about by offering more science courses or nature-study projects but by encouraging students to follow a certain method of thinking.[67] This was to be more than a merely mechanical skill or an empty formal listing of rules for correct thinking. Teachers were to establish conditions in school that were conducive to critical, problem-solving thinking. Such thinking, according to Dewey, passed through five logically distinct steps: "(i) a felt difficulty; (ii) its location and definition; (iii) suggestion of possible solution; (iv) development by reasoning of the bearings of the suggestion; and (v) further observation and experiment leading to its acceptance or rejection."[68] This was the kind of experimentalist or instrumentalist approach to thinking that Dewey was to elaborate on in his later works, and in regard to education most notably in *Democracy and Education* published in 1916.[69] He saw these steps as characterizing reflective experience in general and scientific thinking in particular, and he never ceased to urge that the learning environment be such that genuine problems could arise in the course of the student's own activity and that the student would be expected to come to grips with them and to formulate at least tentative answers.

Dewey's concern for the process of education, for the continuity of experience between home and school, child and adult, for the social dimension of education and the connection of living and learning, and for the importance of scientific problem solving can all be seen as part of his underlying faith in democracy and education. The best environment for the type of participatory activity and problem-solving thinking that he envisaged was one of free discussion and shared possibility. On the other hand, the surest guarantee for such freedom was the very sort of open exchange of ideas and respect for evidence that characterized what he called the scientific attitude. Rather than simply equating democracy with freedom of action, Dewey would have us see its link with freedom of thought. Thus, it is not surprising that he sees a close relationship between democracy and education.

This he extended to the need to preserve democracy *in* education. If we are indeed to recognize and protect the "spiritual basis of democracy, the efficacy and responsibility of freed intelligence,"[70] we must see to it that teachers are given their proper say in the selection of materials for the curriculum, the methods of teaching used, questions of discipline, and so on. It will not do to farm these tasks out to pedagogical experts. How can we justify our belief in the democratic principle if we refuse to put it into practice in our schools? This applies to the role of the students as well. We cannot claim to respect their freedom of intelligence when we seek to impose ready-made subject matter upon them from without. All too often, says Dewey, we let acquiring take the place of inquiring in school; that is to say, we encourage passive and obedient reception of cut-and-dried materials. What we need to do is to allow for the actual problem-solving thinking of the child, to provide materials and situations that will bring about such thinking. We need to make the school "a place for getting and testing experience, as real and adequate to the child upon his existing level as all the resources of laboratory and library afford to the scientific man upon his level."[71]

This is not easily accomplished in a traditional classroom setting. As he was to put it later in *Democracy and Education*: "The physical equipment and arrangements of the average schoolroom are hostile to the existence of real situations of experience. . . . Almost everything testifies to the great premium put upon listening, reading, and the reproduction of what is told and read. . . . There must be more actual material, more *stuff*, more appliances, and more opportunities for doing things, before the gap can be overcome."[72] Dewey describes the difficulty he had in buying the right kinds of desks and chairs for his school. Finally, he says, one dealer, more perceptive than the rest, told him, "I am afraid we have not what you want. You want something at which the children may work: these are all for listening."[73] He also sought to make the school a community in which teachers and students, not ignoring the very real differences in their training, abilities, and temperament, are mutually engaged in inquiring rather than acquiring, in directly experiencing rather than docilely memorizing bits and pieces of second-hand experience and are conscious of and dedicated to the ethical princple upon which democracy rests: "the responsibility and freedom of mind in discovery and proof."[74] This commitment to democracy animated all of Dewey's views on education. Many years later he was to restate it as follows: "Democracy is faith that the process of experience is more important than any special result attained. . . . Since the process of experience is capable of being educative, faith in democracy is all one with faith in experience and education."[75] Let us now turn to the actual operation of his Laboratory School to see whether or not this faith was justified.

DEWEY'S SCHOOL: THE ACTUAL PRACTICE

The children in the school were divided into eleven groups according to age. From the very start, the social aspects of learning were emphasized. The youngest children (ages four and five) were encouraged to talk about their own home life and the various persons helping in the occupations of the household. They discussed the family's dependence upon the daily visit of the milkman, grocer, iceman, postman, and the occasional visits of the coalman and others. They helped to prepare, serve, and clean up after their midmorning luncheon, an activity which was said to afford many opportunities for self-management and initiative.[76]

The six-year-olds spent the first fifteen minutes of the day in group conversation. They took excursions, played floor games, built a farm house and barn out of blocks, and then cleared a small plot of land outdoors to plant their winter wheat. They planted cotton seeds in pots, ginned and baled the cotton, built a train of cars to transport it to market, and then put on a play summarizing the whole process.[77] The seven-year-olds began to study primitive life and did experimental work with the materials that primitive people would use. They tried to work out cave life, with its weapons, utensils, and clothing, in a tangible form, while also reading Stanley Waterloo's *Story of Ab*. They came to some understanding of the use of textiles and the discovery of metals. Museums and books were used as sources. According to Mayhew and Edwards, "This natural setting of man and his occupations, the basis of their future, was clothed with human significance to these little actors of primitive life as they imaginatively wandered in the sand-box hills and valleys of their tribal habitation. In the process, many scientific facts of geology, of chemistry, of physics, or of biology, found their way into the sinews of their intellectual wings."[78]

The eight-year-olds centered their occupational work around the trading and maritime activities of the Phoenicians. This made them directly aware of the need for a system of weights and measurements, as well as the necessity for a more accurate method of written record. One year they made a large map and another year a rough version of a boat. Science was taken up "as involved in the study of cooking, or of history, and not as a subject by itself."[79] They studied the travels of Marco Polo, Prince Henry, and Magellan and kept their own "Journal" of these trips. They studied the life and voyages of Columbus and began to read *Robinson Crusoe*. All of this was in accord with Dewey's desire to avoid what he called "The Primary Education Fetich," which consisted of starting too soon with the teaching of reading and writing. Dewey, not unlike Rousseau before him, would have us hold off until the child has the interest and experience to want to learn to read and write. We must avoid the premature use of the child's analytic and abstract powers. We must start first with activities that engage the child's positive and creative impulses "and direct them in such ways as to discipline them into the habits of thought and action required for effective participation in community life."[80] Language study is needed to provide discipline, organization, and the effective means of communication. It can best be taught when the child has an awareness of this need and seeks for itself such discipline. The child will make the effort to learn to read and write when he or she sees some point in doing so.

The nine-year-olds were divided into two sections and "In order to secure more time for practice in reading and writing, the school day was lengthened an hour in the afternoon."[81] They studied local history and geography, with many visits to local museums and historic spots. They learned about early French exploration and one year built a model of Fort Dearborn. Field trips were frequent, says Ida DePencier in her history of the Laboratory School, "to the quarry on Stony Island where glacial markings were observed, to the cotton mills in Aurora to see the spinning of cotton, and others to Ravinia to see the clay bluffs, to Miller Station to see the sand dunes and desert, and to Sixty-third Street and the city limits to see a typical prairie area."[82]

The children were said to be anxious to attain greater facility in writing and number work in order to carry on their projects to a desired conclusion.[83] Some German and French was introduced. The children were even more involved in the general social activities of the school, helping out with the printing of school materials, the running of assemblies, and indoor and outdoor games. The ten-year-olds studied colonial history and built a colonial room. Here the teachers observed one of the first instances where the children themselves decided on a division of labor by gender: The boys built the furniture for the room and the girls made the fabrics. Heretofore boys and girls had participated in the same activities together.[84] There was much collateral reading on the American colonies, and a relief map was made of the campaigns of the American Revolution. The origin of flax was studied, and its spinning and dyeing were demonstrated to the class by a German woman.[85] Whenever possible the school made use of immigrant workers in Chicago for firsthand information on such occupations.[86] The physiology of digestion was discussed, with some experimental work being done with foods in the cooking laboratory. Many excursions were made to Jackson Park to gather specimens of plant and animal life. Mayhew and Edwards make the claim, "With proper laboratory facilities and proper organization of subject-matter into topics, a group of ten-year-olds, that are shielded from distraction and waste of energy, can make much progress in many directions."[87]

The eleven-year-olds looked at the European background of the colonists. The students were divided into two sections on the basis of previous school experience. One section studied the lives of great men of the period, the other English village life. There was more drill in writing and spelling. Electricity was studied and the working of simple machines. "An account of Faraday's experiment with an iron core and a coil was the starting-point for their construction of a dynamo-motor." As preparation for a visit to the technological displays of the Armour Institute, they reviewed the things they would want to see; there were, in their preferred order: "a motor, a dynamo, a galvanometer (which they called a tester), a storage battery, and an apparatus for telegraphy."[88] The students made a pair of scales. They dissected the heart and lungs of a sheep and examined the circulatory, respiratory, and digestive system of a frog. They worked out the school tax bill and studied taxes in general. More teamwork was stressed in physical education, and with help from the university coach considerable proficiency was developed in basketball.

The twelve-year-olds' activities took on the nature of occupations. They saw more and more clearly their need for certain skills to achieve desired results. Since the child himself saw this need, "his need for skill thus became sufficient to engage himself in its acquisition; he had an impelling motive from within for analysis and mastering rules."[89] They were led to appreciate the importance of a scientific attitude of mind. Throughout their study of changing civilization, it had been brought continually to their attention that "it was always science and scientific method that had broken down physical barriers, conquered disease, and eliminated evils once thought insurmountable."[90] Science was seen as a means to the control of nature and to the perpetuation of social progress. Some of the boys in this and the older groups "were irked by the historical approach to their school subjects and seemed to require a shift in method." In one of their rare admissions of failure, Mayhew and Edwards state, "These boys were finally taken out of the class and allowed to follow their own diverse and individual lines until the general trend of their interest could be determined." Most of them eventually ended up working in the shop.[91]

The thirteen-year-olds, most of whom had been in the school since its beginnings, reviewed U.S. history. "A large number of books were listed and each child was urged to seek out his own sources and to get the help of parents and friends in writing up his topics."[92] They studied photography (the use of the camera, its parts) and made visits to university laboratories to see perfected instruments. This led to the formation of a Camera Club and the subsequent need for darkroom facilities; another club, the so-called Dewey Club for discussion and debating, was also looking for a meeting place. So it was decided that the students would build their own club house. Although Mayhew and

Edwards bemoan the fact that "Lack of a library, lack of quiet, lack of beauty, lack of adequate space for club meetings all made it impossible to carry out many individual and group plans,"[93] they do admit that the project of building the club house drew the whole school into an exciting cooperative effort which turned out to be one of its most memorable accomplishments.

The final group of students were of ages fourteen and fifteen. The oldest were given special tutoring and review courses in preparation for their college board examinations. One visitor to the school says he was initially quite disturbed "when I learned that three or four of the older pupils, whom I saw over in one corner, were being drilled up for college examinations in the old way, the regular work of the school having failed to prepare them to pass such tests. As I considered the matter on my way home, I satisfied myself that the fault lay with the type of examination, rather than with the kind of training which these children had received."[94] Wherever the fault lay, this group of students seemed more difficult for the school to deal with. They were allowed to choose ther own shop work, and "the results were unsatisfactory." Their writing style was clear and fluent but loose and inaccurate in sentence structure. It was thought that their skill in artistic expression should keep pace with their intellectual concepts, but "this was an ideal difficult to attain and more often than not failed of achievement."[95] The pressure of college preparatory examinations made it necessary to drop from the program for the older children a planned course in the techniques of cooking. Despite these shortcomings, Ella Flagg Young noted that they all did well in their later schooling. She said, "It may be well for those who incline to the opinion that philosophy is attractive in theory, but not possible in practice, to know that the valuation put by the high school on the preparation of this class was high."[96]

Throughout the school year, the teachers held weekly meetings to review, discuss, and improve upon the past week's work. They also had almost daily contact at lunch or after school. The teachers came from different backgrounds, but they usually had a college education or training in a technical school such as Pratt, the Drexel Institute, or the Armour Institute of Technology. Most of the teachers were said to be strongly supportive of the school and of what it was trying to accomplish. Over the course of time, the weekly meetings became more structured and more formal, with Dewey himself and later Mrs. Young and Mrs. Dewey present.[97]

Dewey maintained an active interest and involvement in the activities of the school, which he visited almost daily.[98] When it became apparent that a new building would be made available through the generosity of Mrs. Blaine, he sent her a detailed, two-page handwritten letter setting forth his view on the location of rooms, kitchen facilities, work equipment, space for reading and writing in the library, the need for an assembly room, and so on.[99] As mentioned previously, Dewey often gave lectures to parents and friends of the school.

A close relationship was maintained with the University of Chicago. The children made use of many of its facilities, and Dewey enlisted the help of a number of faculty members from outside his department. Robert McCaul notes that there was a substantial core of professors at the university sympathetic to what Dewey was trying to accomplish. "Excluding Dewey and members of the Department of Pedagogy, there were thirty-seven full professors in the arts, literature, and science departments in 1896–7. Of these sixteen had had previous experience as teachers or administrators in subcollegiate schools."[100] Dewey could count on men such as Chamberlin (geology) and Starr (anthropology) for support. Others, for example Small and Vincent in sociology, Coulter in botany, and Hale in Latin, gave occasional lectures to the children, offered teacher education courses in their departments, and showed an active interest in pedagogical theory.[101] Their cooperation and creative help seemed to justify Dewey's criticism of the amount of waste in our educational system owing to the isolation of its component parts. For all his battles over finances, Dewey would have heartily endorsed the view of Mayhew and Edwards that the close relationship of the school to the university "was of incalculable help and importance in maintaining the stability and reality of the experiment."[102]

Despite some notable successes and achievements,[103] outside events began to overtake the noble experiment. Harper succeeded in winning Mrs. Blaine's million-dollar donation to the University of Chicago, and with it came Colonel Parker, his school, and its staff. Dewey and his supporters resisted the amalgamation of the two schools, so Chicago for a time had two University Elementary schools, one heavily endowed and the other struggling to pay its bills. This caused inevitable confusion and not a little bickering, much of it between Dewey and Wilbur Jackman, Parker's aide. Parker died in 1902, and Dewey was made director of the School of Education and the two elementary schools were consolidated under his direction. The administrative task facing Dewey seemed awesome. "His previous administrative experience had been confined to a department of philosophy with seven faculty members, a department of education with four, and a Laboratory School staffed by a coterie of fifteen devoted females and one devoted male. Now he was in command of some one hundred persons and a budget of several hundred thousand dollars a year.[104] Small wonder that he wrote to Mrs. Blaine in August 1902 that although his relations with the staff of the School of Education had thus far been amicable and he sincerely hoped they would continue to be so, "the administrative work is not just in my line."[105]

Things came to a head when Mrs. Dewey was made principal of the newly formed University Elementary School for the year 1903–4. This did not set well with the Parker staff who feared they would lose their identity, if not their jobs, in such a family affair as the Dewey School was becoming. Harper as usual tried to please all parties concerned by interpreting Mrs. Dewey's appointment as being for a one-year period only. She evidently did not think of it this way; when he informed her of this in an interview of March 1904, she was furious and resigned: "Because your attitude toward my position on the Faculty of the School of Education places my work on a personal rather than on an educational basis."[106]

Dewey's reaction was equally swift. He wrote in a letter of resignation to Harper on 6 April that "since the administrative side of the work which I undertook in assuming the Directorship of the School of Education has now been accomplished, and since the conditions as you outline them are not favorable to development upon the educational side," he could no longer continue as director of the School of Education. On 11 April, he also resigned as professor and head of the Department of Philosophy, though he politely thanked Harper for his past support. Such politeness went by the board when Dewey heard that Harper was telling people he had resigned because his wife was not to be allowed to stay on as principal. This was not so, he protested, perhaps a bit too strongly. In a letter of 10 May to Harper he asked that it be made clear to the board that "the question of the alleged failure to reappoint Mrs. Dewey as Principal of the Elementary School is in no sense the cause of my resignation, and that this question had never been discussed between us till after our resignations were in your hands. Your willingness to embarrass and hamper my work as Director by making use of the fact that Mrs. Dewey was Principal is but one incident in the history of years."[107]

"With the resignation of Mr. Dewey and the subsequent dispersal of all save three or four of the faculty of the Laboratory School," says Mayhew and Edwards, "this experiment in education ended."[108] Not, we might add, with a whimper but with a bang. Some say Dewey left with a sense of failure and never again tried to engage in this kind of practical experimentation in the schools.[109] His defenders, such as Mayhew and Edwards, maintain that the experiment worked and that Dewey's basic approach to education was vindicated. In the remaining part of this chapter, I evaluate the experiment and in particular try to trace out the interaction between the theory and the practice. I consider what Dewey thought of it after the fact as well as some recent criticisms that have been made of both the practice and the theory behind it, and conclude with some remarks on what I see as the proper relationship between theory and practice.

DEWEY'S REACTIONS TO THE SCHOOL

From his comments written for the Mayhew and Edwards book, we can see that Dewey was aware of certain problems with the school and the approach it took. Since the principles upon which the school was founded were taken to be "working hypotheses," he had felt that their application, development, and modification should be left largely in the hands of the teachers. After the fact, Dewey speculated that perhaps too much responsibility was imposed upon the teachers. "In avoiding hard and fast plans to be executed and dictation of methods to be followed, individual teachers were, if anything, not given enough assistance either in advice or by way of critical supervision. There might well have been conditions fairer to teachers and more favorable to the success of the experiment."[110]

This is a surprising comment for him to make, given the frequency of teachers' meetings, discussions, and written reports and the active involvement of Dewey himself with the teachers. What happened, says Dewey, was that the discussions tended to revolve around the peculiarities and difficulties of individual children, and the underlying principles "were too much taken for granted as being already understood by all teachers; in the later years an increasing number of meetings were allotted to the specific discussion of underlying principles and aims."[111] Even then one wonders how open and wide-ranging such discussions could be for a young teacher facing the impressive triumvirate of John and Alice Dewey and Ella Flagg Young.[112] One problem with having a coterie of devoted followers is that there is less likelihood of frank assessment of pet theories.

Because they were working comparatively unbroken ground, Dewey realized that much trial-and-error experimentation was required in order to bring the needs and interests of the child into view as well as to determine the desirable components of the curriculum. He admitted that "the school was overweighted, especially in its earlier years, on the 'individualistic' side in consequence of the fact that in order to get data upon which we could act, it was necessary to give too much liberty of action rather than to impose too much restriction."[113] The ideas and policy of the school were modified in light of such experimentation in regard to two points:

(1) The children were originally intended to be mixed together, older and younger, so "the younger children might learn unconsciously from the older." The increase in enrollment made this unfeasible, and the children were grouped, as we have seen, primarily according to age.

(2) The original assumption was that "an all-round teacher would be the best, and perhaps it would be advisable to have one teacher teach the children in

several branches." This was abandoned in favor of having different teachers specialize in different subjects.[114]

No grades were assigned, although there was indication that "some of the children desired external marks as proof of their own development." The ever-present need to prepare the older children for their college entrance examinations often intruded into other school activities for that group. Yet even with them, "Written or oral review on completion of the work to be done took the place of examination."[115]

Without a doubt the biggest problem the school faced, from Dewey's point of view, was the financial one. In one of his reports on the school in *The Elementary School Record*, Dewey reviews the work of the past five years and states that "practically it has not as yet been possible, in many cases, to act adequately upon the best ideas obtained, because of administrative difficulties, due to lack of funds—difficulties centering in the lack of a proper building and appliances, and in inability to pay the amounts necessary to secure the complete times of teachers in some important lines."[116] While we can sympathize with him about meager finances, we should not forget that when the Blaine money became available and Dewey was put in charge of the newly consolidated University Elementary School, things got worse instead of better. While generally praising Dewey's handling of the staff in his school, Arthur Wirth acknowledges that "Dewey was not the perfect administrator. He was far from blameless in the wrangles with Colonel Parker's staff, particularly with Wilbur Jackman."[117]

Even sharper criticisms have been made of Alice Dewey. She was said to be extremely critical of some of the staff of the Parker school and quick to dismiss teachers from her own faculty.[118] Max Eastman, a friend of the family, said that as an administrator she had "the faults of her virtues. She was not a good mixer. She had an uncanny gift of seeing through people who were faking, and made such witty game of them that she alarmed even those who were not faking. . . . And she had a kind of inside-out timidity, a fear of being presumptuous, that because of her obvious superiority looked sometimes like snooty coldness."[119] Here too Dewey may well have erred as an administrator by putting his wife in such an influential position in his own school. It certainly would make it more difficult to bring about radical changes in policy or guiding principles.

A more fundamental criticism that has been made is that the school itself was too much of a special situation to be much of a test of Dewey's ideas. The students were mainly from middle- and upper-class families. Their parents were highly interested in and supportive of the school. The teachers were better trained and more committed to the enterprise than one would normally find. Classes were small,[120] and the vast resources of the University of Chicago were close at hand. No doubt, as McCaul suggests, with a more heterogeneous school population Dewey would have been forced to adapt his theory and approach more to the capacities, interests, and goals of the average child, and as a result he might have achieved "some sort of educational synthesis of theory and practice, of scientific inquiry and direct experience, and of the ideal as prevailing in his school and the actual as existing in the typical schools in which his students would later teach."[121]

Henry Perkinson makes an even more pointed comment about the idealistic nature of the Dewey experiment: "Dewey's educational philosophy depicts a school or school enterprise that never existed and probably never could exist. To carry it out would require superteachers and superstudents." The teachers in his ideal school are expected to have "a thorough understanding of his philosophy plus a knowledge of the subject matter, including its history, its logical structure, and its connection with other subject matters, plus a sociological-psychological understanding of the child and his development." The students, for their part, were learning to be dedicated scientists, "indefatigable in the pursuit of inquiry into the problems of men. . . ."[122] Perkinson doubted whether the entire nation could produce enough such teachers and students to fill a single classroom.

As we have seen, Dewey had not claimed to be setting up a model school of practice turning out materials and methods to be slavishly copied elsewhere. Even Professor Hinsdale, who is often quoted as saying the eyes of the country were on Dewey's experimental school, went on to say that, of course, "No man of sense expects to see the children of the people generally taught in schools like the one that Professor Dewey has set up, but there are many who are hoping that this school may contribute something of value to the progress of elementary education."[123] Dewey realized that in many respects, though hardly in its financial setup, his school operated in nearly optimal conditions. He even admitted, "Like every human enterprise the Laboratory School came far short of achieving its ideal and putting its controlling ideas into practice."[124] Some years after he had severed his connections with Chicago, he dealt with the question of why educational ideals so often fail to be put into practice, speculating that perhaps it is because "the research persons connected with school systems may be too close to the practical problems and the university professor too far away from them, to secure the best results."[125] In his own case he might have added more candidly that the theoretician is not necessarily the best person to enact practical policies. As Plato says, few of us are capable of being philosopher-kings.

Another thing Dewey might have said in his own defense was that the ideals he set for the school were high ones and therefore were going to be difficult to attain under any circumstances. For example, when Mayhew and Edwards claimed that one of the school's goals was to see to it that "the music, the literary and dramatic efforts of the children, and their artistic expression . . . all should represent the culmination, the idealization, the highest point of refinement of all the work carried on," Dewey replied that "the school can justly be said to have failed more often at this point than at any other. This failure, however may be taken as evidence that the difficulty of achievement in this direction is proportionate to its importance."[126] Taking this line of thought, Dewey could defend his "working hypotheses" that the child's experience can be made continuous with that represented by the studies in the curriculum, that the child should be an active member of a democratic, social community in the school, and that the model for all thinking is the scientific, problem-solving method of science; all these he might say are worthwhile objectives, no matter how difficult—or expensive—they may be to reach. Some recent critics of Dewey would challenge these very hypotheses and claim the theory was wrong even before he tried to put it into practice. Let us turn to them now.

SOME RECENT CRITICISMS OF DEWEY'S EDUCATIONAL THEORY

Many contemporary philosophers of education, particularly in Great Britain, have moved away from Dewey's key notion of the unity of knowlege and experience, and from his primary concern with the interests and growth of the child toward an analysis of the component parts of an ideal curriculum and the logical characteristics of the subjects to be studied. Paul Hirst, for example, argues for a return to the Greek ideal of a liberal education based on the nature of knowledge itself.[127] For Hirst, this entails initiating the young into the forms of knowledge. These are "the complex ways of understanding experience which man has achieved, which are publicly specifiable and which are gained through learning."[128] They include mathematics, physical sciences, human sciences, history, religion, literature and fine arts, and philosophy. Each form has its own distinct set of concepts, logical structure, statements and expressions, and ways of testing these against experience. It is by means of the forms of knowledge that experience has become intelligible to man. As educators we want our students to be able to deal with experience in terms of these forms (i.e., to think mathematically or scientifically) and to recognize that they are mutually irreducible (e.g., to do mathematics is not the same kind of activity as doing science), though interdependent (e.g., to do physics requires a knowledge of mathematics). The proper way to learn a form of knowledge is to study its paradigms from someone who has already mastered it.

John White uses Hirst's analysis of the forms of knowledge to construct an argument for a compulsory curriculum.[129] For White, our aim in education is to equip our students to make autonomous choices. This requires that they be made aware of all the possible activities they might choose to engage in for their own sake. But some activities, most notably those of mathematics, science, and philosophy, cannot be understood unless one has engaged in them. That is to say, nothing in a child's prior experience is a sufficient basis for understanding curricular activities of this sort, so we are justified in compelling students to study such subjects in order to be properly equipped to make those autonomous choices. Some external imposition is unavoidable in school because of the very nature of the subject matter, such interference in the child's liberty being justifiable as being in his or her own best interests.

Because of their views of the nature of knowledge, White and Hirst would doubtless agree with Frederick Olafson in his criticism of Dewey's notion of learning as reconstruction of experience. Olafson asserts that education has to do with a process of "internalizing the distinctive procedures of a preexistent discipline . . . , rather than in terms of discovery and reconstruciton."[130] There is a sudden and precipitate jump from the familiar world of common sense to the domain of abstract thought. For Olafson, "the process of mastering, of internalizing a preexistent idiom of thought is very different in respect of the kind of communication and sociality it entails from the form of experience that precedes such a process."[131]

He also charges Dewey with having misconstrued science as a kind of cooperative consensual activity on a par with democratic decision making. This view of science fails to take account of the fact that there are accepted canons of scientific procedure and a special symbolic code and that the processes of scientific inquiry involve a movement to conceptual levels other than those of common sense.[132] Kathryn Morgan echoes this sentiment by charging it is absurd to claim that children have a natural bent for scientific investigation, since they lack most of the features necessary for scientific orientation toward the world, features such as the "detachment of the object from the self . . . ; a capacity for engaging in sustained disinterested speculation; and the systematic naturalization of and deanthropomorphizing of object predicates."[133]

Has Dewey overstated the continuity of experience? Does he illegitimately resolve the dualism between the child and the curriculum by romantically idealizing the capacities of the former while defining away the distinguishing characteristics of the latter? Richard Peters warns us not to forget that the children who come to us to be educated start off as barbarians outside the gates. "The problem is to get them inside the citadel of civilisation so that they will understand and love what they see when they get there."[134] It will not do to ignore, as Dewey does, whole dimensions of the human condition: man's irrationality, his emotional sensitivities and susceptibilities, his life and death predicaments as well as his problems.[135]

Richard Hofstadter calls Dewey's approach to education "anti-intellectual." He claims that Dewey adopts a romantic, primitivist conception of the child, that his notion of growth is nothing but a mischievous metaphor designed to gloss over the need for an externally imposed, adult vision of the good society, that his method of overcoming dualisms is utopian, and his idea that all learning has to be overtly shared in social action is highly questionable. Dewey has placed the child so firmly at the center of things that questions about the content of what is to be taught and the structure of the curriculum are subsumed under those of method and motivation. But, according to Hofstadter, "the moment one admits that it is not all of life which is presented to children in school, one also admits that a selective process has been set up which is determined by some external end; and then one has once again embraced the traditional view that education is after all not a comprehensive attempt to mirror or reproduce life but a segment of life that is specialized for a distinct function."[136]

Dewey would not deny that the school is a special environment. He called it a simplified, purified, broadening kind of environment.[137] Simpler than our complex civilization and our numerous social relationships, in school we select features of life and thought that are "fairly fundamental and capable of being responded to by the young" and proceed toward those that are more complicated. This occurs in what Dewey calls a "purified medium of action" in which we have weeded out what is antisocial, immoral, or downright perverse. School seeks to reinforce the power of the best. Finally, by bringing children into contact with a larger, more diverse social group, school aims to create a new and broader environment in which to grow.

This was not meant simply to mirror or reproduce life; Dewey's term is "reconstruction." We help the child develop from relatively crude and narrow experience into the more critically refined, socially responsible experience of the adult. The way to accomplish this is not to center all our attention on the child[138] any more than it is to be so enamored of the logical features of the curriculum that we fail to appreciate the need to "psychologize" the material so it can be learned by the child. Dewey sought to strike a balance between both factors in the educative process. He set up a school in which the attempt was made for the child to interact with the curriculum in a new and creative way. To those who chide him for neglecting what was to be learned, I would throw back his own challenge of how *they* proposed to teach it. In real life one seldom has the luxury of settling all philosophical differences before commencing to educate. Dewey at least attempted to practice what he preached.

But did the practice have any lasting effect upon his theory of education? We have seen how the leading ideas were meant to direct and clarify the work; but in what important ways did the actual work serve to "criticize, modify, and build up the theory"? In a recent review of Dewey's writings from 1899 to 1909, J. O. C. Phillips remarks that for all Dewey's talk about the value of the scientific method, he himself was never really an exponent of it. He did not dirty his own hands with experiments in psychology laboratories, and his school "functioned far more as a public demonstration of his views than as a genuinely experimental laboratory." Even his writing does not appear to us now as very scientific. "The research seems thin, the factual evidence impressionistic. Statistics are rare; most of the conclusions are based on deduction."[139]

A similar appraisal was given by Lawrence Cremin in the course of a generally favorable review of Dewey and his school: "Actually, there were few dramatic changes in Dewey's pedagogical theory as a result of the Laboratory School. Rather, he was able to state his initial hypotheses with ever greater confidence and specificity."[140] According to Joe R. Burnett, the lack of direct influence of Dewey's educational practices upon his theory is not so surprising in light of the fact that by 1900 he was already moving away from a direct concern with practical pedagogy and becoming a philosopher of culture. "Within four years," says Burnett, "he stopped discussing matters of practical pedagogy at any length. Even *Democracy and Education* . . . is a work of social, political, and educational philosophy rather than of practical pedagogy."[141]

This is not to say that none of Dewey's ideas were vindicated by the school. His belief that teaching should be a profession and teachers trained in their subject matter, the latest teaching methods, child psychology, and the history of education, as well as be given the opportunity to practice in a real school situation, seems to be almost taken for granted today. We should not forget how radical some of these ideas appeared to be at the turn of the century. I think his experience with the school also supports his point about the amount of waste in our educational system caused by the isolation of its parts. He showed how much the elementary level of education could gain by interacting with the university level. It might be added that universities would likewise benefit from this exposure to the practical problems of educating children.

Finally, whatever the shortcomings of his notion of the role of social occupations in the curriculum, Dewey did establish the point that children will learn more readily if we can overcome the distance between them and the subject matter. This should involve making them aware of the origins of much curricular material in the lives and experiences of human beings. The approach to the school as a kind of community in which teachers and students are active participants is another way to overcome an unproductive conflict between the child and the curriculum. Democracy itself he saw as a working hypothesis to be tested in our educational activities. He wanted it not simply to be studied but to be lived.

SOME CONCLUDING REMARKS ON THEORY
AND PRACTICE IN EDUCATION

Some conceptual problems remain with theory and practice in education. Do they refer to distinct domains of thought and action? Is there a dualism here that cannot be overcome? Or is the problem that they do not normally interact in the same person? Perhaps we all suffer from a kind of split between what we say and what we do. Is this because of some ingrown tendency in ourselves or is it part of the very nature of things?

Perhaps there is something about education that promotes a division between theory and practice. We tend to espouse very high educational ideals. Education is an act of faith and hope, as well as love: faith in the future of the human race, hope that the young will carry on what we have accomplished and go beyond us, love in the sense of an active concern for their growth and a willingness to sacrifice for their welfare. It has been said that what we want in education is what all good parents want for their own children. If so, then it is not altogether surprising that our aspirations often exceed our accomplishments. Failure to achieve our educational ideals in practice usually serves to prod us to try harder rather than to modify or abandon the ideals altogether.

Another problem has to do with the evaluation of practice. How is it to be evaluated, by whom, and when? There are long-term as well as short-term results in education. Which are we to judge and and in what fashion? Not even the great advances by the social sciences since the days of Dewey's school have completely resolved the old issues of the relative importance of nature and nurture in the upbringing of a child, what methods are most effective for teaching various individuals or a class full of them, what content is most worthwhile from the point of view of society and from the individual student's own point of view. Is it obvious that massive increases in equipment and personnel will improve the quality of education? Do we seek to produce happy individuals or good citizens? What things do the young need to learn and how can they best be taught?

Clearly, Dewey's experiment in education has not answered such questions. If anything it has added to our perplexities. This can be seen in a positive light as a stimulus to the kind of thinking about the problems involved in educating the young that Dewey felt was so crucial. In Dewey's eyes this is an ongoing inquiry where the answers are tentative at best. Whatever theoretical conclusions we might reach, we must also take account of their practical consequences. The most lasting lesson from his experiment may well be that if we are to make progress in education, the duality between theory and practice is one that must be overcome.

CHAPTER THREE

Bertrand Russell and the Beacon Hill School

Children go to school with the belief that they have a right to be happy, that God will give them a good time. This is the perversion of true religion, self-denial and obedience.[1]

Rumors were rife of godless orgies. When a pastor visited Beacon Hill, a naked teenage girl was supposed to have answered the door. "Good God," gasped the astonished cleric. "There is no God," she replied, slamming the door in his face.[2]

THESE TWO QUOTATIONS EPITOMIZE the social and cultural atomsphere in which Bertrand Russell and his second wife, Dora, set up their school in 1927. The Russells had two young children, John and Kate, and were quite concerned they receive a proper education. State schools would not do, for they had "the vices characteristic of the modern world: nationalism, glorification of competition and success, worship of mechanism, love of uniformity and contempt for individuality." Church schools were no better, since they aimed at "producing submission to authority, belief in nonsense through the hypnotic effect of early and frequent repetition, respect for superior individuals rather than for the spirit of the herd."[3]

The Russells briefly considered sending their children to one of the new, experimental schools then being established. They took John and Kate to spend half a day at the Margaret McMillan open-air nursery school "while we talked with her and studied her ideas in action." They considered the very latest educational methods and materials. Although they saw much they approved of, they were not altogether satisfied with what they found. They disliked what they took to be the rigidity of the Montessori approach to the teaching of number, reading, and writing.[4] "All of us found the Montessori apparatus too restrictive of the children's imagination," says Dora.[5] They thought that the experimental school run by Geoffrey Pyke and Susan Isaacs at the Malting House School went too far in allowing children "very great freedom, in order to see what they would do and what they would find out for themselves."[6] They agreed with A.

Russell on the grounds of Beacon Hill School with his own two children and other pupils.
Associated Press photograph.

S. Neill that a psychological approach to the education of small children was
needed, although Neill himself recognized that he placed more emphasis on
handwork in his school, while the Russells seemed more interested in thought
and ideas. Russell later wrote to H. G. Wells that "hardly any other [i.e. besides
himself] educational reformers lay much stress upon intelligence. A. S. Neill,
for example, who is in many ways an admirable man, allows such complete
liberty that his children fail to get the necessary training and are always going to
the cinema, when they might otherwise be interested in things of more value."[7]

The Russells also read widely in educational psychology. Dora said they
knew about "Freud, Adler, Piaget, Pestalozzi, Froebel, Montessori, and Margaret McMillan."[8] Russell found the behaviorist approach of John Watson too
confining; and while he was in sympathy with some of the ideas of Freud, he felt
that the tendency of some psychoanalysts to see sexual symbolism in children's
play was "utter moonshine. The main instinctive urge of childhood is not sex,
but the desire to become adult, or, perhaps more correctly, the will to power."[9]
None of what they read and saw was quite what they wanted, so they decided to
set up their own school.

Russell describes their decision in his *Autobiography:*

> [W]e did not know of any existing school that seemed to us in any way
> satisfactory. We wanted an unusual combination: on the one hand, we
> disliked prudery and religious instruction and a great many restraints on

freedom which are taken for granted in conventional schools; on the other hand, we could not agree with most 'modern' educationists in thinking scholastic instruction unimportant, or in advocating a *complete* absence of discipline. We therefore endeavoured to collect a group of about twenty children, of roughly the same ages as John and Kate, with a view to keeping these same children through their school years. [10]

For this purpose they rented Russell's brother Frank's house, known as Telegraph House, situated on 230 acres[11] on West Sussex Downs, the highest point of which was called Beacon Hill. The school came to be called the "Beacon Hill School" or simply the "Russell School."

An ad in the *Nation* of 16 March 1927 somewat bravely announced this new educational venture to American readers. Headed "To Modern Parents," it deserves to be quoted in full:

We offer to educate, from babyhood to university age, in ideal country surroundings (with large wooded private grounds), a group of boys and girls who, in September, 1927, when the school opens, are between the ages of two and seven years. Later admissions according to vacancies or extension. Distance from London, two hours.

For terms and prospectus, write to Bertrand or Dora Russell, 31 Sydney Street, London SW3.[12]

The original prospectus of the school, drawn up by the Russells, stated that "this school has been planned to meet the needs of parents who desire to break with traditional educational methods, not only during the early years of a child's life, but throughout education." The house and grounds were then described, followed by comments on the need for proper diet and exercise. Two women teachers, one Swiss and the other English, would initially be in charge, under the supervision of the Russells, who would also do some teaching. "Methods will be on the lines of Margaret McMillan, Dr. Montessori, some Froebel and individual work." Domestic practice was to be extended to boys as well as girls; and music, art, and dancing were to be developed, as well as the production of plays. Above all, argument was to be encouraged in the interests of promoting free thinking. "At all ages, every question, on no matter what subject, will be answered to the best of our knowledge and ability." Although everything possible would be done to prepare the children for university examinations and scholarship competitions, the approach would be international in history and largely experimental in science. "Knowledge will not be viewed as mere knowledge, but as an instrument of progress, the value of which is shown by bringing it into relation with the needs of the world." Finally, the aim of the school was not to produce "listless intellectuals, but young men and women filled with constructive hopefulness, conscious that there are great things to be done in the world, and possessed of the skill required for taking their part."[13]

The school opened, as advertised, on 21 September 1927. One of the two initial teachers departed at the end of the first year "on account of some differences of approach in methods." Two new teachers were appointed, "fresh from Froebel training," one of whom, Betty Cross, "became a remarkable mainstay" and was, in Dora's opinion, "one of the best teachers we have ever known."[14] There were originally twelve boarders and five day pupils,[15] and they paid yearly fees of £150 and £50 respectively. David Harley points out that fees were meant to maintain a support staff that included "a cook, housekeeper, three maids, two chauffeurs, and a gardener" and a teaching staff that eventually consisted of "a matron, assistant matron, science, art and language instructors, a visiting part-time music teacher, a doctor who came up to the school regularly to give periodical examinations of the children, and finally Russell's private secretary."[16] Small wonder that Russell was to report that in its first twelve months of operation the school had already lost £1,847![17]

Adding to Russell's financial problems was the fact that not all parents paid even these low fees. In a letter to A. S. Neill of 31 January 1931, Russell bemoans the sorry state of the school's finances and admits that "Parents owe me altogether about £500 which I shall certainly never see." He goes on to say, "I have sometimes attempted in a mild way to get a little financial support from people who think they believe in modern education, but I have found the thing that stood most in my way was the fact which leaked out, that I do not absolutely insist upon strict sexual virtue on the part of the staff. I found that even people who think themselves quite advanced believe that only the sexually starved can exert a wholesome moral influence."[18] Dora echoes these sentiments by saying how surprised and disappointed they were that their school was treated in either a frivolous or hostile manner within their own country. Many of the Bloomsbury set, for example, "treated the school as matter for merriment, making up tales about it for dinner table conversation, which got repeated as true, thus catering for adverse comment in the Press, who delighted in headlines describing the 'Go as you Please School.' "[19] How right she was can be seen from a *New York Times* report of 18 April 1937, which mentions that Russell once ran a school "where the children could do just what they pleased—go naked when they felt the urge, swear and attend classes as the spirit moved them."

With expenses rapidly outstripping income, Russell had to find other ways of bringing money in to support the school. He did this mainly by writing and lecturing. He wrote what he called "potboilers," books on popular topics, not very technical, dictated in a single draft to a secretary. Among these were *On Education* (1926), *Marriage and Morals* (1929)—a book that was later to get him into the imbroglio with the City College of New York, *The Conquest of Happiness* (1930), and *Education and the Social Order* (1932). One need not shy away from these books on account of their hasty composition, for each of them contains a number of valuable insights, clearly expressed. As we shall see, Dewey wrote a favorable review of *On Education*, and Russell himself was said to have claimed that he won the Nobel Prize for Literature expressly for *Marriage and Morals*.[20] Russell, moreover, was *not* prone to answer criticisms of the ideas set forth in these books with the excuse that they were after all mere potboilers, not meant to be taken very seriously.

The lecture tours to the United States had begun in 1924, and Russell continued them in 1927, 1929, and 1931.[21] They no doubt interfered with his devoting full or even consistent attention and energy to the running of the school. The timing was also unfortunate; Russell was away on a lecture tour of America during the first term the school was open, while Dora herself was off to America to promote her book, *The Right to Be Happy*, after Christmas that year, when Russell had returned. This created some difficulty, as Russell later remarked, for "throughout the first two terms there was never more than one of us in charge. When I was not in America, I had to write books to make the necessary money. Consequently, I was never able to give my whole time to the school."[22] When he was there, Russell was actively involved in the running of the school, sharing with Dora some of the decisions on staffing and admission, presiding at the weekly staff meetings, and occasionally teaching history or geography classes in his study in the tower of Telegraph House.[23]

Having traced the motivation behind their setting up of the school and some of the initial and ongoing problems that arose, we should now examine the theory of education behind Beacon Hill School, drawing upon Russell's writings before its founding and supplementing these with Dora's work either in collaboration with him or on her own. Much of our attention is focused on the book *On Education*. We then proceed to a consideration of the actual practice of the school, attempting as we did with the Dewey School to delineate any interaction between the theory and the practice. The chapter concludes with a discussion of the relative success or failure of the school.

BEACON HILL SCHOOL: THE THEORY BEHIND IT

Russell had written about education long before he and Dora hit upon the idea of starting their own school. Two chapters in his early books merit special attention. The first is his chapter on education in the book *Principles of Social Reconstruction*,[24] written at the end of World War I, a period which saw Russell go to jail for his pacifist beliefs; this chapter, according to his daughter, Kate, was "written before he had any hope of children of his own or any personal reason to concern himself with the subject. A large part of his educational theory was set out here, a good six years before he had a child to try it out on: an intellectual ideal of how one ought to treat children in order to have them turn out well."[25]

In his Preface to the book, Russell says he is attempting to state a philosophy of politics "based on the belief that impulse has more effect than conscious purpose in moulding men's lives." He divides impulses into those which are possessive and aimed at acquiring or retaining something which cannot be shared, and those which are creative and seek to bring into the world something valuable such as knowledge, art, or goodwill. Russell sees the state, war, and property as the chief political embodiments of the possessive impulses, and education, marriage, and religion as the proper embodiment of the creative impulses. The best life is to be based upon these.

What was needed in education, then, is a liberation of the child's creative impulses. This may well entail allowing the child more liberty than we are accustomed to, says Russell, although "some departure from complete liberty is unavoidable if children are to be taught anything, except in the case of unusually intelligent children who are kept isolated from more normal companions."[26] Despite this disclaimer in regard to the unusually intelligent, Russell's own unhappy, solitary childhood led him to believe that his children should have the companionship of others their own age. Later on in *On Education,* he refers to some boys and girls who ought not to go to school because they combine abnormal mental powers with poor physique and great nervousness; but even these exceptional cases, he thinks, might be better handled with greater care during infancy so that nearly all of them "would grow into boys and girls sufficiently normal to enjoy the company of other boys and girls."[27]

This early statement on the inevitability of adult authority and discipline in education already sets Russell apart from some of the more radical freeschoolers or deschoolers. Such authority must be coupled with a sense of responsibility and "reverence" toward the child, a feeling of imagination and vital warmth toward something sacred in the child: "indefinable, unlimited, something individual and strangely precious, the growing principle of life, an embodied fragment of the dumb striving of the world." There is to be a sense of both "unaccountable humility" and trust as the teacher tries to further the creative impulses of the child and equip and strengthen it "for the ends which the child's own spirit is obscurely seeking."

It is precisely this spirit of reverence that is so conspicuously absent in the education conducted by states and churches. Feeling themselves in competition with other points of view, they seek to consolidate their own position by instilling a kind of unthinking loyalty in the young who are being educated. "Every State," says Russell, "wishes to promote national pride, and is conscious that this cannot be done by unbiased history."[28] He suggests that all teaching of history be submitted to an internatioal commission whose task it would be to produce "neutral" textbooks free from patriotic bias.[29] Similarly, the teaching of religion should be carried out in a spirit of free inquiry rather than indoctrination. In all our instruction, "Instead of obedience and discipline, we ought to aim at preserving independence and impulse." We should spend the money necessary to free our teachers from long hours and mechanical teaching. We should treat discipline in the classroom as a necessary step toward individual achievement rather than as a necessary evil required to keep order. The desirable kind of discipline is the kind "that comes from within, which consists in the power of pursuing a distant object steadily, forgoing and suffering many things on the way."

Russell gives credit to traditional higher education for having achieved some measure of success in producing mental discipline. He feels that this cannot be achieved "except by compelling or persuading active attention to a prescribed task." Thus, while admiring the methods of Montessori for teaching the young child, he does not think they are applicable to older children. In a passage conveniently ignored by those who charge him with advocating a go-as-you-please type of education, Russell insists, "Many things which must be thought about are uninteresting and even those that are interesting at first often become very wearisome before they have been considered as long as is necessary. The power of giving prolonged attention is very important, and it is hardly to be widely acquired except as a habit induced originally by outside pressure."[30]

By outside pressure Russell does not mean a constant stream of examinations, degree requirements, or grades for admission into a higher program of studies. Nor does he want to inculcate a habit of passive acceptance or a fear of thinking for oneself. Rather, there should be a concerted effort to "rouse and stimulate the love of mental adventure." Russell is unshaken in his belief that "no institution inspired by fear can further life" or develop the child's creative impulses. He concludes that "education should not aim at a passive awareness of dead facts, but at an activity directed towards the world that our efforts are to create."[31]

Russell's other early writing on education worthy of our notice appears in the book *The Prospects of Industrial Civilization,* written in collaboration with Dora in 1923. In a chapter on "Education" he begins by granting the point that since most of the evils of the present system of education are the result of the economic system of our industrial civilization, we will not radically cure such evils until we have changed the economic system. Prior to such a radical economic change, however, we can take steps "to make education less harmful in the meantime"; and he proposes to deal with "what can be done here and now to prevent the grosser evils of education as it is at present." Such a sense of priorities will no doubt annoy radical educational reformers and political revolutionaries alike, but Russell seems intent on offering practical advice for dealing with current educational problems.

Once again we are given the division of elementary education into that conducted by the state and that run by the church. After detailing the flaws inherent in either approach, Russell observes, "It is difficult to say whether the State or the Church does the greater damage to the minds and hearts of children." In any case, he decides that he will concentrate on state education in particular. "The best hope is with the teachers." They should insist on freedom of expression. "The best teachers are not impartial," he claims; "they are men of strong enthusiasms, to which they wish to give expression in their teaching. The impartiality of the learner is best secured by exposing him to teachers with opposite prejudices. . . . If the result is skepticism as to all violent opinions, so much the better; that is the very attitude of mind that the modern world most needs in the mass of mankind."[32]

What should be the ideals that a teacher sets for himself? Harking back to Rousseau, Russell states that an educational system can endeavor to make good citizens or good human beings. He sees our twentieth-century nationalistic approaches to education making this into a kind of either/or dualism whereby whatever is favorable to our own country is presented and whatever is unfavorable is suppressed, even if, for the individual learner, it means neglecting the need to know the truth. To counteract this tendency, Russell renews his call for history textbooks to be drawn up by an international authority. Here he adds the notion that such an authority should also direct the training of teachers. Somewhat playfully, he suggests that if he were ever to be put in charge of the training of teachers (not a very likely prospect, to say the least), he would impress upon them two things: "First, that a man's public duty is towards mankind as a whole, not towards any subordinate group such as a nation or a class; secondly, that a good community is a community of good men and women . . . who live freely but not destructively or oppressively." Such men and women would be taught to approach problems impartially and to acquire the habit of searching for impersonal truth. They would recognize the interconnection of different parts of the world. Russell ends up on an optimistic note: "if we could abolish wars and armaments and advertisement and the waste of commercial competition, we could all subsist comfortably on about four hours' work a day." One of the important tasks of education should be to prepare us for the intelligent use of all such new-found leisure time.[33]

So we have the beginnings of Russell's view of education. We should seek to develop the creative impulses of children by allowing them the freedom to engage in certain pursuits but providing the authority and discipline necessary to inculcate good work habits. We should respect the sacred uniqueness and individuality of each child while encouraging free and impartial thinking. Teachers can hold strong opinions so long as the child is also made aware of other points of view. Toward this end history textbooks should take on an international perspective and religious instruction an open-mindedness seldom found in either state or church schools. If we can ever get human beings to stop competing and fighting with one another, we can begin to educate them for the best use of their leisure time.

In an article entitled "Freedom or Authority in Education," published in 1924, Russell reiterates some of these themes. We cannot reasonably defend absolute freedom in education, he says, because some children will do harm to themselves or others by swallowing pins, drinking poison, falling out of upper windows, going unwashed, overeating, smoking until they are sick, getting chills, or even plaguing elderly gentlemen! We must have some authority in schools, but who should exercise it? Ultimately the teacher should exercise authority over his or her pupils but in a way that attempts to utilize their natural desires and impulses. We can see such an approach at work in a child's learning how to talk, according to Russell, where all that grownups do is provide opportunity and praise.

Similarly, in teaching a child mathematics we should make the problems pertinent to his or her interests. "There should be nothing hypothetical about the sums that a child is asked to do," says Russell in a passage suggestive of Whitehead. Overall, Russell's ideal scheme of education would see to it that every child at twelve would have some instruction in classics, mathematics, and science; and by the age of fourteen, those who wanted to would specialize. The ideal of an "all-round" education is out of date, Russell asserts; "it has been destroyed by the progress of knowledge."[34] Again he emphasizes the need to promote thinking in our children by teaching them truthfulness, or what he terms "the habit of forming our opinions on the evidence, and holding them with that degree of conviction that the evidence warrants." Such an approach is taken by the scientist who has to rely solely on the strength of his case.

Subjects such as history must not be taught to further any special point of view. Harking back to his familiar plea for a more international approach to the teaching and learning of history, Russell suggests that it might be taught by Frenchmen in England and Englishmen in France so that "there would be no disagreements between the two countries, because each would understand the other's point of view." This recurring theme is not as radical as it may seem.

Russell is merely restating the Platonic faith in the rational good, the view that once someone knows the truth, he or she will perforce act in a virtuous manner. But are national rivalries and personal enmities simply the result of a lack of knowledge, an ignorance of all the facts? I think that history itself shows to what an extent men and countries can carry on vindictive policies despite the evidence. Surely not an ideal situation, but if Russell feels he is making a practical pedagogical suggestion here, it is difficult to take him seriously. And since he does not put historical knowledge on the same level of certainty as that achievable in science or mathematics, it is not clear exactly what would constitute the evidence in such disputes. Historians still argue about the causes of the First World War, for example, the actual outcome of its major battles, the justice of its settlement, the wisdom of American involvement, the relationship of the war in the trenches to that discussed by the press and the politicians. What exactly hearing both sides would mean in such a case is unclear. Russell seems to have a strong feeling toward the international perspective he would like children to adopt, but he does not seem to have given much thought to the practical implications of his suggestions for the teaching and writing of history which are supposed to further this end.

He closes the article with a renewed plea for educators to regard children as ends in themselves with their own rights and personalities. "Reverence for human personality," he writes, "is the beginning of wisdom in every social question, but above all in education."[35] The need for reverence in the education of the young became more than an academic question for Russell with the birth of his son John (November 1921) and his daughter Kate (December 1923). All his previous considerations of educational ideals and methods were given greater urgency in the very practical matter of finding the proper school for his own children. This culminated in his writing *On Education,* published in 1926, the work Russell himself called "my chief book on the subject."[36] Since the Russells opened their school in 1927, this book might well be called "the handbook of Beacon Hill—at least during the period in which Russell was affiliated with it."[37] It was a book that had a very large sale both at home and abroad and even succeeded in drawing a number of inquiries from interested parents about Russell's school.[38]

John Dewey reviewed the book for the *New Republic,* calling it "a fine contribution to the literature of education as religion." Although he does not find the book to be strikingly original, Dewey praises it for displaying a strong faith in the possibility of achieving a better world through education. This faith Dewey attributed to the fact that Russell now has two children of his own to educate.[39] In a letter to Dewey, Russell acknowledged the accuracy of this observation: "the book is addressed to parents as ignorant as I was when I first became a parent, and is only intended to give common sense. What you say about the effect of my children on me is quite just. I am as pessimistic as ever about politics, but I have now something else to think about."[40] Indeed, in his Introduction to the book, Russell advises the reader that "What I have to say is the outcome of perplexities in regard to my own children."

One of the appealing aspects of the book is its combination of common sense, wit, a sceptical yet caring attitude, and a concern to share his own experiences with raising two children. Russell deals with practical educational problems (e.g., whether day schools are preferable to nursery schools) and more general topics (e.g., the postulates of modern educational theory), and gives specific bits of advice (e.g., how he cured his son John of his fear of the water) as well as formulating various educational principles (e.g., the four characteristics that form the basis of an ideal character). He does not see this as a work of technical philosophy[41] but as that of one conscientious parent addressing other parents who have a "sincere desire for the welfare of their offspring." This is not to say that one cannot find in the book ideas and ideals that might be evaluated against the actual practices of the Beacon Hill School. Indeed, we shall compare his views of education before and after the running of the school to see in what ways they have changed. In this sense, we treat Russell's views on education as what Dewey liked to call "working hypotheses." Their lack of philosophical technicality need not preclude our taking them seriously; in fact, it may simply mean they are somewhat easier to understand.

ON EDUCATION

Russell divides his book into three parts: educational ideals, the education of character, intellectual education. "The ideal system of education must be democratic," he insists. Even though this ideal may not be immediately attainable, Russell hopes to propose changes in education that are capable of being universal. He states that "we cannot regard a method of education as satisfactory if it is one which could not possibly be universal." Given the large number of correctable physical evils in the world, the subjects taught should have some utility; but the humanistic elements are also important, for they help to show us what the world might be. We should divide what is to be learned into suitable stages so that "every stage can be made agreeable to the average child." In this way we can supply the right amounts of freedom and discipline so that the child will develop self-discipline. Children are not naturally either good or bad; they are born with reflexes and instincts out of which, by the action of the environment, habits are produced. Every normal child possesses a "spontaneous wish to learn" which should be "the driving-force in education."[42] This is an item of faith in Russell's educational outlook that he never bothers to substantiate.

The aims of education depend upon the kind of person we wish to produce. Such a person, for Russell, should have the "scientific temper," that is, be someone who believes that knowledge is attainable, though with difficulty; that mistakes in our beliefs can be rectified by care and industry; and that we must act upon our beliefs, despite their lack of absolute certainty. The teacher should treat the child as an end in itself and seek to develop certain characteristics in the child. In an often-quoted passage, Russell maintains that there are "four characteristics which seem to me jointly to form the basis of an ideal character: vitality, courage, sensitivity and intelligence."[43]

Vitality involves a "pleasure in feeling alive, quite apart from any specific pleasant circumstances. . . . It makes it easy to take an interest in whatever occurs, and thus promotes objectivity, which is an essential of sanity." Courage is the absence of irrational fear; it involves a combination of self-respect and an impersonal outlook on life. We can even overcome our fear of death if we are able to be taken beyond our self through love, knowledge, and art. Sensitiveness means "being affected pleasurably or the reverse by many things, and by the right things." It also includes a capacity for abstract sympathy whereby we can be sensitive to the pains and tribulations of those we do not know or will never meet. Finally, intelligence entails both actual knowledge and the receptivity to knowledge. To train intelligence we must impart information as well as technique, working with the child's instinctive curiosity. The development of intelligence also promotes desirable intellectual virtues such as open-mindedness, courage, and a sense of cooperation. Like Dewey and like Aristotle, Russell believes that the cultivation of such virtues "should result from intellectual education: but they should result as needed in learning, not as virtues pursued for their own sake. Among such qualities the chief seem to me: curiosity, open-mindedness, belief that knowledge is possible though difficult, patience, industry, concentration, and exactness."[44]

The middle section of his book combines common sense and child psychology in dealing with the education of character. Dewey characterized the book as exhibiting "enlightened empirical common sense" very much in the spirit of Locke's writings on education. Such topics as fear, play and fancy, constructiveness, selfishness, truthfulness, punishment, the importance of other children, and sex education are discussed with accompanying examples of Russell's handling of such things with his own children. We should treat sex as "natural, delightful and decent" and deal with sex knowledge as we would with any other type of knowledge. All of the child's questions about sex should be answered truthfully, and no prudery should be shown in regard to the human body. Russell also discusses the importance of nursery schools, with ample references to the thought and work of Margaret McMillan.

In the last part of the book, Russell makes some suggestions in regard to the curriculum. Concentration, exactness, and the voluntary control of attention are all especially valuable and can be enhanced through physical as well as mental activity. For example, he suggests learning poetry by heart, acting, singing, and dancing. Geography and history could be made more interesting by making full use of the cinema, field trips, and the child's natural curiosity; They could be taught as part of man's ongoing battle against Chaos and Old Night. "Good" literature should be read; not silly sentimental books written expressly for children, but books that happen to suit the child although written for grownups (such as *Robinson Crusoe*) or books written for children but also delightful to grownups (such as the verses of Edmund Lear and the stories of Lewis Carroll). Like many another educator when proposing an ideal curriculum for young children, Russell extrapolates from his own interests and tastes and seems to assume that any right-minded youngster would share them.

If modern languages are to be taught, they should be taught by native speakers.[45] Mathematics and science, that is to say, the formal teaching of geometry, algebra, physics, and chemistry, begin only at the age of twelve or so. Russell assumes that the child already has learned to count and has some direct experience of nature. He grants that not everyone will have an aptitude for mathematics and science but urges that these subjects be presented in sufficient detail so that by fourteen the child will know whether or not he wants to specialize in them. The same holds true of the classics. Throughout the whole period of education there should also be what Russell calls "education in outdoor things," which includes "knowledge of agricultural processes, familiarity with animals and plants, gardening, habits of observation in the country." It is not clear whether Russell assumes here that every school will be similarly situated on 230 acres of virgin forest as was Beacon Hill.

At fourteen Russell would have the child begin to specialize. He would make three broad divisions in school: (1) classics, (2) mathematics and science, (3) modern languages, history, and literature. He urges schools to have ample library and laboratory facilities and would have the students taught in a scientific spirit with a sense of intellectual adventure. "In my school," he asserts, "no obstacle to knowledge shall exist, of any sort or kind."[46] The book closes with two short chapters; one is on the question of day versus boarding schools (the latter he finds better for health reasons, the former for maintaining family relationships) and the other on university education.

Universities are not for everyone, acording to Russell. He is convinced that "at present, only a minority of the population can profit by a scholastic education prolonged to the age of twenty-one or twenty-two." Those qualified to go to a university should not be excluded for financial reasons. At the university the students should be encouraged to engage in individual work, and the teachers should be engaged in research. Perhaps assuming that all universities can or should be on a par with Trinity College, Cambridge, of his own youth, Russell proclaims, "In university teaching, skill in pedagogy is no longer important; what is important is knowledge of one's subject and keenness about what is being done in it." Russell wants more, not less, "disinterested investigation" to take place in universities, for he feels that "All the great advances are at first purely theoretical, and are only afterwards found to be capable of practical applications." This is to reassert his basic belief that "the understanding of the world is one of the ultimate goods."[47]

Although Russell's earlier suggestions about educating young children can be seen as a negative reaction to his own upbringing, his remarks here on university education are clearly in support of the kind of experience he had as a student at Cambridge. It does not seem to have occurred to him that not all university students have the time, money, or interests of a prospective lord. This also represents another departure from the more pragmatic views of Dewey and Whitehead. Russell is more like Plato in his approach to knowledge as hierarchical and learning as culminating in a speculative contemplation of the whole of reality. There are some similarities with Whitehead's notion that university should be the great period of generalization, but the details are too sketchy to warrant a thorough comparison. All in all, Russell strikes me as a born aristocrat who desperately wants to be democratic in his educational outlook, but never fully succeeds.[48]

The book concludes with Russell's most-quoted statement about education: "Knowledge yielded by love is what the educator needs, and what his pupils should acquire."[49] Psychology has shown us the vital importance of loving, respecting, and revering the child as an end in itself with rights, impulses, needs, fears, and desires. Knowledge is what the child needs to pursue its goals. Education should supply the facts, techniques for acquiring information and ideas, discipline, and the means to develop one's creative impulses. With these goals in mind, Bertrand and Dora Russell opened their school. Let us now look at what happened.

BEACON HILL SCHOOL: THE ACTUAL PRACTICE

As we have seen, the Russells opened their school on 21 September 1927 to twelve boarders and five day pupils. For first-hand information on the actual running of the school, we have several accounts by Dora Russell, supplemented by those of her daughter Kate and by some articles written at the time by Russell. There are also a number of secondary reports and appraisals which should help to give us a fairly clear idea of how the school was run.

In a description of the school published in 1934, Dora explained its organizational structure (it had at that time twenty-five pupils, boys and girls, the oldest being twelve years old). Children under five were kept "as a separate group for sleeping and eating and classroom play." Their playroom was filled "with a variety of material, so far as possible of a malleable or adaptable nature." They were given quite a bit of freedom in the use of things like saws, hammers, and scissors. The guiding rule was not to interfere with what someone else was trying to do. Those between the ages of five and seven were given the opportunity to learn reading, writing, and doing sums but only when they saw some reason for wishing to learn them. They did much nature work, discussed how people make houses and clothes, and, according to Dora, "they learn much orally and from pictures about the practical life of human beings at different periods of history."[50] The school had a complete twenty-six-volume set of the *Encyclopedia Britannica,* and the children were shown how to use it and write about the things they learned from it.[51] From the age of five on, the children were given brief exposure to French and German, mainly in the form of games and conversation. From eight onward, they progressed in academic work with the study of history, geography, literature, play writing, mathematics, science and laboratory work, and arts and crafts in the workshop.

The students displayed a strong interest in the functioning of the human body. In an interesting parallel to Dewey's tale of his difficulty in finding the kind of desks he wanted for his Laboratory School, Russell relates, "When we were equipping our school, we were looking one day for diagrams suitable for the teaching of physiology. We found some which were admirably made, one showing muscles, one nerves, one veins and arteries and so on. But unfortunately, in all of them the sexual parts were omitted."[52] Just as Dewey's commitment to learning by doing was put to the test in his struggle to find desks for his students that were suitable for more than listening, so too Russell's concern for sexual honesty in the classroom was highlighted by his unsuccessful attempts to obtain an anatomically correct chart of the human body. Both cases illustrate the kinds of practical problems faced by educational reformers.

Perhaps the most notorious aspect of the school was the fact that the Russells did not insist on the children's wearing clothing out of doors. This naturally caught the public's attention more than anything else going on at the school. For example, when James Wedgewood Drawbell reported on his visit to the school, he constantly referred to naked tots of two and three playing outside.[53] He seems so astonished at the sight of toddlers "without a stitch of clothing" that one begins to wonder more about him than about the moral climate of the school. Dora favored exercise and dance *au naturel* out of doors when the weather permitted, but she took pains to make it clear that "all of our children were well under the age of puberty."[54]

It strikes the modern reader as rather bizarre, how much notoriety these small naked children caused, culminating in the hysterical tone of the comments made by those who opposed Russell's being allowed to teach logic at the City College of New York in 1941. Mrs. Jean Kay had petitioned the New York State Supreme Court to rescind and revoke Russell's appointment by the Board of Higher Education. A supporting affidavit by her attorney charged that Russell was unsuited to teach because of his irreligious and immoral views and character. To substantiate this charge, it was claimed, among other things, that he had "conducted a school in England, where he taught that children need not respect their parents. He also conducted a nudist school for both sexes of all ages, children, adolescents and adults. He participated in this nudist colony and went about naked in the company of persons of both sexes who were exhibiting themselves naked in public."[55] The thought of the puckish Russell sauntering about in the nude and thereby posing a danger to public morals would be laughable if it were not for the fact that Mrs. Kay and her cohorts won the day, and Russell was left in desperate straits without a job in the United States and unable to return to Britain because of the War.[56] As so often happened during Russell's lifetime, he obviously touched a sore spot in a number of people, and their vehement protests lent support to the very point he was trying to make; that is, we are overly concerned with keeping sexual matters hidden from children, and this only serves to stimulate their curiosity and leads to an unhealthy attitude toward sex later in life.

The Russells hoped not only to divest the children of their inhibitions in regard to covering up their bodies, they also tried to be honest in answering questions about sex and in allowing for "dirty" language. As quoted by Allan Wood, Russell observed, "When children are left free as regards their language, they say from time to time such things as Freudian textbooks assert they must be thinking." Thus, on a walk a child might be heard to comment that the shape of a tree resembled a penis, or words to that effect. Russell felt that this was certainly preferable to a hush-hush policy that could lead to repression and personality disorders.[57]

After the age of eight, more time was devoted to the study of history and geography, not as distinct subjects but rather as "the whole life of a people in relation to climate and soil, and the conditions of life obtaining for the people of that place or time."[58] Both Russells favored the reading of H. G. Wells's *Outline of History*.[59] They were pleased to discover a great deal of Roman pottery on the school grounds, which occasioned a lively interest among the students in archaeology. All along, stress was laid on the oneness of the human species in order to give children the kinds of international perspective that Russell desired.

Science was taught in a laboratory that had been set up in one of the summer houses Frank Russell had built in the woods. According to Kate Russell, the long, low building had been provided with work benches, shelves, a sink, a Bunsen burner, and all kinds of laboratory equipment. A young Russian teacher, Boris Uvarov, led the children through experiments in such a fascinating manner that Kate felt "it was a privilege to know those facts and to try those experiments, not a chore to memorize the stuff and write up the results in notebooks. Science class was as exciting as a magic show in which one is allowed to discover the secrets and practice the tricks."[60] Unfortunately for the Russells, this particular teacher proved to be so good that he was eventually noticed and weaned away at a higher salary by the Dartington Hall School.

The children were also encouraged to take a creative approach to literature and art. The young ones would dictate stories to their teachers, while older pupils would write their own as well as compose plays and poems. Russell saw this as yet another benefit from sustaining an atmosphere of free speech. In an article written for the *New Statesman and Nation* in 1931, he summarized his four-year experience with the school. "At Beacon Hill School . . . my wife and I are putting into practice our theories of education." He was proud of the fact that the children were given complete freedom of speech: "There is no check upon irreverence towards elders and betters, and no check upon scientific curiosity, and no check upon the choice of words." This allows the staff to know what the children are thinking, and it gives the children a "robust sense of reality." The absence of sex taboos serves to free their natural scientific curiosity and, especially in the case of the girls, allows them to pursue interests in biology, anatomy, and physiology that might otherwise be closed off by sexual ignorance and inhibition.

"As regards literature," Russell continued, "the children's diction is exact and impressive; their emotions clothe themselves spontaneously in appropriate language, and they do not acquire that bookishness which is the bane of artificial culture." To prove his point, Russell quoted in full two poems, "The Deserted Farmhouse" and "In the Graveyard," written by a group of the children. These should dispel the idea that a scientific attitude is inimical to the imagination, he said. His conclusion was perhaps his most positive assessment of the results of the school and should be kept in mind when we consider his later admission that it was an utter failure: "I firmly believe that our methods enable a child to acquire knowledge without losing the joy of life and to become scientific without ceasing to be spontaneous. I hoped that this might be the case when we founded the school, and my hopes are now confirmed by nearly four years' experience."[61]

Some of the readers of the *New Statesman and Nation* found all this a bit hard to swallow. Stephen Schofield wrote that Russell claims not to allow the children in his school absolute freedom, yet to give them complete freedom of speech. How can he do both? In the same issue, W. E. Williams challenges Russell's views on the communal authorship of poetry. He suggests that the group's activity is suggested or arranged by a teacher and the poem initiated by one child. He feels that group authorship cramps the really creative personality and that they should leave the children alone to create their own works of art. He closes with the suggestion that the poems indicate the children have been reading Walter de la Mare.[62]

Russell was quick to reply. The only limitations to freedom at Beacon Hill are those necessary for the health of the children. Thus, they are cleaned twice a day and given enough time to sleep. Neither of these affects their freedom of speech. As regards the group poems, he admits that he was surprised to see how successful such a cooperative venture turned out to be, but he insists that the group did indeed write the poems. This may not seem so unusual, he adds, if we keep in mind the fact that "Homer and the Authorised Version [of the Bible] were not products of individual genius, and that the individualism of the artist is perhaps overemphasized in modern times."[63]

This did not quite remedy the situation. In the next issue, there were two more letters. One, from Barbara Low, criticized Russell's main thesis that "the human being in the state of childhood is perfectly capable of, first, *knowing* his own thoughts and feelings; secondly, *expressing* those thoughts and feelings in appropriate fashion" (Low's italics). Russell seems to think that all that is required is that we free the child to do so by removing all external barriers. This tells of a meager knowledge of psychology as well as a naive experience of life. She quotes Samuel Butler to the effect that we all carry with us former selves that tend to act as a check on what we say and do. Russell might look to psychoanalysis to find just how repressive such aspects of our selves really are, no matter what amount of external freedom is provided. The other letter, from M. R. LeFleming, speaks on behalf of the "ordinary teachers" who have read Russell's writings on education and expect, in all fairness, that he stop generalizing from his own unfortunate educational experiences of the past and pay attention to the efforts of teachers nowadays. They are trying to inculcate "a fair-minded and unprejudiced outlook on social and international affairs" just as much as he is.[64]

Russell, as usual, has the last word. He chides Miss Low for her reference to psychoanalysts. "Psycho-analysts, in the main, derive their ideas of childhood from the reminiscences of neurotics; those whose impressions are derived from direct contact with children, combined with careful observation, are regarded by the psycho-analysts as unscientific outsiders." He rebuts the quotation from Butler by sarcastically referring to his views on heredity as wholly unscientific (and thus seems to take some of the sting out of his own criticism of the psychoanalysts). He sympathizes with Mr. LeFleming's efforts to instill an international outlook in children but says that the textbooks on geography and history that he is acquainted with seem woefully inadequate for this task. He has attempted to find suitable films for the students but they too seem to be inspired by "national, imperialist or commercial propaganda." He ends with a plea for teachers like LeFleming to join in his denunciation of the manufacture of prejudiced matter for children.[65]

Besides poetry, the children also wrote and produced their own plays. Dora boasts, "The children have never yet acted a play that they had not written themselves."[66] She had a number of the plays collected and printed in a separate volume[67] and reprints some of them in the second volume of her autobiography. Kate Russell recalls that the "theme of enlightened youth in conflict with hoary superstition was common in our plays, as it was common in our thoughts, but it was rarely a straightforward conflict of good and evil." They did plays about the crusades, Japan, the ancient Greeks, the Romans in Britain, a farce about the French Revolution, and a play about British India. Each play required a fair amount of research. For example, in a play about Egypt, "we had to find out about the beliefs of ancient Egypt, the names of the gods and people and the kind of clothes they wore." The children consulted the *Book of the Dead* and the encyclopedia, then "sewed the clothes and painted the scenery, learned our parts and rehearsed diligently, until at last we were ready to perform for the parents at the end of term."

"The plays were a form of group therapy as well as learning," Kate goes on to say. Each child made up his or her part, which the teacher wrote down as they went along; and "everyone was free to offer suggestions to anyone who seemed at a loss. There was tremendous satisfaction in creating one's own role and putting into it all kinds of secret aspirations one was otherwise ashamed to acknowledge."[68] This observation would seem to lend credence to Barbara Low's point that there is more to freedom of speech among children than removal of external restraints. Indeed, in an article in *The Spectator*, which appeared right in the midst of Russell's dispute in the *New Statesman and Nation* about communal authorship, Russell does acknowledge that allowing children free speech from the moment they can first speak tends to confirm many of Freud's hypotheses about their nature.[69] He points to experiments done along this line at Malting House School and reported by Susan Isaacs[70] and calls for more public support for the scientific observation of the behavior of young children.

The educator, of course, should seek to do more than merely observe behavior. The educator wants actively to influence it in a certain direction. For Russell, this entailed "moral qualities which I regard as important to produce during the early years" such as "freedom from hatred, fearlessness, a scientific attitude towards reality, and the possession of such habits as are essential to health and to a tolerable social life." He repeats his injunction against allowing children compete freedom, since good habits are not spontaneously formed; and after the age of eight, "children need to acquire more knowledge than most of them will acquire if they are allowed free choice between lessons and play. Neither should we tolerate the bullying of younger children by older ones. True freedom of speech will enable children to express their inner feelings, fears, and hostilities and will supply them with a purely "laryngeal" way of discharging their emotions. "The same kind of hatred which will lead a man prevented from speech to murder his enemy," says Russell, "may lead a thoroughly verbalized man to be content with a biting epigram." He claims to see this pattern emerging among the students in his school.[71] Unfortunately, not all of us have attained either the level of verbalization or acquired the biting wit of a Russell, and so we seem doomed to settle some of our emotional upsets in nonverbal ways.

Besides their studies and other activities, the children participated in a form of self-government through a School Council. "The government of the school is in the hands of the School Council," says Dora. "Everybody belongs to this, from the principal to the gardener, and every child who is 5 years old and over. Each person has one vote, and may attend and speak."[72] The meetings were held on request by any of the members, and the Council made rules about bedtimes, rest, washing, cleaning up, bullying, destructive acts, and so on. The idea is strikingly similar to that of A. S. Neill at Summerhill—that is, by letting the children have a hand in formulating the rules, they will come to see the point of having them and be more inclined to follow them.[73]

An example of the School Council in action relates to the problem of the hitting of smaller children by bigger ones. A resolution was passed disapproving of such "sloshing" as a method of settling disputes. "Thereafter," says Dora, "when two started a fight, others would be seen runnning up chanting the Council resolution. It was quite effective. And how like the relation of the United Nations to the rest of the world at the present day."[74] Russell gives a different perspective in his *Autobiography* when he admits that many of the children who came to the school were cruel and destructive, "and I found myself, when the children were not at lessons, obliged to supervise them continually to stop cruelty." He soon realized that not merely creative impulses were being manifested and "sometimes really sinister impulses came to light." He mentions the girl who put a hatpin in her brother's soup and the two children who set a large fire in order to burn the rabbits that had been given to an unpopular comrade.[75] All in all, the School Council seems to have been about as effective as the United Nations.

Russell seemed to blow hot and cold in this matter of discipline. In his article "In Our School," he takes a rather jocular view of childish high jinks, excusing them with the remark, "A certain waywardness in self-expression and rollicking movements are as necessary to young children as to puppies." He stresses that in his school "there are no prizes, and no competition except an occasional test or class game. Their time table is posted up, and they are free to attend or not, but cannot go and annoy others if they want to be idle." He grants that such a free education will probably not work with those who have already been over-disciplined in conventional schools, nor with those who are severely disturbed psychologically. He does believe that starting early with a child (recall that the original advertisement for the school called for children between the ages of two and seven) and caring for his or her health, emotions, and initiative, we can enable that child to educate itself as a social being and make use under expert guidance of opportunities suiting its talents.[76]

Whatever the case, corporal punishment as a means of instilling correct habits of behavior was ruled out entirely. Evidently this rule was not always followed by harried staff, and Russell complains that "however often and however meticulously our principles were explained to them, [some of the staff] could never be brought to act in accordance with them unless one of us was present."[77] This is another instance of Russell's naive belief that knowledge is both a necessary and a sufficient condition of virtuous action. In defense of the staff it might be added that the children were often unruly, the Russells often away, and the rules not always self-evidently correct. For example, Dora felt she had to dismiss the matron at one point "because she had caught her giving the children 'a WC complex' by telling them not to use their pots in public."[78]

On another occasion, Dora returned from a trip to be confronted by her Irish cook Hannah, who tearfully informed her that Russell was sleeping with the children's governess while she was away. Dora's reaction was to explain to Hannah that "though I loved her for her loyalty, we did not feel she and 'the Masther' could hardly get on after this. And to the governess, who was a charming girl, I simply said that her job at the school was *not* cancelled."[79] Is it any wonder that the staff often seemed not to act in accordance with the Russell's guiding "principles"? The fact that Dora for her part proceeded to give birth to two more children, Harriet in 1930 and Roderick in 1932, fathered by Griffin Barry, an American journalist and occasional visitor to Beacon Hill, and not by "the Masther," must have added to their perplexity.[80] Add to this that both Russells took it for granted that they were entitled to large amounts of hard work and forbearance on the part of their staff with very little required in the way of financial return.

Despite her feelings about not giving the children a "WC complex," Dora paid strict attention to hygiene. She saw to it that the chidren were to get "the very best that we could manage for mind and body." This included specially constructed beds, brightly colored rooms, and a diet of fruit and fresh milk. The children were showered (in cold water) morning and night.

Mealtime manners and choice of clothing were far less regulated. Kate Russell recounts how they would amuse themselves at mealtime by putting a dab of butter on the end of a knife and flicking it onto the ceiling.[81] Alan Wood speaks of the contrast that struck visitors to the school between the fastidious neatness of Russell himself and the general impression of untidiness at the school.[82] Indeed, in the series of pictures that appear in H. W. Leggett's book on the school, one is immediately struck by the contrast between the rough-and-tumble kids and the impeccably clad Russell, pipe firmly in his mouth, always looking as if he were in but not fully of the group in each picture.[83] James Wedgwood Drawbell tries to draw a positive picture of the school but is forced to admit "They are not, however, the kind of children that a kind parent would bring into the drawing-room at just this hour of tea and parade proudly in front of visitors. No parents, unless the understanding ones who send their children to this and similar schools, would acknowledge this bunch of Scallawags in pullovers and bathing suits. In any ordinary home they would be hustled off to the bathroom to have some of the grit taken off before changing into fresh clean linen."[84]

Although they had entered into this educational experiment with mutual enthusiasm and for a time saw it as a truly joint enterprise, various strains began to appear in the relationship of Russell and Dora which were eventually to have a devastating effect on the school. As already noted, Dora had a child by Griffin Barry in 1930, at about the same time Patricia (Peter) Spence was hired as governess (she was later to become Russell's third wife). Russell went away on another lecture tour to America in October 1931. By this time he had become the third Earl Russell; his brother Frank had died earlier in the year, with the result that Bertrand succeeded to the earldom. He also inherited the alimony payments for Frank's wife Molly, which amounted to £300 a year for life; and, as he ruefully notes in his *Autobiography*, she lived to be about ninety. Undaunted by Russell's increasing financial woes, Dora had a second child by Barry in 1932. This proved more than even he could tolerate, if not for his wounded pride then for the sake of preserving the continuance of the Russell line. To Dora's apparent surprise and disappointment, he filed for a Deed of Separation in 1932 and left the school. She commented that "it is a sad fact that, when, in 1932, he left the school and me for good, it had just begun to look like breaking even."[85] A Petition for Divorce was filed in 1934, and Dora was forced to vacate Telegraph House and move the school elsewhere. Kate and John were sent to the Dartington Hall School. Dora managed to keep the Beacon Hill School operating until 1943 when it was closed during the war. Thus ended an episode which Russell has characterized as "one of the most personally unhappy and unfortunate of my life."[86]

SUCCESS OR FAILURE?

The general impression is that Beacon Hill School was a failure. The main source of this impression is undoubtedly Russell himself. For example, in his book *Bertrand Russell on Education,* Joe Park states, "The evidence is overwhelming. Bertrand Russell believed the school to be a failure . . . he feels he wasted his effort and wishes he had never undertaken the school. . . . He made it quite plain that he did not wish the present writer to go into the subject of Beacon Hill: 'It wasn't at all the sort of place that I had imagined it would be.' "[87] Park lists three reasons why Russell felt the school failed. First, he was a poor administrator. "It is not my style of thinking at all," Russell said. Dora remarks, "When we started the school Bertie and I underestimated how much the time and energy of both of us would be consumed by administration."[88] One can sympathize with their being overcome by administrivia, although their insistence on complete control of the school may have contributed to this difficulty.

The second reason Russell gave was that the teachers agreed with him concerning his theory of education or pretended to agree with him simply to keep their jobs. "When my back was turned," he told Park, "they did just the opposite." This is a strange complaint, coming from such a strong advocate of complete freedom of speech. Did Russell not countenance criticism of his theory? Was speech to be free for the children but not for the staff? This sounds like a bad climate in which to test one's theories and hardly befits the scientific temper that Russell urged upon one and all.

The final reason given seems more straightforward: some of the children at the school were problem children.[89] Alan Wood expands upon this point: "What really made the school impossible . . . was that it became a natural receptacle for specially difficult children, ejected from more conventional establishments; and with them the attempt to allow free development could only lead to pandemonium."[90] Even Dora, then and now the school's staunchest supporter, admits that they had their share of difficult children but adds that they had to eject only one pupil.[91] Ronald Clark sums up the problem by saying, "Beacon Hill accumulated an undue percentage of children from broken homes, illegitimates, and children with one or more American parents, sometimes separated. Thus the cross-section on whom Russell and his wife tried out their educational ideas was more caricature than fair sample." Nonetheless, Clark attributes the failure of the school to the behavior of the Russells rather than that of their students, "From 1927 onwards, both Russell and his wife were themselves becoming entangled in the practical application of their beliefs in free love."[92]

In his *Autobiography,* Russell cites several causes for the failure of his school: the problems of finance, which were only partially alleviated by his writings and lecture tours; the staff, some of whom could never be brought to act in accordance with the school's underlying principles unless one of the Russells was present; and the "undue proportion of problem children." Russell realized after the fact that his sort of school would draw such children and that "the parents who were most inclined to try new methods were those who had difficulties with their children." Although Dora's opinion is that "our clients and supporters came mainly from people of original minds,"[93] Russell put it more bluntly and said the school was meant for the middle classes, "that is, for those who can pay for their children's education."[94] Neither of them expected such lively and often destructive children, and they were not properly prepared to handle them.

Another cause of problems with the school, according to Russell, was that in order to avoid showing any favoritism toward their own two children, he and Dora "had to keep an unnatural distance between them and us except during the holidays," with the result that "the complete happiness that had existed in our relations to John and Kate was thus destroyed, and was replaced by awkwardness and embarrassment." With the benefit of hindsight, Russell felt that "something of this sort is bound to happen whenever parents and children are at the same school."[95] It should be noted that there is no evidence such a division between parents and children occurred with the Deweys at their school, through, as we have seen, there were difficulties for the teaching staff which accrued to the fact that husband and wife were jointly involved in the running of the school.

Russell goes on to discuss mistakes in the principles upon which Beacon Hill School was conducted. "Young children in a group cannot be happy without a certain amount of order and routine." Left to their own devices, they will turn to bullying or other destructive behavior if only out of sheer boredom. Better to have an adult on hand to suggest activities and "to supply an initiative which is hardly to be expected of young children." Then, too, he felt that there was "a pretence of more freedom than in fact existed" in the school. There were strict rules about hygiene, diet, and bedtime. Children who had heard their parents talking about freedom of the school would test it by seeing how far they could go. Russell somewhat ruefully notes, "As we only forbade things that were obviously harmful, such experiments were apt to be very inconvenient."[96]

Still others reasons for the failure of the school have been given. Leggett claims that Russell was not a good organizer and his wife not interested in the domestic side of the undertaking.[97] From Dora's and Kate's accounts of the school, the latter criticism seems unjustified. We do get from Kate a more realistic picture of the difficult position the staff were placed in: "The teachers led a strenuous life. Not only did they have to know their material and make it interesting enough for us to learn without compulsion; they also had to accompany us on hikes and supervise our meals and play. And in their free time, if they had any, there was really nowhere to go and nothing to do except more of the same." The real cause of their distress lay deeper, however, and related more directly to the very principles underlying the school. "Without a formal structure of authority to back them up, the teachers had only the strength of their own personalities to rely on in the face of children trained and encouraged to ask constant questions, to accept nothing on mere adult say-so. Those who survived and succeeded won our respect and affection; the others departed in shame and despair.[98]

Robert Dearden has defined the teacher-student relationship as an authority relationship. According to Dearden, the teacher should be *an* authority (i.e., more knowledgeable on the subject to be learned) as well as be *in* authority. (i.e., have the formally recognized right to keep order and to make judgments about the work of the students).[99] At Beacon Hill the former criterion was usually met, but the latter not at all. The teachers were placed in a learning environment touted to be free and were clearly seen to be subservient to the Russells in the day-to-day operation of the school. Is it any wonder that they did not last? Russell felt strongly that children could not learn unless they were free. He might well have asked whether anyone can effectively teach unless they are given structural authority to do so.

This may be a problem endemic to child-centered schools; the children are happy but the staff are either exhausted or despondent. In any case, the Russells carried on with their joint and private ventures seemingly unaware of the pain and suffering of many of those around them. This too may be part of the curse of the crusader, one who is so concentrated on tackling the big problems of man and society that the less dramatic, more personal difficulties close to hand are not recognized. Kate Russell has conveyed to us how lonely and unhappy she felt at the school. We can be sure that at the time both of her parents would have been quite surprised to hear that.

A less personal but perhaps more telling criticism of the school was made by C. E. M. Joad. Joad had written a favorable review of a book entitled *The Case for Examinations,* by J. L. Brereton, a review which extolled the virtue of examinations and discipline in school. W. B. Curry of Dartington Hall School did not like what Joad said, and responded in a letter to the editor in which he quoted Whitehead and mentioned Russell and his school. Joad replied by saying, among other things, that Russell did not manage to keep his school going and that "it was a common criticism of children educated there: (i) that they did not know dull facts, e.g. irregular verbs; (ii) that they had not the technique for acquiring such knowledge." He added, "I have yet to meet a teacher who does not think that competition with other children helps, that examinations are a stimulus to effort . . . that some incentive is desirable and that some degree of discipline must be exercised in order to subdue the untrained mind to the mastering of what is difficult and dull."

Dora, in her turn, was not long in responding. She admitted that an independent, progressive school such as Beacon Hill had to make do with uneconomic fees and private sacrifices by the staff and parents, but she stoutly insisted that it still managed to provide its children "with teaching, books, equipment and facilities far and away beyond those to be found in the average elementary school backed by State funds." Some of the pupils showed academic brilliance, others did not. Since the age range was from two to twelve years, Joad's criticisms of their scholastic attainments "are somewhat fantastic and exceed even those of the State scholarship examinations." As for not meeting any teachers who oppose competition and examinations, Joad had only to talk to her. She concludes that for all its supposed academic shortcomings, "we were not weak in social arithmetic at Beacon Hill: we knew that co-operation between human beings is the basis of social cohesion and that fostering the competitive spirit is one of the preludes to war."[100]

Dora has proved to be the single most vociferous defender of the school. She chides Russell for criticizing after the fact what he seemed to think was working well at the time.[101] Both volumes of her autobiography contain extended treatments of the school. She is not alone in her feeling that it did not fail. David Harley sums up his thorough investigation of the school and its early pupils by saying that "throughout my research, I have not encountered a single individual connected with the school who thought it was a failure"[102] Even Kate Russell acknowledges, "Though I have been among the school's critics, I believe that it performed an invaluable service, both to the children who learned there and as what is now known as a 'pilot project' for others."[103]

As we saw with Dewey's Laboratory School, the judgment of the success or failure of an educational experiment to a large extent depends on what one's expectations were for it in the first place. Dora sees Beacon Hill as a success. It set out to produce autonomous individuals and in many cases it did. The children "learned to live in democratic freedom, and, with free speech, to handle their own and other languages, both spoken and written; they were able to practice various arts and to take the first steps in science. They studied their own bodies and the natural world and what happened in human history, including the events actually taking place around them. They were not fed illusions, but neither did they lack ideals." She concludes that "so equipped, children should be able to adapt to whatever kind of life the future might bring."[104]

Some authors contend that although Dora and Bertrand Russell had similar views on education, they were not identical. Alan Wood claims that Dora's approach to freedom was much more extreme. If we take the case of nudity in the school as an example, it does seem to have gotten far more flagrant under Dora's sole leadership than it was when they ran the school together.[105] Terry Philpot says they differed on the aims of education as well; while Russell's main preoccupation was the education of the individual, Dora also believed "that education should stress how human beings could live together in harmony. She wanted the child to be allowed to develop as an individual and as a social being so that a truly *living* democracy might be created."[106] It is difficult to fully accept this judgment, since Russell wanted to education the citizen as well as the individual, though it was to be a citizen of the world free from nationalistic or doctrinal biases. This was to be accomplished, according to Ronald Jager, by trying to create almost from scratch the kind of human being that he supposed the world needed. Thus, Beacon Hill School took in very young children and proposed to educate them from babyhood to university age. Russell sought to reform society by means of "an educational reform of the psychological structure of mankind." He saw philosophy as envisioning and education as molding loyalties to the world and to mankind.[107]

The question of how to educate the citizen looms large in Russell's second book on education, *Education and the Social Order,* which was published in 1932.[108] It is a problem, he admits, since what constitutes the good of the individual is often directly at odds with the characteristics that states wish to promote in their citizens. Thus, traditional education is usually conservative and reactionary and runs counter to the scientific frame of mind which holds that although truth is discoverable, one's own beliefs should be held as tentative and undogmatic, "as approximations subject to future correction." We need to promote such an attitude in the young and cultivate in them a sense of loyalty to the world itself. To do this more freedom is required in education, though with certain limitations such as what is necessary in regard to health and hygiene, some sense of punctuality (which Russell sees as a quality bound up with social cooperation), honesty and the respect for the property of others, and the importance of routine. The last-mentioned is important because children become nervously exhausted when faced with too much uncertainty, and, like all of us, they benefit from the security of knowing more or less what is going to happen day by day.

Routine also involves providing a sense of direction and discipline for the child's activities. "The capacity for consistent self-direction," says Russell, "is one of the most valuable that a human being can possess. It is practically unknown in young children, and is never developed either by a very rigid discipline or by complete freedom." Children will be interested in learning concrete facts, but they may also have to be compelled to gain more abstract knowledge. "Very few children have a spontaneous impulse to learn the multiplication table," for instance, yet it is such abstract knowledge that makes a civilized community possible.[109]

A primary concern must be to teach them the scientific attitude which will demand evidence for what is believed and follow it regardless of the direction in which it leads. This attitude will be at variance with religious beliefs as they are usually taught, traditional sex and moral education, and the teaching of nationalism which inevitably entails the teaching of false propositions. Russell feels strongly that "Education could easily, if men choose, produce a sense of the solidarity of the human race, and of the importance of international co-operation." Competition should be avoided as much as possible as well as trying to get all students to fit the same mold. Having issued a call for human solidarity, he quickly reverts to his own perspective as the third Earl Russell, and loftily intones, "A great deal of needless pain and friction would be saved to clever children if they were not compelled to associate intimately with stupid contemporaries. There is an idea that rubbing up against all and sundry in youth is a good preparation for life. This appears to me to be rubbish. No one, in later life, associates with all and sundry."[110]

Once again the aristocrat peers out from behind his democratic facade and reminds us all to keep in our proper place. Dewey would reject such an attitude as running counter to the goals of democratic society as well as the nature of educative experience. Russell managed to temper his feelings for humanity with a positive acceptance of some of the features of the class structure of his own society, and apparently never saw any inconsistency in doing so.

He closes with a favorable account of education in Soviet Russia (he was later to become outspoken in his criticism of Russian policies) and issues stern warnings about the increased use of propaganda in education, whether it be for advancement of political parties, creeds, or nations. Again our best defense against one-sided propaganda is the development of the scientific attitude. He makes a plea for the establishment of an international authority strong enough to impose its settlement of disputes on recalcitrant states. Ours is a mad world, and the only cure is to make men sane by educating them sanely. We need not despair, he concludes, for "the means of happiness for the human race exist, and it is only necessary that the human race should choose to use them."[111]

This combination of a critical diagnosis of society's ills together with a hopeful prognosis for future remedy through education runs through most of Russell's other writings on education. Usually he calls for more freedom but always with some limits. Thus, in "Education and Discipline" (1935), he calls for more cooperation among children developed within a context of adult guidance and authority. Having learned his lesson at Beacon Hill, he now informs us, "Consideration for others does not, with most children, arise spontaneously, but it has to be taught, and can hardly be taught except by the exercise of authority."[112] The time and energy required of the teacher can be greatly fatiguing and produce irritation, so he advocates that teaching be undertaken for at most two hours a day by teachers who can then spend the rest of the day away from children. Judging from Kate Russell's comments quoted earlier, most of the staff at Beacon Hill would have enthusiastically supported this proposal.

In an article entitled "The Functions of a Teacher" (1940), he repeats the idea that teachers are overworked.[113] Most teachers have too many demands upon them and not enough freedom to decide what they want to teach and how they want to go about doing it. The teaching profession needs more opportunities for self-determination and more independence from interfering bureaucrats and bigots. Like the artist, the philosopher, or the person of letters, the teacher needs to be directed by an inner creative impulse, rather than by an outside authority.

In his "Proposals for an International University" (1942), Russell again addresses the problem of promoting an unbiased treatment of subjects such as history. He proposes the establishment of a postgraduate institution of higher learning that would screen textbooks, do research, and train teachers in a way that would avoid narrow nationalistic concerns and inspire universal human loyalty. This school would be open to people of all ages, races, and religions, "except such as reject the idea of international government." It would act as a kind of final authority in the selection of texts: "Every author of a textbook would have to seek the *imprimatur* of the international university before his book could be used in the schools."[114]

One cannot help having the uncomfortable feeling that Russell wants to replace bigotry and narrow-mindedness with an intolerance of his very own. As an example of this in practice, there is the statement by Kate Russell that at

Beacon Hill "there was never a cogent presentation of the Christian faith . . . from someone who really believed in it."[115] And what would be the response to this from the advocate of complete freedom of speech, the advocate of hearing all the evidence and seeing both sides of contentious issues? Probably what he said when describing the first year of the school's operation: "Certainly, for my part, I am not prepared to tell children anything I do not believe."[116]

A change of heart toward some of the practices at Beacon Hill (and perhaps another indication of how his views differed from Dora's) can be found in his article "As School Opens—The Educators Examined" (1952). Here he points out good and bad features of the progressive approach to education. Among the latter are the overencouragement of the child's initiative. Children need order, direction, and discipline even in their play. In regard to artistic creation, they should not be misled into thinking that their own little works are on a level with that excellence which can only come with rigorous training. As a matter of fact, says Russell (*pace* Dora), "I would rather have children act some good play than spend the time learning by heart what they have co-operatively produced."[117] He would insist upon good manners; the child's freedom of speech should not extend to being rude to parents or teachers.

Finally, in "Education for a Difficult World" (1961), he argues that although scientific skill is necessary to develop a better world, it is by no means sufficient. It can help us know the means, but it is no substitute for the wisdom of knowing which ends to pursue. That comes from the study of great literature or history. One of the major things that education should give is "the power of seeing the general in the particular, the power of feeling that this, although it is happening to *me,* is very like what happens to others, what has happened through many ages, and may continue to happen."[118] This kind of impersonal, objective attitude with an openness to all of one's fellows and a loyalty to the world itself is the only way that Russell can see for people to live together in harmony and our world to survive.[119]

CONCLUSION

We have recounted Russell's views on education before, during, and after his practical involvement with the Beacon Hill School. Some of them remained virtually unchanged (e.g., the need for a truly international approach to the teaching of history), others were tempered by the actual experience of having tried to run a school (e.g., on the amount of adult supervision needed by young children), and still others seemed to distinguish themselves from the views of Dora once their partnership had broken up (e.g., on the value of spontaneous group authorship and performance of plays). I think a case can be made for the claim that Russell was less radical in his approach to freedom in the school than was Dora and certainly that he was unfairly treated by the press and by various critics of his educational thought and practice.

He was evidently depressed by that whole episode of his life, which ended in the splitting up of his family, and he was discouraged by the fact that the school did not seem to be producing the world reformers he had hoped it would. One reason for this failure might be, as Kate Russell has pointed out, that being taught to see two sides to every question (except perhaps for religion) tends to dampen one's crusading spirit.[120] Both Russells seemed at times incredibly naive about the impulses of small children, and often oblivious to the sagging morale and hardship imposed upon their teaching staff. At their best, their views on education tended to complement one another. She was willing to limit the child's freedom in regard to health and hygiene, he when it came to the acquiring of knowledge. Perhaps the most positive judgment we can make is that together they attempted to put into practice Russell's belief that education at its best is based on knowledge wielded by love. At times neither the knowledge nor the love seemed very prominent at Beacon Hill. In the end, this may have been their greatest failure.

Curiously enough, Russell displays almost the obverse of the shortcomings usually associated with philosophers of education. He does not shy away from practical difficulties and is eager to put his ideas to the test; on the other hand, his ideas often lack intellectual rigor and overall cohesion. He tells us in so many words what he dislikes in our schools (nationalism, religious indoctrination, sexual hypocrisy) and what he would like to see developed (international understanding, a scientific outlook, sexual frankness) but gives little underlying argument or set of principles upon which to ground his specific educational proposals. He speaks from strong personal feelings, but is easily dissuaded from the more painstaking task of clarifying and revising his thoughts in light of their practical consequences.

This is no doubt because of the highly emotional connections that existed between his being the husband of Dora, the father of John and Kate, and the "Masther" at Beacon Hill. Unlike Dewey, his views on education were not part and parcel of a philosophy of human experience. Unlike Whitehead, he was unable to give us a set of basic categories or provide us with a fresh way of seeing the process of education. What we do get from Russell on education comes as much from his heart as from his head, from his lifelong desire to ameliorate the ills of mankind. He may have failed to accomplish what he set out to do at Beacon Hill; nonetheless, he serves to remind us of the vitally important need to educate the young to be socially cooperative, peace-loving, morally responsible citizens of the world. We can learn from his mistakes and perhaps also absorb some of his fervor for justice and mutual understanding.

What Russell has to offer as philosopher who was also an educator is very much what he had to offer as a man driven, as he tells us in his *Autobiography,* by three passions: the longing for love, the search for knowledge, and pity for the suffering of mankind. His achievement can best be summed up in his own words:

> Love and knowledge, so far as they were possible, led upward toward the heavens. But always pity brought me back to earth. . . . the whole world of loneliness, poverty and pain [that] make a mockery of what human life should be. I long to alleviate the evil, but I cannot, and I too suffer.[121]

It is to Russell's credit that he made the effort. His life and thought should challenge us to reaffirm our faith in education as a means toward perfecting man.

CHAPTER FOUR

Alfred North Whitehead and the Rhythm of Education

[B]eing tackled at Rugby, there is the Real. Nobody who hasn't been knocked down has the slightest notion of what the Real is . . . I used to play in the middle of the scrum. They used to hack at your shins to make you surrender the ball, a compulsory element—but the question was *How you took it*—your own self-creation. Freedom lies in summoning up a mentality which transforms the situation, as against letting organic reactions take their course. [1]

Education is not merely an appeal to the abstract intelligence. Purposeful activity, intellectual activity, and the immediate sense of worthwhile achievement, should be conjoined in a unity of experience. . . . My own experience, which is a large one, in the educational requirements of the population in London has convinced me that the sharp distinction between institutions devoted to abstract knowledge and those devoted to application and to handicraft is a mistake. [2]

ALFRED NORTH WHITEHEAD was born in Ramsgate, Kent, in 1861. As he tells us, his grandfather, father, uncles, and brothers were all engaged in "activities concerned with education, religion, and Local Administration." His grandfather was head of a private school in Ramsgate, as was his father. Even when his father gave up the school and became an Anglican minister, he "never lost his interest in education, and daily visited his three parochial schools, for infants, for girls, and for boys. As a small boy . . . I often accompanied him."[3] Because he was considered to be a frail boy, Whitehead was educated at home by his father until he was fourteen. This teaching was supplemented by a steady exposure to many of the leading men of the day who happened to be visiting his family and by his geographical location which enabled him to travel to historical sites and gain a first-hand experience of the glories of the past.

In 1875, he attended Sherborne School in Dorsetshire where he received a predominantly classical education, with some time off from Latin to do extra work in mathematics.[4] Besides playing rugby and cricket, and being named

Whitehead and the staff of the Department of Mathematics and Mechanics, University of London, 1922–1923; Whitehead is fourth from the left in the front row. Photograph courtesy of Imperial College Archives.

Captain of the Games, he was also put in charge of discipline outside the classroom. In this capacity he once had to cane a boy before the whole school for stealing.[5] His spare time was spent reading poetry and history.

Whitehead's adult life is usually divided into three periods corresponding to the three different places where he lived and worked: Cambridge, where he began as a student at Trinity College in 1880 and left as a Fellow in 1910 "chiefly from a desire to preserve by a change to the more varied life of London the necessary freshness for my work"[6]; London, where he was Professor of Applied Mathematics at the Imperial College of Science and Technology at Kensington from 1914 to 1924, and was actively involved in educational administration; Cambridge, Massachusetts, where he taught at Harvard from 1924 to 1937 and remained until his death in 1947. A common thread through these three periods is his abiding interest in mathematics and science and the most effective ways of teaching them. At Cambridge, England, he wrote a dissertation on Maxwell's theory of electricity and magnetism and published his first book, *A Treatise on Universal Algebra, With Applications* (1898).

His interests were by no means narrowly specialized, however. Although all his lectures heard as a student were on pure and applied mathematics, as a member of a student society known as the Apostles and through "incessant conversation" with friends, students, and faculty, he managed to acquire a thorough grounding in the humanities as well. He later depicted this Cambridge period of his life as having supplied him with a kind of Platonic education, "with its emphasis on mathematics and on free discussion among friends," an education well suited for the nineteenth-century leisure class but otherwise very limited in its application to life.[7]

Two people who were to have a continuing influence on Whitehead's life and thought stem from this period: Evelyn Willoughby Wade, who was to become his wife and the mother of his three children; and Bertrand Russell, who started as his student and eventually became a colleague, collaborator, and friend. Of Evelyn he has said, "The effect of my wife upon my outlook on the world has been so fundamental, that it must be mentioned as an essential factor in my philosophical output. . . . Her vivid life has taught me that beauty, moral and aesthetic, is the aim of existence; and that kindness, and love, and artistic satisfaction are among its modes of attainment."[8] Russell attended Whitehead's lectures on statics in 1890 and was quickly recognized as an outstanding student. When Evelyn took him to task for the severity of his criticism of Russell's fellowship dissertation, Whitehead is said to have defended himself by saying that it was the last time he would be able to speak to Russell as a pupil.[9]

Russell and Whitehead continued to discuss mathematical topics. In 1903, when Russell's *The Principles of Mathematics* appeared, Whitehead ceased working on a second volume of his *Universal Algebra* and began collaborating with Russell on a second volume of the *Principles*. This led to a ten-year effort culminating in the three-volume *Principia Mathematica* (1910–1913). It was a truly joint effort, with each commenting on drafts written by the other. Russell characterized Whitehead as more patient, accurate, and careful than he was, but also more complicated. "Neither of us alone could have written the book," he said; and "even together, and with the alleviation brought by mutual discussion, the effort was so severe that at the end we both turned aside from mathematical logic with a kind of nausea."[10] Outside of this attempt to deduce mathematics from logic, the philosophic interests of the two proved to be quite divergent, and their collaboration came to an end. They remained friends, even through a difficult period when Whitehead's youngest son was killed in action in France in 1918 and Russell refused to modify his pacifist views. Even in these disagreements, Russell admits that "he was more tolerant than I was, and it was much more my fault that these differences caused a diminution in the closeness of our friendship."[11] Russell, although often faced with financial problems of his own, surreptitiously lent Evelyn Whitehead money from time to time to help pay for bills that Whitehead would run up but not be able to settle.[12]

Whitehead left Cambridge for London in 1910 and did not have an academic position there until 1911, when he taught mechanics and astronomy in the Department of Applied Mathematics at University College, London. He applied for a chair in the department in 1912 but did not get it.[13] Instead, he was appointed to a Readership in Geometry in the Department of Pure Mathematics. In 1914, he was appointed to a chair of Applied Mathematics at the Imperial College of Science and Technology at Kensington, a position he held until 1924. It was during this period in London that Whitehead became aware of the practical problems of education in a big city, and became increasingly involved with committees and administrative work which were part of the attempt to resolve them. His book *An Introduction to Mathematics* (1911) had been a popular addition to the Home University Library Series. He became president of the Mathematical Association in 1916. He was governor of the Borough Polytechnic Institute at Southwark, a member of the Senate and Dean of the Faculty of Science at the University of London, chairman of the Academic Council which managed the internal affairs concerning education in London, and chairman of the Delegacy administering Goldsmith's College, one of England's major institutions for the training of teachers.[14] From 1919 to 1921 he was a member of the National Committee to inquire into the position of the classics in the educational system of the United Kingdom.

Whitehead says, "There were endless other committees involved in these positions. In fact, participation in the supervision of London education, University and Technological, joined to the teaching duties of my professorship at the Imperial College constituted a busy life."[15] In his study of Whitehead's views on education, Harold Dunkel maintains that we should not overestimate the importance of his practical involvement in education. Dunkel concludes, "Though Whitehead served on many educational boards, councils and committees, he was never a professional administrator or student of the educational system. His interest stemmed from being an educator in the same sense as are all professors who are sincere and conscientious about their professional duties."[16] Since this is an important counterclaim to my own analysis of the relationship of theory and practice in Whitehead's educational thought, it is worthwhile to take a closer look at the kind of involvement we are talking about. I would like briefly to describe Whitehead's membership on the Surrey Education Committee from 1921 to 1924.[17]

The Surrey Education Committee was established by a resolution of the Surrey County Council on 10 February 1903 in order to bring the Education Act of 1902 into operation. This act empowered such councils to be the local educational authority for their area with full financial control. Education committees were set up to carry out this function. Their membership was drawn from council members and other persons "with experience in education or those who had intimate knowledge of the needs of the various kinds of schools in the district."[18] Whitehead was appointed to serve as a selected member of the committee representing the Imperial College; he was also appointed to serve on the Scholarships Sub-committee and the Educational Reports Sub-committee, as well as being a member of the Standing Committee on Higher Education.[19]

The Standing Committee on Higher Education dealt with very practical matters. Their report of 26 July 1921, for example, deals with the provision of secondary school accommodation, courses, personnel, admissions, fence and buildings, tuition fees, teachers' salaries, scholarships and exhibitions, the training of teachers, and even such mundane but necessary items as lavatory facilities at the Guildford Technical Institute. From all I can tell, Whitehead was present at that meeting.[20] Whitehead's involvement with the committee is difficult to document, and his attendance at committee meetings was sporadic at best.[21] Upon completion of his term, he was replaced as the representative of the Imperial College by Professor W. W. Watts, F.R.S.[22] There is no record of any communication between Whitehead and Watts in regard to the activities of the committee.

So it seems that Whitehead had a diminishing interest in the educational affairs of Surrey County. His poor attendance in the last two years of his term might be attributed to his impending move from England to America. Or it might be that he had by then sized up the committee and its work and decided nonattendance was the better course. Whatever his eventual feelings toward the committee, I merely point to this as one of the many instances where he participated in the practical consideration of educational problems. He was also apparently known to have had such an interest by being named representative of the Imperial College on the committee in the first place.

I grant Dunkel's point that Whitehead's educational activities can no way be described as those of a professional administrator, but I think they show far more interest in such practical matters than is the case with professors who are simply being "sincere and conscientious about their professional duties." Whitehead's membership on bodies such as the Surrey Education Committee or his role as an administrator at the University of London strike me as the natural outcome of his general approach to abstract ideas, his impatience with mere linguistic expressions of "the Real," his dislike of divorcing headwork from handicrafts. I believe that in the same way as did Dewey and Russell, Whitehead sought to put his educational ideas into practice and that, in turn, his practical experiences served to modify and amplify the ideas. He himself said that "this experience of the problems of London, extending for fourteen years, transformed my views as to the problem of higher education in a modern industrial civilization."[23] The same enthusiasm for practical education can be seen years later in his strong support for the newly established Harvard Business School. The importance he attached to his practical involvement in education has been attested to by Victor Lowe, who says, "he never gave his research priority over his educational work; one cause of his failure to complete the fourth volume of *Principia Mathematica* in the post-war years was his participation in administrative affairs at the University of London."[24]

Lest this convey the impression that Whitehead perhaps had his heart in the wrong place and should have dropped the committee work and stuck to his research, Lowe points out that instead of finishing the *Principia*, Whitehead, as necessary preliminaries to the latter task, did write three books on the foundations of physics: *Enquiry concerning the Principles of Natural Knowledge* (1919), *The Concept of Matter* (1920), and *The Principle of Relativity* (1922). He had visited the United States in 1922 and given a lecture at Bryn Mawr.[25] Soon after came an invitation to join the Philosophy Department at Harvard. Although he was sixty-three years old, he accepted the invitation with obvious relish, writing to a friend that "the post might give me a welcome opportunity of developing in systematic form my ideas on Logic, the Philosophy of Science, Metaphysics, and some more general questions, half philosophical and half practical, such as Education."[26] Whitehead was given a five-year appointment to Harvard, which was eventually extended until his retirement in 1937. As Russell put it with only slight exaggeration, "In England, Whitehead was regarded as a mathematician, and it was left to America to discover him as a philosopher."[27]

Indeed, it was while at Harvard that Whitehead produced his major philosophical works: *Science and the Modern World* (The Lowell Lectures for 1925), *Religion in the Making* (1926), *Symbolism, Its Meaning and Effect* (1927), *The Function of Reason* (1929), *Process and Reality: An Essay in Cosmology* (1929), *Adventures of Ideas* (1933), and *Modes of Thought* (1938). In 1929, he collected together a number of his talks and essays on education ranging from 1912 to 1928 and published them under the title *The Aims of Education and Other Essays*. A remarkable output for an English mathematician who first came to America when he was nearing retirement age!

John Smith argues that in his adherence to the belief that thinking is primarily an activity aimed at solving problems, that ideas and theories must make a difference in the conduct of the people who hold them, and the belief that the earth can be civilized and obstacles to knowledge overcome by the application of knowledge, Whitehead can quite properly be classified as an American philosopher in the spirit of Peirce, James, Royce, and Dewey.[28] I concur with that assessment, particularly in regard to Whitehead's views on education. In what follows I try to summarize his educational views while indicating their practical applicability. I concentrate on his thoughts on the teaching of mathematics but also consider the question of the overall aims of education, the Report of the Committee on the Classics and Whitehead's likely contributions to it, and the insight that there is a rhythm of education. Some remarks are made on his approach to university education; and, where appropriate, an evaluation of some of the criticisms that have been made of his views is offered. In all this we look for that interplay between the practical and the theoretical that we found operating in the thought of Dewey and Russell.

THE TEACHING OF MATHEMATICS

Whitehead's earliest writings on education have to do with the teaching of mathematics. In *An Introduction to Mathematics* (1911), he explains the nature and methods of mathematics and its symbolism, generalizations of number, geometry, trigonometry, and the differential calculus. He begins the book by noting that "the study of mathematics is apt to commence in disappointment" because its fundamental ideas are not presented to the student "disentangled from the technical procedure which has been invented to facilitate their exact presentation in particular instances."[29] The student is overwhelmed with technical details unilluminated by any general conception. What is needed is an explanation of the basic ideas done as simply as possible and with some indication of how they orginated and how they apply to our everyday lives.

Throughout the book, Whitehead gradually introduces the reader to the more abstract elements of mathematics while referring to the history of their development to show which individuals formulated the ideas and in what manner. Thus, we have Archimedes leaping from his bath, Galileo dropping weights from the leaning tower of Pisa, Newton and Leibniz quarreling over who invented the differential calculus. All this serves to humanize the abstractions, to make them more vivid, and to convey a sense of the adventure and advance of ideas.

Whitehead also tries to connect the mathematical ideas he is explaining to situations from everyday life. For example, in talking of the graphical representation of vectors by straight lines, he asks the reader to consider a moving steamer with a man walking across its deck. In his discussion of continuous and discontinuous functions, he speaks of a train in its journey from Euston station passing a certain number of stations in a certain amount of time. A train also serves to illuminate his explanation of the differential calculus. The examples are often wittily given, as in his discussion of the mathematical idea of a series where he asks us to consider "the series of English Prime Ministers during the nineteenth century, arranged in the order of their first tenure of that office within the century." The series, he points out, "commences with William Pitt, and ends with Lord Roseberry, who, appropriately enough, is the biographer of the first member."[30]

For all of his references to the applicability of mathematical ideas, Whitehead is not one to slight the importance of seeking to know things for their own sake. "The really profound changes in human life all have their origin in knowledge pursued for its own sake," he claims. As an instance of this he mentions the origin of conic sections. "No more impressive warning can be given to those who would confine knowledge and research to what is apparently useful, than the reflection that conic sections were studied for 1800 years merely as an abstract science, without a thought of any utility other than to satisfy the craving for knowledge on the part of mathematicians" before they were found to be "the necessary key with which to attain the knowledge of the most important laws of nature."[31] On the other hand, some abstract ideas originate from practical concerns. Trigonometry, for example, was invented because it was needed for astronomical research. Its importance, "both to the theory and the application of mathematics, is only one of innumerable instances of the fruitful ideas which the general science has gained from its practical applications."[32]

Mathematics is therefore depicted by Whitehead as an abstract science with an interesting history of development and an ongoing practical utility. The student is encouraged to pursue the subject further but warned not to expect to attain complete mastery of it since "the science has grown to such vast proportions that probably no living mathematician can claim to have achieved this."[33] Whitehead displays sound pedagogy here by judiciously combining enthusiasm with realistic expectations. His advice seems singularly appropriate today given the tremendous advances and specializations in mathematics.

Many of these aspects of his own introductory book on mathematics can be found in his essays and talks on the teaching of mathematics. In "Mathematics and Liberal Education" (1912), he proclaims that we are in the midst of an educational revolution which will see the end of the absolute dominance of classical ideas in education. This revolution reflects fundamental changes in our daily lives whereby science has entered the very texture of our thoughts, mechanical inventions have transformed our industrial system and the social structure based upon it, and we now have a worldwide sense of human affairs. What these momentous changes portend for educators is that we must now show our students how logic applies to life.[34]

This can best be accomplished by the proper teaching of elementary mathematics. It is one of the most characteristic creations of modern thought "by virtue of the intimate way in which it correlates theory and practice." We should see to it that our course in elementary mathematics has a threefold character.

First, our pupils should be left with "a precise perception of the nature of the abstractions acquired by constant use of them, illumined by explanations and finally by precise statements." Second, "the logical treatment of such ideas is to be exemplified by trains of reasoning which employ them and interconnect them." And third, "the application of these ideas to the course of nature conceived in its widest sense as including human society is to be made familiar." This is to be done in order to avoid making mathematics into "a silly subject with silly applications." Far from it, we want to generate in our pupils "a capacity to apply ideas to the concrete universe." To this end, Whitehead maintains that through the study of statistics and the reduction of these to graphs "half of the teaching of modern history should be handed over to the mathematicians." Statistics can help us study social forces by giving us a grasp of such quantitative factors as these are found in trade, railway traffic, harvests, health, prices, population, crime, weather, and taxes. "The reduction of these to graphs, the careful study of the peculiarities of these graphs, the search for correlations among them, and the study of the public events which corresponded in time to peculiarities in graphical form, would," Whitehead asserts, "teach more mathematics and more knowledge of modern social forces than all our present methods put together."[35]

Whitehead's main point is that modern times require a modern approach to mathematics; "the elements of mathematics should be treated as the study of a set of fundamental ideas, the importance of which the student can immediately appreciate." To achieve this we should "simplify the details and emphasize the important principles and applications."[36] It is only by giving mathematics such a "breath of reality" that we will secure for it a place as an important element in the liberal education of the future.

Whitehead pursued this theme in a paper he read to the Educational Section of the International Congress of Mathematicians held in Cambridge in 1912. Here he asks, "What are the qualities of mind which a mathematical training is designed to produce when it is employed as an element in a liberal education?" and his answer is that "the object of a mathematical education is, to acquire the powers of analysis, of generalisation, and of reasoning."[37] This entails the power of grasping abstract ideas. The only way to acquire the habit and power of using such ideas, says Whitehead, is to do so habitually. We should start with the most obvious general ideas, such as in geometry the ideas of volumes, surfaces, lines, and straightness and curvature; or, in elementary algebra, the idea of functionality. The method used is "continual practice in the consideration of the simplest particular cases" and the goal is power of use.

The power of logical reasoning involves acquiring the habit of thinking logically, and the study of elementary mathematics trains the mind in deductive logic. This power of concentrated logical thinking does not exist in the mind ready-made; it must be developed gradually. Whitehead would have the student "initially to learn the meaning of the ideas by a crude practice in simple ways, and [then] to refine the logical procedure in preparation for an advance to greater generality."[38] It is a mistake to start with ideas in their refined, analyzed, and generalized forms. This is our goal. What we start with are the relatively crude, uncivilized ideas of the child. Whitehead compares the schoolmaster to a missionary who must deal with the "savages" which are "the ideas in the child's mind."[39]

This approach to the teaching of mathematics is made even more explicit in his presidential address to the London Branch of the Mathematical Association in 1912. If mathematics is to retain a position of importance in the curriculum of today, he says, it must be taught so as to relate clearly to the modern world. Most people think of mathematics as the paradigm case of an abstruse subject, one whose ideas are "of highly special application and rarely influence thought." This is largely owing to the way in which mathematics has traditionally been taught, "by teaching innumerable special results from general ideas, each result more recondite than the preceding." To counter this tendency, Whitehead would have the basic ideas in mathematics presented as "the simple study of a few general truths, well illustrated by practical examples."[40] Students should be led to see how mathematical ideas are essential to the precise formulation of the mechanical laws of sciences. For example, "the analytical and geometrical ideas find immediate application in the physical laboratory where a course of simple experimental mechanics should have been worked through."[41] It should be noted here that Whitehead himself was not a regular frequenter of scientific laboratories. As Lowe tells us, "No history of the Cavendish Laboratory mentions Whitehead when naming the young men who worked there. In my biographical research I have not found any evidence that he ever participated in any experimental investigation. His concern was always with mathematical ideas, their symbolization and logical structure, *and* their explanatory power."[42]

Besides this awareness of the experimental implications of mathematical ideas, Whitehead stresses that the more intelligent students can be shown how the fundamental properties of quantity in general have led to the introductions of the kinds of numerical measurement they have been studying. He saw the reading of Euclid's fifth book as an excellent way to accomplish this. Another important use of mathematics is its role as "the chief instrument in logical method." Geometry is especially useful in this regard because in it "the essence of logical method receives immediate exemplification." In geometry we can also make practical applications to plans and maps. In his proposed scheme of things, the actual amount of mathematical deduction at each stage would be slight, but "much more explanation would be given, the importance of each proposition being illustrated by examples, either worked out or for students to work, so selected as to indicate the fields of thought to which it applies."[43]

THE AIMS OF EDUCATION

In his presidential address of 1916 to the Mathematical Association of England,[44] Whitehead expanded upon his view of the aims of education as a whole. He continued his protest against reconditeness by alluding to the necessity of avoiding "inert ideas"—"ideas that are merely received into the mind without being utilized, or tested, or thrown into fresh combinations." An educational system overladen with such inert ideas exhibits mere pedantry and routine and is not only useless but downright harmful. Whitehead would have us prevent such "mental dryrot" by showing our students that the ideas we are asking them to learn are indeed useful. Rather than allowing them to remain inert, he would have us utilize ideas. "By utilizing an idea," he says, "I mean relating it to that stream, compounded of sense perceptions, feelings, hopes, desires, and of mental activities adjusting thought to thought, which forms our life."

For Whitehead, education is "the acquisition of the art of the utilisation of knowledge." In a statement reminiscent of Dewey, he says, "There is only one subject-matter for education, and that is Life in all its manifestations. Instead of this single unity we offer children—Algebra, from which nothing follows; Geometry, from which nothing follows; Science, from which nothing follows; History, from which nothing follows; A couple of Languages, never mastered; and lastly, most dreary of all, Literature, represented by plays of Shakespeare, with philosophical notes and short analyses of plot and character to be in substance committed to memory." After this depressing recital of the contents of the typical school curriculum, he asks, "Can such a list be said to represent Life, as it is known in the midst of living it?"[45]

If so much of our subject matter is recondite, inert, overly abstract, and disconnected, is it any wonder that we face so many problems with student motivation and discipline? Whitehead again turns to the teaching of mathematics as a way out of this dilemma. Consider, he says, quadratic equations. They should be taught because our world is through and through "infected with quantity." If we are to make sense of our social, political, and historical situation, we must make use of quantitative information. The idea of the variable, the function, the rate of change, equations and their solutions need not be presented solely to pass an examination or because someone (usually not the student) finds them to be intrinsically interesting, but rather to exhibit the quantitative flux of the forces of modern society. "If this course be followed," he concludes in a manner strikingly similar to Dewey's encomium on the teaching of weaving, "the route from Chaucer to the Black Death, from the Black Death to modern Labour troubles, will connect the tales of the medieval pilgrims with the abstract science of algebra both yielding diverse aspects of that single theme, Life."[46]

While allowing for a certain amount of rhetorical hyperbole to make his point, Whitehead seems to be correctly emphasizing the need to connect the subject matter of the curriculum to life. This is not to say that all subjects have to be shown to have an immediate practical outcome, but they can each be seen as contributing to our understanding of life. And what, he might ask, could be more useful than that? The overall aim of education should be to establish such a connection. As he put it elsewhere, "The aim of education is the marriage of thought and action—that actions should be controlled by thought and that thoughts should issue in action. And beyond both there is the sense for what is worthy in thought and worthy in action."[47] Along these lines he applauds the applications of geometrical drawing being made in connection with machinery and workshop practice in the London Polytechnics.

We are not to neglect the specialist side of education which conveys a sense of style. Style is the last and most useful acquisition of the educated mind. Whitehead calls it "the ultimate morality of the mind." It involves a sense of restraint and appropriateness as well as duty and reverence that go to make up a truly educated person. Someone with style need not be crammed with soon-to-be-outdated information or forced to submit to arbitrary requrements. He or she will have that sense for what is worthy in thought and action that makes for a happy individual and a productive citizen. Whitehead sums up his approach to the aims of education as follows: "What education has to impart is an intimate sense for the power of ideas, for the beauty of ideas, and for the structure of ideas, together with a particular body of knowledge which has peculiar reference to the life of the being possessing it."[48]

Whitehead tried to carry this message to institutions which specialized in practical training. In 1917, in his address at the Prize Distribution at the Borough Polytechnic Institute in Southward, he urged the students to maintain a standard of excellence in their work and to see it as connected with other important aspects of life and happiness such as art and recreation. An engineer will love the beauty of his machines; "he loves also the sense of foresight and of insight which knowledge can give him." This love of order and appreciation for the power of knowledge constitutes the sense of style we have seen him advocate. Again he appeals for the interconnectedness and vitality of ideas, urging the graduates to become aware of the great revolution in painting that is taking place and to recognize the beauty that their own technological knowledge can bring about. He closes by affirming, "People say that machinery and commerce are driving beauty out of the modern world. I do not believe it. A new beauty is being added, a more intellectual beauty, appealing to the understanding as much as to the eye."[49]

His next presidential address to the Mathematical Association, also in 1917, continues in the same vein. He sees the ideal of technical education to be that of the Benedictine monks of the Middle Ages who rejoiced in their labors. In the same spirit, we should try to transfuse our work with intellectual and moral vision and turn it into a joy. The way to accomplish this is to conceive of technical education in a liberal spirit, "as a real intellectual enlightenment in regard to principles applied and services rendered. In such an education geometry and poetry are as essential as turning lathes."[50]

Whitehead contrasts the Benedictine ideal with the so-called Platonic ideal of a liberal education for thought and aesthetic appreciation, the type of education which sought to prepare one for the cultivated life of a leisured aristocrat (cf. his remarks on his own education at Cambridge). Here one seeks to attain a large discursive knowledge of the best literature and a kind of disinterested intellectual appreciation of works of art. But, Whitehead argues, "culture should be for action." Education should impart technique and vision, something the student knows well and something he or she can do well. "This intimate union of practice and theory aids both," and to bring it about he proposes a national system of education which will combine the elements of a literary, a scientific, and a technical curriculum.

Literary studies can provide the techniques of verbal expression and the aesthetic appreciation attendant upon the successful employment of language. Science trains us in the art of observation and in the knowledge and deduction of laws concerning the sequence of natural phenomena. A technical education involves using knowledge for the manufacture of material products. For Whitehead, they are all interconnected, and the study of each will be of benefit in the study of the others. He insists upon the reciprocal influence of brain activity and material creative activity. "If you want to understand anything, make it yourself" is for him a sound rule of education, because by attempting to put your ideas into practice they will "gain that reality which comes from seeing the limits of their application."[51]

Surprisingly, it is this English mathematician with the gentleman's education who advocates so strongly that all students be exposed to technical education. This will provide creative experience while they think and will teach them how to coordinate thought and action. It will give theory "and a shrewd insight as to where theory fails." It must not be relegated to the status of a second-best education for those who cannot make the grade in literary or scientific studies. Science and mathematics can supply the general ideas of techniques to be applied; literature can give creative stimulus and relaxation, as well as vision. Technique and vision culminating in material creative activity represent the Benedictine ideal which saved the vanishing civilization of the ancient world and may well, says Whitehead (remember that this was in the days of World War I), be called upon to perform the same task today.

Several points in this address are major elements in the later development of Whitehead's educational thought. One is the need to connect what he liked to call headwork and handiwork. This was to be a means of overcoming the reconditeness of ideas as well as to supply a unity and vitality to education. His defense of the Benedictine ideal might be taken as a principle that motivated much of his own practical involvement with educational administration and committees like the Surrey Education Committee. He shares with Dewey a respect for the vocational, as well as the technological, side of education and is equally disdainful of the isolation of different subject matters from one another and from life itself. The need to develop both thought and action is a frequent refrain in his educational writings.

A subsidiary point worth noting in this address has to do with the value that was often attached to having children learn to read great works of Greek and Latin literature in the original. Whitehead complained that there was no necessary connection between literature and grammar. On the contrary, "the great age of Greek literature was already past before the arrival of the grammarians of Alexandria. Of all the types of men today existing, classical scholars are the most remote from the Greeks of the Periclean times."[52] These harsh remarks about the teaching of the classics are further sharpened in a talk he gave to the British Association for the Advancement of Science in 1919. There he called for an end to the fallacious belief that the best means to get a literary education is through classical learning. Actually, says Whitehead, this is going about things backward: "You must not go on to a dead language until a modern one has gripped the imagination. Classical learning is the superstructure of a literary education, not the foundation. Classical learning has had its chance with the well-to-do-class, and has failed—failed to impress upon them that learning should mould life, a failure which originates in a lack of relevancy in the subject-matter of education." What is needed in the postwar period, he goes on to say, is a general education "compact of material which will enter into the habitual lives of its recipients, a doctrine which applies alike to language, literature, history, natural science, and to mathematics."[53]

These blasts against classical learning make it all the more interesting that in 1919 Whitehead was appointed, as the only scientist, to be one of the nineteen members of a national committee to inquire into the position of the classics in the educational system of the United Kingdom. Archival material on the committee[54] reveals that a meeting of four school inspectors considered the desirability of setting up such a committee and in a memorandum of 24 July 1919 drew up some terms of reference for it and appended a list of prospective members. Whitehead's name does not appear on this list. A subsequent memorandum of 13 September 1919 indicates the grounds for the establishment of the committee and contains a revised list of prospective members which does include Whitehead. The terms of reference and list of members were accepted, and the committee was officially created by a memorandum of 27 November 1919 signed on behalf of Prime Minister Lloyd George by the historian, H. A. L. Fisher, president of the Board of Education. Let us now consider its Report and then deal with the question of Whitehead's possible contributions to it.

THE COMMITTEE ON THE CLASSICS

The committee was established "to inquire into the position to be assigned to the Classics . . . in the Educational System of the United Kingdom, and to advise as to the means by which the proper study of these subjects may be maintained and improved."[55] It sat for 85 days and interviewed 140 witnesses, including officials of the Civil Service Commission, representatives of universities, members of Local Educational authorities, persons connected with the Working Men's College, the Labour Party, the Workers' Educational Association, members of leading commercial firms, and journalists. Many other individual witnesses appeared before the committee, and still others submitted memoranda. Questionnaires were sent to "the Modern Universities and University Colleges, the Women's Colleges of Oxford and Cambridge, and all the Schools of the Headmaster's Conference and of the Incorporated Associations of Head Masters and Head Mistresses," while information was contributed unofficially by individual members of Oxford and Cambridge universities.

The committee acknowledged right from the start that the position of exceptional privilege the classics held in European education was owing in some measure to historical causes no longer valid, and they made clear their belief that "the place occupied by the Classics in our national education ought to be determined by their educational value and nothing else."

The Introduction to the Report considers various arguments for and against the study of the classics. A person who has successfully completed an honors course in classics would be likely to defend the study by claiming 1) to have gained access to prose and poetry that many judge to be the noblest in the world; 2) to have studied a civilization in which many of the fundamental problems were like those of the present day but in vastly simpler forms and on a much smaller scale; 3) that training in the classics provides a superb exercise for the different powers of the mind by combining memory training, imagination, aesthetic appreciation, and scientific method. Such a fully trained classical scholar would thereby be better able to enjoy, understand, and master the world he or she lives in.[56]

Many students, of course, are not capable or interested in pursuing the classics to these lofty heights. Some will study them until they enter university. This will give them an excellent preparation for the study of such subjects as history and English and even natural science. Others will stay in school only until they are eighteen. They too would benefit from a classical course, though admittedly one "less exacting on the linguistic side," perhaps learning Latin and Greek "for the purpose of reading only, with no composition at all." The large number of boys and girls who will drop the study of the classics altogether at about the age of sixteen should at least take a course which gives some general knowledge of the ancient world "based both on modern histories and on translations." Even for them the classics can be an important preliminary to the pursuit of other studies, for instance, journalism. The committee asserts somewhat optimistically, "The better classical scholars our writers are, the more precise should be their statements and the more lucid their thought; the better scholars their readers are, the more they will look for precision and be repelled by the lack of it."[57] When one recalls Whitehead's scathing remarks about classical scholars, one can well imagine his squirming in his seat when comments like this were endorsed by the committee.

Another line of defense for the study of the classics is that the languages involved are "sufficiently unlike our own to compel attention to every step in the mechanism of linguistic expression." From this perspective, translations simply will not do, because they cannot capture the "untranslatable quality" of poetry and the higher type of prose. The committee so puffs this up as to make the unrealistic assertion that for students in school a good English translation of Plato will be very inadequate, and "a student who wishes really to understand the Authorised Version of the New Testament must go to the Greek if he is not to be misled." Recall that they are speaking of the majority of students here, not just a select few who seem destined to become the classical scholars of the future. Gilbert Murray sat on the committee and listened to all this, but there is no indication of how he felt about it. Whitehead, as we shall see shortly, had quite a different view about the value of translations. Whether these opinions acted as a kind of counterforce to the majority view is unclear, but it is noteworthy that the committee did come down to earth sufficiently to recommend that subject to the rule that translations can never be a complete substitute for original texts, their use in classical education should be greatly extended provided a teacher be present "who is a competent scholar and knows the text in the original." This seems a rearguard action at best, since the committee admits that fewer and fewer young people have the time, interest, or capacity to pursue classical studies as a career, and thus one could well expect the number of competent scholars to dwindle and the use of translations to increase.

One final comment is in order on the Introduction. There is a definitely Whiteheadian type of suggestion made that there need be no natural antagonism between science and the humanities, neither in aims nor in methods, because both set forth, "in different fields, the aim of enlarging the confines of human knowledge: both pursue knowledge by observation of facts laboriously gathered, wisely selected and carefully tested; and both in their several ways appeal to the aesthetic sense."[58] Later on in the Report, the proposal is made that such commonality might be brought out by incorporating into the study of the classics the history of Greek scientific thought and discovery. Members of the science staff could be invited to take part in the discussions and "Lectures open to the whole upper school might also occasionally be given on such subjects as Greek mathematics and mechanics."[59]

Robert S. Brumbaugh speculates that this proposal was probably "inspired by Whitehead, and probably written by him or copied from a memorandum."[60] The general idea of establishing a connection between science and humanities courses might well have come from the Report of the Proceedings of the Council for Humanistic Studies, entitled *Education, Scientific and Humane*. The committee refers to this Report, and in an Appendix lists resolutions which were passed at a Conference of the Sub-Committee on Education of the Board of Scientific Societies and the Council for Humanistic Studies. Incidentally, Gilbert Murray, the distinguished Hellenist, also sat on this Council for Humanistic Studies, as did H. A. L. Fisher of the Board of Education. The council solicited briefs from various associations; one, dated November 1916, was signed by Whitehead on behalf of the Mathematical Association.[61] Perhaps this was the circuitous route by which his name came to the surface as a prospective member of the Committee on the Classics.

The next part of the committee Report consists of a historical sketch of classical education in England from the Middle Ages to 1920, followed by statistics illustrating the present position of the classics in the schools. The Report admits that classical studies are not exactly flourishing but insists that "Latin or Greek or both are assigned a substantial position in the general education of pupils in Secondary Schols and . . . that full opportunity is given to selected pupils everywhere to carry their study of them to the highest point of which their capacity will admit." Then comes a detailed discussion of some of the practical problems to be faced in implementing this policy, together with a consideration of appropriate texts and "material aids." The latter should include visits to museums and archaeological sites whenever possible.

The Report goes on to deal with the teaching of Latin and Greek in the universities. It takes note of the fact that compulsory Greek has been abolished at Oxford and Cambridge, which is not altogether a bad thing since "no schools will any longer be forced to devise means of teaching their best Science and Mathematical pupils the required modicum of Greek." Again, one detects the unseen hand of Whitehead in the committee's deliberations. In treating of the role of the study of the classics in postgraduate professions, the point is made that they can be highly beneficial since "in the higher branches of industry and commerce what is demanded is character, breadth of view, judgment, grasp of principle, and the power of clear thinking and clear expression." Those parents who refuse to allow their children to learn Latin and Greek because they feel other subjects have greater utility are sadly mistaken, according to the committee. "Such parents, if their children show linguistic capacity, are really depriving them of one of their best chances for success."[62]

The Report concludes with 14 pages of recommendations, ranging from general (e.g., "whenever it is impossible under existing conditions to introduce Greek into a curriculum, everything should be done to strengthen the position of Latin") to very specific (e.g., "the Civil Service Commissioners should be asked to reconsider their Regulations for admission to the Home Civil Service"). Various appendices were attached, many of a statistical nature. All in all, the Report, which appeared in 1921, was 308 pages long—a substantial piece of work for any committee.

Once Fisher had received the Report, he set up an Office Committee to study it and three similar reports commissioned on the position of natural science, modern languages, and English, in order to see how the recommendations might be worked into the practice of the schools. This Office Committee concluded that one could not realistically adopt all the recommendations made on behalf of their individual subjects by the four Reports since there were literally not enough hours in the school day to accommodate them! They did acknowledge the validity of the recommendation that the classics should be taught with reference to their historical and social context and that special attention be paid to recent archaeological work. They also agreed with the Committee on the Classics that under present circumstances the most likely means of guaranteeing students access to the study of Greek could well be simply to transfer them to the few remaining schools that still offer such courses. Other than that, very few changes in the educational system of the United Kingdom were made as a result of the Report of the Committee on the

Classics.[63] This may not have been an unwelcome result, if one can judge from a letter from Crewe (as chairman of the Committee on the Classics) to Fisher (as president of the Board of Education) dated 22 July 1921, where he speaks of his determination "that the document should not be a tract advocating the use of Greek and Latin in and out of season."[64]

Whitehead's exact involvement with the committee and his contributions to the Report are obviously hard to determine. In 1968, Victor Lowe interviewed Dame Dorothy Brock, then the only surviving member of the committee, and "she remembered Wh[itehead] as one who listened quietly and whose questions, not very frequent, were always clear and relevant; and, she said, he never squashed a witness."[65] Lowe maintains that although Whitehead's own defense of the classics differs from that of the committee, this should not be taken to indicate his disagreement within the committee, for "he did not often take stands against the majority."[66] Brumbaugh, on the other hand, makes the case that Whitehead's article "The Place of Classics in Education" (1923) is in effect "a one-man minority report, in which he presented his dissent from the conservative consensus of the classicists who made up a large majority of the Commission."[67]

Indeed, in this article Whitehead makes several points in regard to the study of the classics that are directly at variance with the committee Report. "The future of classics in this country is not going mainly to be decided by the joy of the classics to a finished scholar, and by the utility of scholarly training for scholarly avocations," he begins. Nor is it legitimate to criticize those who would turn away from the classics as being overly concerned with the likelihood of the pecuniary rewards of such study. "As a member of the Prime Minister's Committee on the Place of Classics in Education it was my misfortune to listen to much ineffectual wailing from witnesses on the mercenary tendencies of modern parents. I do not believe the modern parent of any class is more mercenary than his predecessors. When classics was the road to advancement, classics was the popular subject for study." We must face the fact that "in the future ninety percent of the pupils who leave school at the age of eighteen will never again read a classical book in the original."[68]

What can be defended, says Whitehead, is the study of the classics as an introduction to the analysis of thought and to philosophic logic and the vision of the unity of civilization that they provided. Translations are to be used for proper pace and adequate coverage. As if to rub this point in more deeply in light of the committee's enthusiastic praise of the joys of reading texts in the original, Whitehead describes a child laboriously struggling, with constant reference to the dictionary, to translate an epic line word for word. Both scale and pace can be achieved by a judicious blending of translations with reading the work in the original. This should be supplemented by making the child aware of the art and science of Greece and Rome by means of models, pictures, "and sometimes the very objects in museums." In short, "the whole claim for the importance of classics rests on the basis that there is no substitute for first-hand knowledge." Since Greece and Rome are the founders of European civilization, a knowledge of history requires above all a first-hand knowledge of the thoughts of Greeks and Romans. "The history of Europe is the history of Rome," he adds, and "the vision of Rome is the vision of the unity of civilization."[69]

So we have Whitehead's own defense of the classics, departing at significant junctures from that of the committee. It does strike me as a minority report of sorts, the kind of thing a gentle, polite member of a committee might mull over and produce after the fact. His approach to the classics is not as reverential, and his emphasis on the need to develop technique and vision is one we have seen him make before. His experience as a member of the Committee on the Classics no doubt broadened his perspective about the current state of the educational system in the United Kingdom and heightened his interest in the problems of teaching subjects so that ideas are alive and utilized. This led to the next stage of his thinking about education, the attempt to trace out a rhythmic cycle of learning.

THE RHYTHM OF EDUCATION

In a talk on "Science in General Education" (1922), Whitehead again bemoans the fact that in the past there was no unity to what was taught and that "the subjects in the curriculum were taught as incomplete fragments." Science, for example, though deemed useful as a source of practical information was rarely considered in terms of its possible modification of one's character. The latter was assumed to be derived from the study of literature or the humanities. But by eliciting the habit of controlled observation and developing a facility of the imagination which issues in a stimulus for creativeness, science can indeed change the individual for the better. In addition, some of the underlying impulses of scientific investigation, such as the impulse for browsing or the collector's instinct, are held in common with other subjects.

The danger in science teaching is not that we abolish the hard work and exact knowledge but that we "organize genius out of existence" by forgetting the less efficient but more romantic roots of scientific inquiry. Whitehead worries that we will fail to keep in mind the fact that "science and poetry have the same root in human nature." The teaching of science, then, should contain both a hard element of factual information, laboratory work, and experimentation leading to "the attainment of exact knowledge based on first-hand information" and a soft element which encourages the imaginative and fanciful impulses. Those who go on to further study in the university should be made aware of the more general aspects of science such as the notion of the conservation of energy or the theory of evolution. Furthermore, the applications of science should not be neglected: "machinery and its connections with the economic revolution at the beginning of the nineteenth century, the importance of nitrates and their artificial production, coal-tar, aeronautics, and other topics."[70]

This talk was followed by an address in 1922 to the Training College Association of London on "The Rhythm of Education." Here Whitehead spells out his most famous contribution to educational thought—the idea that learning is best accomplished if it proceeds through a rhythmic cycle of stages of romance, precision, and generalization.[71] This is what occurs in the things we learn naturally. Consider the small child learning to speak. Initially there is intense excitement and a tremendous rush to find out what sounds attach to which objects. Anyone who has raised a young child will likely recall the almost feverish delight by which the child continues to ask "What's that?" while eagerly pointing to one object after another. This is what Whitehead calls the stage of romance, where the subject matter is first apprehended as vivid and novel and "holds within itself unexplored connexions with possibilities half-disclosed by glimpses and half-concealed by the wealth of material."[72] This is the stage of Robinson Crusoe, alone on his island and suddenly coming upon a human footprint in the sand. Only a footprint, we might say, but consider the exciting possibilities it portended for Crusoe!

Children learning to speak are in a similar state of exciting discovery. They want to find out more, to gather more information, more facts, to organize them and study them to see if they make sense. So the child begins to develop a vocabulary and some elementary rules to put words together into sentences in order to express his or her feelings, questions, beliefs, and so on. The ferment of romance leads naturally into the request for precision, the stage of exactness of formulation. This is the time for learning grammar, rules and procedures, definitions and techniques. The student gains more facts and a way of analyzing them. But the precision should never be sought as an end in itself; the rules are to be *used*. The child learns how to express himself or herself and to use words to refer to things more generally and even to refer to what is not at hand or not directly experienced. Precision paves the way for entry into the more abstract realm of generalization, which, in turn, brings about a new sense of wonder and a new awareness of possibilities. And so the cycle continues.

"Education should consist in a continual repetition of such cycles," Whitehead asserts. We should realize that the incredibly difficult task of learning a language is by and large successfully accomplished by the small child who can speak, classify ideas, sharpen perceptions, and enlarge the range of experiences by means of language. Considering the difficulty of the task and the extremely young age of the child, the best explanation of the success of this learning process is that "nature, in the form of surrounding circumstances, sets it a task for which the normal development of its brain is exactly fitted." We educators should try to follow a similar pattern and stop postponing the teaching of some subjects because they are thought to be too difficult or imposing others because it is thought that our students might someday need them. What we must do is take account of the fact that the student is alive and has an active mind. In short, "education must essentially be a setting in order of a ferment already stirring in the mind."[73]

What we are after is not the sharpening of a dull, lifeless instrument or the packing of objects into a container or trunk but the rhythmic growth of the human mind. This requires that we seek to find and tap that initial romantic excitement which will then motivate the child to acquire the tools of precision which in turn will lead to a stage of generalization and a new sense of romantic excitement. The idea is a simple one but singularly appropriate to our large, impersonal educational systems where we must overcome the apathy, hostility, and even stupidity of the young in order to "educate" them. Look at how much a child accomplishes in learning to speak, says Whitehead. Why not try to follow a similar pattern in formal education?

I find his idea of the rhythmic stages of learning an extremely suggestive one and have myself proposed it as a model for teaching introductory philosophy.[74] It is, however, mainly a suggestion of a general way of proceeding; the specific details are left to the particular teacher in his or her own situation. Whitehead warns us that the stages are not fixed or distinct. They overlap, and we can speak only of a distinct emphasis or pervasive quality in each stage. Also, the student progresses in certain subjects at different rates. The time for precision in language may well be the time for romance in science. The main point is to recognize the active state of the child's mind and his or her interests and try to channel these on to precision and generalization. The importance Whitehead attached to precision should be noted. He criticizes the Montessori system, because although it quite effectively employs romance and encourages vivid freshness, "it lacks the restraint which is necessary for the great stages of precision." This is a surprising departure from the view of Russell, who thought that there was too much order and regimentation in a Montessori school, and Dewey, who found the Montessori approach guilty of imposing adult distinctions and refinements of thoughts upon a child too young to see them for itself.[75]

The specific examples Whitehead gives of how one might follow the rhythm of education in school are clearly the product of his own time and circumstances. By the age of fifteen, he says, the ordinary child "should have command of English, should be able to read fluently fairly simple French, and should have completed the elementary stage of Latin." More gifted children can begin their study of Greek at this time. Some history would have been learned but science would remain in the stage of romance with the child experimenting for itself. Toward the end of this year, the child enters into a stage of generalization in language and precision in science, the latter involving work covering the main principles of mechanics, physics, chemistry, algebra, and geometry. In language we move from grammar and composition to the reading of literature and the general history in which it is embedded. Those who go on to university will enter the great period of generalization. Familiar with details and procedures, students at university should "start from general ideas and study their applications to concrete cases." Here they can shed details in favor of principles. "The really useful training yields a comprehension of a few general principles with a thorough grounding in the way they apply to a variety of concrete details."[76]

Whitehead also takes up this idea of the rhythmic cycles of learning in his article "The Rhythmic Claims of Freedom and Discipline" (1923). This time he equates romance with freedom, precision with discipline, and generalization with a wider freedom achieved in the presence of knowledge "by discipline in the acquirement of ordered fact." We are reminded that the pupil's mind is a growing organism and that interest is "the *sine qua non* for attention and apprehension." We must construct our formal system of education so that enough freedom is allowed for natural growth, yet enough discipline is provided for true development. We are enjoined to avoid "barren knowledge" and to seek active mastery and the utilization of what is known. If we build upon freedom and romance, the discipline will be sought and "the habit of cheerfully undertaking imposed tasks" will be enhanced.[77]

He admits that it is difficult to provide discipline and precision without dulling interest, but insists that "a certain ruthless definiteness is essential in education." The secret is to adopt the right pace: "Get your knowledge quickly, and then use it. If you can use it, you will retain it." Education should begin and end in research. Begin with the freedom and romance of initial encounter and discovery, carry on through a disciplined acquiring of precise means of expression and understanding, and reach a new stage of excitement over general principles and ideas. A university professor should exhibit himself or herself as "an ignorant man thinking, actively utilising his small share of knowledge." The professor seeks to inculcate in students an active wisdom, "the habit of the active utilisation of well-understood principles."[78]

For Whitehead the teacher performs a double function; the teacher elicits the student's enthusiasm "by resonance from his own personality" and creates "the environment of a larger knowledge and a firmer purpose." In a sense, the teacher personifies all three stages of rhythmic growth: romantic enthusiasm for the subject (which Whitehead hopes will prove to be contagious); mastery of the techniques of precise analysis; the ability to deal with general principles, to rise above rules and details and actively utilize ideas. This could also be represented as an evolving pattern of freedom, discipline, and then greater freedom. The wise man is most truly free, as we can see from the argument and example of Socrates in the *Crito*. The good teacher avoids reconditeness and barren knowledge by respecting the active minds of the students and helping them grow in wisdom through a rhythmic interplay of freedom and discipline. In another essay Whitehead describes education as an art which, like any other art, attempts to turn the abstract into the concrete and the concrete into the abstract.[79]

UNIVERSITY EDUCATION

Whitehead's schema is also useful for depicting the stages of formal education running from elementary, with the emphasis on romance and imagination, through secondary, where the stress is placed on precision and discipline, to university, the great period of generalization. In his own educational writings, the consideration of university education begins to loom ever larger, particularly during his period at Harvard. In an address on "Universities and Their Function" (1927), he looks at the newly developed Harvard Business School and sees it as a vital part of the growth of universities. Contrary to those who feel that universities should remain isolated centers of learning concerned only with the pursuit of truth for its own sake, Whitehead appeals to the history of universities to show that from the very beginning they have been concerned to train clergy, medical men, lawyers, and engineers. Business fits into this series quite nicely. It certainly exemplifies the wedding of thought to action that we have seen him espouse.

Universities are places for research and education. Neither function, he says, requires such an expensive outlay for faculty and materials. "So far as the imparting of information is concerned, no university has had any justification for existence since the popularization of printing in the fifteenth century." We can bring his remarks up to date by including the role of the computer as a source of information in our own time. What universities at their best accomplish comes from the bringing together of young and old in the "imaginative consideration of learning."[80] The teachers should be scholars who have a thorough understanding of their subjects. They encounter the students whose zest for life and youthful imagination and energy help to transform this knowledge and keep it alive. The young lack discipline and experience but possess enthusiasm and imagination. Ideally they should complement their teachers who possess the knowledge and experience but may have lost the excitement and curiosity.

This is another way of using his notion of the rhythm of education. Encourage your teachers to do research and then "bring them into intellectual sympathy with the young at the most eager, imaginative period of life." The scholars will have to explain their ideas to "active minds, plastic and with the world before them," while the young will benefit by coming into contact with "minds gifted with experience of intellectual adventure." Both young and old will gain from this encounter. Thus, Whitehead sees universities as "homes of adventure shared in common by young and old."[81] The complexity of the modern business world requires just such a meeting of freedom and discipline, of romance and precision in order to achieve understanding and generalization. He praises the establishment of a school of business at Harvard as both the continuation of the tradition of universities trying to meet social needs and as an indication of some of the exciting possibilities for learning in the future.

So strongly does Whitehead feel about this that his last published article on education is entitled "Harvard: The Future" (1936).[82] This was occasioned by the tercentenary celebrations at Harvard. He starts with the grandiose claim that the center of gravity for civilization has shifted and the fate of intellectual civilization now resides in "Harvard," or the university system throughout the eastern states of America—a fairly extensive grouping since by eastern he means "from Charlottesville to Baltimore, from Baltimore to Boston, and from Boston to Chicago." This shift corresponds to a change in our approach to knowledge. Today we have less apparent ground for certainty than did Plato and Aristotle. Even in mathematics, "the very citadel of the doctrine of certainty," we find new perplexities. "Every single generalization respecting mathematical physics, which I was taught at the University of Cambridge," Whitehead avows, "has now been abandoned in the sense in which it was then held." We fall short of certainty in regard to the foundations of mathematics; and even in logic, "the chosen resort of clear-headed people, severally convinced of the complete adequacy of their doctrines," there are sharp disagreements.[83]

The proper response to this lack of complete certainty should not be complete scepticism, which he sees as self-destructive, but rather a sense of the progress in clarity needed and an appreciation of the suggestiveness in what we do not know and what we have gotten wrong. "Knowledge is a process, adding content and control to the flux of experience. It is the function of a university to initiate its students in the exercise of this process of knowledge."[84] And this is what "Harvard" does so admirably. It combines the simplicity and orderliness and clarity of knowledge with the suggestiveness and excitement of discovery and revelation. It introduces the freedom of nature into the orderliness of knowledge.

"Celibacy does not suit a university," he claims. "It must mate itself with action." He supports the presence within universities such as Harvard of schools of law, religion, medicine, business, art, education, government, and engineering. "The main advantage to a university of this fusion of vocational schools with the central core of theoretical consideration is the increase of suggestiveness." The close association of universities with practical concerns helps to overcome the abstruseness of ideas that Whitehead has criticized through all his educational writings. It is a means to the active utilization of knowledge, a blending of thought and action in order to bring unity to our understanding of experience. The ideal of the university is the ideal of the good life, of civilization itself, and that is to serve as an agent of unification seeking "the discovery, the understanding, and the exposition, of the possible harmony of diverse things, involving and exciting every mode of human experience."[85]

As a university professor, Whitehead combined the qualities of being able to elicit enthusiasm from the students while creating an environment of larger knowledge and firmer purpose. Russell remembers him as an "extraordinarily perfect" teacher who took a personal interest in his students, knew both their strong and weak points, and managed to elicit from them the best of which they were capable.[86] J. E. Littlewood, the mathematician who succeeded Whitehead at Trinity in 1910, recalls taking a stimulating course from him at Cambridge on the foundations of mechanics, as well as attending his lectures on the foundations of mathematics. The latter he enjoyed, although he characterized them as "solid and unexciting."[87] Whitehead's philosophy students at Harvard pointed to his benevolent manner and obvious erudition as a teacher. Most of them found him enthusiastic about the subject matter and concerned that they master it.[88]

CONCLUSION

We have examined Whitehead's writings in some detail, tracing a pattern from his thoughts on the teaching of mathematics to the question of the aims of education and the idea of rhythmic stages of learning. Other issues, such as the place of the classics in the curriculum, the value of technical education for all, and the proper function of university education were treated as well. We also attempted to indicate the relevance of his practical involvement in education, ranging from his presidency of the Mathematical Association to his participation in university administration to his membership on local and national committees of education. Although he did not, like Dewey and Russell, have to face the everyday problems of running his own school, I think a case can be made for his intense concern for what was actually being done in the schools. This reflected his theoretical commitment to the union of thought and action and the importance of avoiding inert ideas in the classroom.

I see his practical involvement as an attempt to utilize what he said and wrote about education, to make it less recondite, to test his ideas. There are no radical changes apparent in his educational views as a result of this practical experience, but there is a widening of outlook and a more concrete concern for the problems of teaching and learning which can be seen through the course of his writings. He would certainly share Dewey's animosity toward those who merely pontificate about education without getting involved. Technique and vision are called for if we are to deal realistically with actual school situations. It is to Whitehead's credit that, in his own characteristic way, he so immersed himself in what was going on that his insights still illuminate and stimulate our thinking about education.[89] He is a prime example of the "ignorant man thinking, actively utilizing his small share of knowledge."

CHAPTER FIVE

The Philosopher as Educator Today

Observe, too, that prudence is something more than a knowledge of general principles. It must acquire familiarity with particulars also, for conduct deals with particular circumstances, and prudence is a matter of conduct. This accounts for the fact that men who know nothing of the theory of their subject sometimes practise it with greater success than others who know it.[1]

The research persons connected with school systems may be too close to the practical problems and the university professor too far away from them, to secure the best results. The former may get too entangled in immediate detailed problems for the best work. Minor problems for immediate solution may be put up to him and not leave him time for investigations having a longer time-span. The latter may not have enough first-hand contact to discriminate the important problems from the secondary and the conditions which render them problems.[2]

What, then, are we to make of the practical involvement of these three philosophers in education? It cannot be said that any of them proved to be an outstanding practitioner. Russell, for one, seemed to treat the problem of the education of his son and daughter and the other young children at Beacon Hill as a pressing issue for several years. After that, his interest waned, his marriage broke up, and he moved on to other causes. He began to speak quite disparagingly about Beacon Hill School and in later years refused to discuss it at all. He was thoroughly dismayed with this part of his life. Some of her father's anguish (and her own as a young child seeing her parents drift farther and farther apart) is conveyed by his daughter Kate when she says in her book that at Beacon Hill she began to feel more and more that she was being driven out from the gates of paradise forever.

Dora Russell remains adamant in her defense of what the school accomplished. She helps to balance our view of the school by pointing to Russell's favorable attitude toward it at the time. She continued to operate the school and was actively involved in educational reform organizations such as the New

Education Fellowship.[3] Russell did retain a critical interest in the problems of education, and throughout the rest of his life he wrote about such topics as the ideal university education and the role education must play if we are to avoid a nuclear holocaust. It is not clear that he radically altered any of his theories because of the Beacon Hill experience.

Dewey was the thinker most insistent upon the need to test one's theories in practice. This was supposed to result in sharper, more realistic ideas, as well as better directed, more thoughtful practices. For all his talk of maintaining a scientific, problem-solving attitude and engaging in a community inquiry that featured much trial and error, Dewey shared with Russell an impatience with failure. Both men tended to regard undesirable or unforeseen results as the fault of the practitioners rather than the theory. When things did not work out as planned, the response was usually to increase the effort to get the staff to understand what it was they were supposed to be doing. There are few indications of Dewey's having revised or reconstructed his educational theories because of the findings of the Laboratory School experiment.[4]

This steadfastness in the face of difficulties undoubtedly had an inhibiting effect on the critical attitudes of the teaching staff. Both Dewey and Russell tried to run their schools in their own way. Neither seemed eager to enlist the aid of staff (other than a chosen few, such as Ella Flagg Young for Dewey) as coinvestigators in a project which was to test various hypotheses about education. Weekly discussions among the staff at the Laboratory School were often "entangled in immediate detailed problems." At Beacon Hill, Russell and his wife were often away and left things up to the staff; upon returning, they quickly made it clear when they felt that things were not being done properly.

The major involvement of their wives in these educational ventures could only further the impression that each man was determined to be completely, unassailably in charge. Although neither Dewey nor Russell claimed to have a good head for administration, there is little evidence that either made much of an effort to seek outside help in this regard. Dewey, in fact, seemed too distrustful of the Parker staff in general and Wilbur Jackman in particular to gain the kind of assistance he needed to run the school more efficiently. Perhaps the lesson to be learned here is that the claim that theory and practice should interact does not entail any assurance that a single individual will necessarily be both the best theoretician and the best practitioner. There seem to be various psychological requirements for being a successful educational practitioner that need not be present in a leading educational theorist. Dewey's point is perhaps best understood in terms of a community of inquirers whose relative talents can be brought together into some kind of organic unity. The fact of the matter is that he (and

Russell as well) could have done more to make his experiment in education into a joint inquiry of this sort.[5]

Having made this criticism, I must in fairness add that both the Laboratory School and the Beacon Hill School had a number of conspicuous successes with pupils and developed a core of dedicated teachers. Whether this is due to the correctness of the underlying theories or to some other factor is not so clear. Being part of a self-styled educational experiment run by a famous philosopher might have drawn out that strong sense of commitment and plain hard work shown by some of the staff. An additional positive element in the Laboratory School was the intellectual and financial support of the parents. There is little worrying in Dewey's writings about having to deal with problem children and problem parents of the kind Russell had to contend with at his school. Being part of the University of Chicago meant that Dewey had resources at his disposal that would have been the envy of any elementary school principal in the country. Russell, too, with his brother Frank's house and the surrounding countryside, had a congenial setting for the kind of free-spirited education he hoped to promote. The special locale and unusual student group at each school make it even harder to extrapolate from the results of these experiments to today's large, inner-city public schools.

Whitehead's practical concern for education took quite a different turn from that of Dewey and Russell, though by his own admission it was very time-consuming. Few details are available about his tenure as dean and member of the Academic Senate in London. From all reports he was a good committee member: observant, patient, critical yet cooperative. His appointment to a national committee and his work on local education committees show more than a typically professorial interest in education. He may well have seen these as opportunities for avoiding "mental dryrot" in his own ideas of how, why, and what subjects the young should be taught. Even at Harvard, where his philosophical writings turned to more cosmological topics, there are still traces of this more concrete, pragmatic outlook. His role in the establishment of the Junior Fellows Program and his enthusiastic support for the aims and activites of the Harvard Business School can be taken as examples of this.[6]

Because he thought it important that men and women of ideas concern themselves with the practical problems of education, Whitehead is included in this study of the philosopher as educator. As a contributing member of an education committee or actively working within an administrative structure, he was kept aware of what was actually going on in our schools and also given the opportunity to offer his own point of view on what ought to be done. Consequently, his successes as well as his failures as an educator are harder to document; but his concern with the practice of education is certainly consistent with his dicta that "knowledge does not keep any better than fish" and that "theoretical ideas should always find important applications with the pupil's curriculum."[7] Like Dewey, he saw education as a good place to test or utilize one's ideas. The fact that some contemporary thinkers still make use of some of Whitehead's educational ideas, such as the rhythm of education, is some indication of their freshness, part of which may be attributable to his taking care to find out what really was taking place in education.[8] He shares with Dewey and Russell the desire to theorize about education and to consider the practical ramifications of one's theory.

What has all this to do with the philosopher of education today? The purpose of my detailed examination of these three philosophers as educators has not been to set them forth as model practitioners; nor has it been to promulgate any specific pedagogical techniques they may have advocated; nor has it even been to defend any one of their educational theories. My intention throughout has been to suggest a way out of the current impasse in the philosophy of education by reopening a conversation regarding a more productive role for philosophers to play, rather than merely analyzing concepts and policing arguments. My claim has been that philosophers of education can learn from their past, that we can see in Dewey, Russell, and Whitehead instances of a productive approach to educational problems through thought and action.

Each of them took a philosophical look at educational theories and practices. Any theory of education rests upon certain assumptions, such as a view of the nature of man, what knowledge is most worth having, and how it might best be taught. Most fundamental of all is a notion of the ideal society. For Dewey, this was to be a truly democratic society wherein individuals contributed their own special ideas and opinions and shared in the joys and frustrations that form part of the common experience of human beings living together. Problems were to be dealt with in a scientific manner: gathering the pertinent information, framing a hypothetical solution, putting one's ideas to the test. Thinking of this sort required and reinforced his view of the school as a miniature community whose members participated in a joint inquiry. The process of education was to develop in our students those dispositions of thought and feeling which would promote the growth of full, humane experience throughout the rest of their lives.

Russell was suspicious of the indoctrinating tendencies of state and church schools and sought to encourage an international perspective in the young based on an open-minded consideration of differing points of view. Like Dewey, Russell saw the school as an environment in which we can attempt to create our ideal society in miniature and thereby train the individuals who will go out and reform society as a whole. Unlike Dewey, he seemed quite naive about the way children actually behave in groups; further, once his experiment in education was underway, he stayed somewhat aloof from the whole proceeding. Russell quickly tired of his idea that the way to world peace was through the proper education of small children and eventually shifted his concern to rousing citizen protest against nuclear arms and the critical roasting of politicians for not acting in the best interests of mankind. His practical experience served to shift the focus of his energies but did not dampen his fervor for world peace.

Whitehead stressed the need to utilize our ideas lest they wither away in abstraction from life. He fully appreciated the importance of precision in thought but saw it as most fruitful when it stemmed from a stage of romantic excitement and led on to a stage of the generalized use of rules and procedures. His local and national educational contacts provided him with the background and quite often the occasion for spelling out his views on the necessity for hand- as well as head-work in our schools and the desirability of achieving a style of thinking and a reverence for life. It may well be that Whitehead's long exposure to the practical problems of inner-city schools accounts for the fact that his ideas on education seem to have a more solid basis and a greater relevance than do Russell's.

All three men had a general awareness of how an educational scheme should function to promote an ideal society. To varying degress, each tempered his theory with an acknowledgement of what was actually taking place in the schools. At their best, as educational philosophers, Dewey, Russell, and White-head struck a reasonable balance between the theoretical and the practical, avoided many of the untenable dualisms that accrue to a hard-and-fast distinction between thought and action, and managed to convey in their generalizations some of the romantic excitement of possibilities and the precision of thought that Whitehead advocated. These characteristics would go a long way toward rehabilitating the philosophy of education today.

Dewey was by far the strongest proponent of such an approach to the philosophy of education. He constantly inveighed against the study of philosophy "in itself," where it is taken as "so much nimble or severe intellectual exercise—as something said by philosophers and concerning them alone." For Dewey, theory should not be divorced from practice, especially in education. "If a theory makes no difference in educational endeavor," he said, "it must be artificial." That is to say, if the auditing of past experience and the program of values set forth by a philosophy did not (or indeed could not) take effect in conduct, then for Dewey it was merely symbolic or verbal or arbitrary dogma, or "a sentimental indulgence for a few." All too often in reading or listening to the latest batch of research by philosophers of education, I get the feeling I am an observer at a meeting of an elite chess club whose members regularly congregate to talk of new opening gambits and winning strategies and comment on each other's moves. If you do not see the point or do not want to play that particular game, then you are reminded that you are free to go elsewhere. Little effort is made to relate what is said and written to what is actually taking place in the classroom. Abstractness is taken as a sign of rigorous thinking.

What distressed Dewey so much about such a state of affairs was the fact that he believed education provided the philosopher with an ideal opportunity to connect thought with action. It offered "a vantage ground from which to penetrate to the human, as distinct from the technical, significance of philosophic discussions." The connection between philosophy and education was so intimate in Dewey's eyes that the one tended to merge into the other. Thus, he claimed that "if we are willing to conceive education as the process of forming fundamental dispositions, intellectual and emotional, toward nature and fellow-man, philosophy may even be defined *as the general theory of education*."[9] A far cry indeed from the more aloof contemporary view which locates philosophy safely on a higher level gazing down upon educational theories and activities in search of unclear concepts and faulty reasoning.

I have great sympathy with Dewey's notion that philosophy should *matter* to more than one's fellow professional philosophers and that education is an area of human experience especially well suited for philosophical scrutiny because it provides a context where it is very difficult to ignore the demands of practical applicability. He strikes me as overstating his case, however, when he tries to equate philosophy with the theory of education. Surely there are legitimate branches of philosophy, such as decision theory or formal logic that have little to do with the formation of dispositions toward nature or one's fellow humans. Then, too, not all philosophic considerations of nature and human beings need be of the applied, problem-solving type that Dewey espouses. As Israel Scheffler has pointed out, theory is rightly connected with practice but "it is also autonomous; it has its own career and life." For Scheffler, "theories serve not simply to guide practice, but to afford us an intelligible and coherent representation of fundamental natural processes." Scheffler would modify Dewey's view by insisting upon the value of maintaining a kind of theoretical distance in education. He argues that in searching for deeper insights and broader perspectives the theoretician "may need to back away from the detail of phenomenal change, and practical urgency in order to strive to 'see through' to underlying elements and patterns." Dewey was right to stress the importance of problem-solving, but Scheffler criticizes him for down-playing the value of problem-finding. Even in science, says Scheffler, "scientific thought of the highest significance is expended in seeking, formulating, and elaborating questions that have not yet intruded on practice."[10]

I agree with this criticism of Dewey, who seems to want us to go from one extreme to another, thereby positing a kind of dualism of his own; that is, either philosophy takes education seriously and concentrates all its critical attention on practical problems, or it sinks to the level of trivial mental gymnastics. My own view of philosophy is that it is a persistent attempt by man to understand himself, his fellow man, and the world around him. Such an attempt can be both critical and comprehensive. The philosopher is critical of arguments, seeks clarity in concepts, and wants to make presuppositions more explicit. He also tries to spell out in a general way how he sees things, to incorporate the data from more specialized disciplines into an overview. All the while, the philosopher displays a loyalty to reason in though and practice.[11] This loyalty to reason is displayed dramatically in those men from Socrates to Russell who have gone to jail for their beliefs, but also less dramatically by those who, like Thomas Aquinas, will criticize arguments by their fellow Christians and turn to "unorthodox" sources such as Aristotle, Avicenna, or Maimonides in the quest for truth. In doing so, Aquinas spurred the bishop of Paris to condemn some of his ideas as heretical.[12] Loyalty to reason has never made for overwhelming popularity.

It would be foolish to depict philosophers as having any kind of monopoly on information and insight pertinent to education. What they can contribute at their best is this dedication to thinking things through. Perhaps we can adopt from Dewey the notion of community inquiry and see the philosopher as a working member of a team of investigators looking at education. Dewey insisted that he be made the chairman at Chicago of a Department of Philosophy, Psychology, and Pedagogy. He was familiar with the research being done on education by nonphilosophers and wanted to utilize all these resources for education. Dewey also decried the waste in education due to isolation, with different parts of the educational system operating in ignorance of the other parts. I would extend this objection to the academic disciplines themselves. Within philosophy we disagree about what we are doing and about the worth of what we have done in the past. And yet so often do I find the ideas of past philosophers to be relevant to current issues in education that I am inclined to agree with the view of one's intellectual forebears that was expressed in the twelfth century by John of Salisbury: "We can see more and further than our predecessors, not because we have keener vision or greater height, but because we are lifted up and borne aloft on their gigantic stature."[13] I have argued at some length elsewhere that philosophers should stop treating the history of our own discipline as a liability and come to appreciate the sense of continuity of ideas and fruitful suggestions that flow from thinkers who have come before us.[14]

We need not work in isolation, cut off from our fellow philosophers, from the history of our discipline, from those in other disciplines, and from what is actually happening in the classroom. Contemporary philosophers of education should make more of an effort to find out the facts and to acknowledge the relevance of the work of other thinkers to the investigation of questions about the aims, methods, and content of education. A notable exception to this tendency to neglect the ideas and findings of social scientists as they pertain to education is the work of Robert Brumbaugh and Nathaniel Lawrence, who take a serious look at Freud, Skinner, Piaget, Bruner, and Erickson. [15] Richard Peters has displayed a similar appreciation for the work being done in psychology [16] and has issued a call, largely unheeded by some of his devoted followers, for the development of a new phase in educational theory in which contributing disciplines such as philosophy, psychology, sociology, and history are integrated around concrete problems. [17]

Participation by philosophers with social scientists and educators in a joint inquiry would certainly be in the spirit of Dewey's call for the wedding of thought to action. The commitment to thinking things through, the sense of logical rigor, the ability to generalize from more specialized information to a comprehensive overview, these would be some of the assets the philosopher could bring to such an enterprise. Lest we be too faint-hearted about resuming traditional tasks and engaging in general theorizing, we should recognize the fact that social scientists seldom share these qualms. Psychologists such as Bruner, Maslow, Rogers, Kohlberg, and Piaget do not hesitate to move beyond their experimental bases and propound general theories about the nature of man or the ideal society or the best kind of education for everyone. At times they even make explicit reference to philosophical positions from the past which suit their own outlook. Why, then, should philosophers whose training and tradition seem so useful for this type of thinking about education politely back off on the grounds of "professionalism" or even hostilely reject all such attempts at general theorizing as fantasy or nonsense? [18]

Dewey himself was led to wonder why philosophers in general, although they were usually practicing teachers, did not take education sufficiently seriously to appreciate the fact that "any rational person could actually think it possible that philosophizing should focus about education as the supreme human interest in which, moreover, other problems, cosmological, moral, logical, come to a head." [19] My contention in this book has been that Dewey, Russell, and Whitehead brought to their consideration of education a general perspective not often found in studies by psychologists and sociologists. By attempting to locate educational ideas and practices within the context of the development of an ideal society, they are not bound to any specific experimental technique or explanatory model. By rising above details while still taking account of them, they can supply us with an educational philosophy we can utilize in our own thinking and acting about education. As such, I find them good role models for a revived philosophy of education.

Some recent books in the field may well signal a return to these more fruitful tasks.[20] Especially welcome is *The Aims of Education Restated* (1982), by John White, a leading member of the so-called London school headed by Richard Peters. White states that little has been forthcoming from philosophers on this important topic because they have been engaged in more piecemeal, analytically oriented studies in which they have been "chary of saying what they think aims ought to be because they have felt this kind of question lies outside their discipline." To his credit, White feels that the question of the development of overall aims of education is too important to remain untouched by philosophical thinking.[21]

Another move in the right direction is the recent *Paideia Proposal* of Mortimer Adler.[22] Even though I disagree with some of his conclusions, I applaud Adler's efforts to reopen the debate on the general objectives, worthwhile content, and appropriate methodology for educating citizens in a democracy. He has traveled extensively throughout the United States, defending and explaining his proposals to groups of educators, businessmen, politicians, students, professors, and the public at large and has urged school boards to take steps to implement his suggestions and put his ideas to the test. This concern for translating thought into action may well account for the fact that Adler dedicates his book to John Dewey, among others. Their overall philosophical views are quite different, but they share a questioning spirit about the foundations of education and a determination to take their ideas to the public.

This is not to say that no respectable work will be forthcoming from contemporary philosophers of education unless they are willing to mount the public podium, engage in popular debates, or be interviewed on television. Nor do I insist that philosophers set up small experimental schools to test their theories. I am not so naive as to believe that those who seem temperamentally so inclined toward abstract theorizing can (or should) be miraculously transformed into world-shaking activists. My point has rather been in support of a change of attitude to the whole endeavor of philosophizing about education, along the lines followed by Dewey, Russell, and Whitehead. By paying more attention to practical problems in education and by participating with other investigators in the analysis and discussion of their causes and the implementation of proposed solutions, we can avoid the abstruseness in our own ideas that Whitehead warned against and achieve the meaningfulness of philosophical inquiry that Dewey promoted.

One way to accomplish this might be to follow the lead taken by recent work in ethics, making extensive use of "case studies."[23] Particular cases of ethical decision making are presented for comment by philosophers, social scientists, health care professionals, and other professionals. The cases are based on real events and the commentators are forced to apply their ethical theories to real-life, day-to-day problems, as well as to become aware of alternative approaches to these problems. They discuss what they would do when faced with such dilemmas and give the reasoning behind their decisions. The goal of the enterprise is "the pursuit of reflective, well-thought-out solutions to real human moral dilemmas based upon more systematic ethical analysis."[24]

Something like this could be done in education with examples drawn from actual classroom situations, as well as depictions of teaching and learning experiences from works of literature or proposals of goals and means from government reports. Whitehead's participation on the many educational committees was an instance of such an interdisciplinary approach to specific cases as well as to general objectives and the reasoning behind them. I contend that the philosopher has much to offer and to gain from such an inquiry. It is a way out of our current impasse. Once freed of the shackles of the interminable disputes about our proper "professional" role, we can move on to more pressing matters. There are topics that have arisen in modern-day education that would indeed benefit from philosophical analysis and the broader view. I briefly list some of these as a kind of agenda for a newly revived philosophy of education.

AN AGENDA FOR THE PHILOSOPHY OF EDUCATION TODAY

Computers and Education

It is quite clear that computers will play an increasingly large role in education. They have become legitimate objects of study, as well as being touted as the most efficient means of education. Even in these days of tight budgets, school boards invariably find the funds to purchase the latest in computer hardware and software; and whole new courses have been created to deal with the programming, servicing, and selling of the computer. Computer literacy now ranks alongside the traditional three R's as part of the minimal level of achievement that every student can reasonably be expected to attain. The media bombard us with futuristic scenarios in which virtually all our waking and sleeping hours are to be made more joyful and productive thanks to the computer. As philosophers of education we should be concerned that this growing enthusiasm for the computer as the newest educational panacea be tempered by some further reflection on what it is we are trying to accomplish in education, what knowledge is of most worth, and how we might best set about teaching it.

We need to raise once again the perplexing questions about the nature of man, the structure of knowledge and reality, and the construction of an ideal society, questions that have no easy answers. The fact that the computer has become so versatile, portable, inexpensive, and easy to use should not lull us into thinking that it can solve all our educational problems. Too many educational innovations have come and gone in the past twenty-five years to justify such a sanguine attitude.[25] The widespread use of educational technology in the classroom can generate new problems for the people already operating in the present system. We must get clear as to what the computer can do for us and then what tasks we want to assign it in the context of teaching and learning.

A useful introductory study shows how the computer can function as tutor, tool, and tutee.[26] As a tutor, the computer can be the kind of teacher that not even Rousseau dreamt about: ever-patient, all-knowing, constantly on call, rigorously logical, inexhaustible. Ivan Illich, a radical educator who might be seen as a spiritual descendant of Rousseau, advocates the use of the computer as a means of returning the initiative of learning to the student and overcoming the limitations of a particular physical plant or the restricted access to educational resources. The computer constitutes a powerful new force in the instructional domain, but will it serve or rule the human beings who are presently teaching there?

Eric Hoyle suggests that many educational innovations have failed in the past because they have run afoul of the prevailing values of the teachers. Most teachers are what Hoyle calls "restricted professionals" who derive their job satisfaction from "the personal encounter with pupils, the here-and-now urgency of the classroom, the autonomy which allows them to respond to the particular nature and needs of a class."[27] Such teachers are less interested in making instruction more efficient than in keeping it more personal. They rely more on intuition and personal interaction with their students, less on objective-oriented aids and programs. They cherish the immediacy of classroom life and resist intrusions from without, even when these are well-meant and rationally defensible. It is on the values of restricted professionals, says Hoyle, that so many educational innovations have foundered, among them programmed learning, team teaching, and resource-based learning. He concludes that we should see the computer as a solution in search of a problem, that is, we should first make an honest effort to find out what our teachers see as problematic before we foist the computer upon them as a pedagogical cure-all.

Nor should we minimize the importance for the learner of face-to-face contact, the vividness of the human encounter, and the value of spontaneity and improvisation. Much of our learning is social in nature; we learn from and with other people. In a classroom we learn from what the teacher says and does, but we also learn from the kind of person he or she is. A teacher conveys facts, ideas, questions, criticisms, suggestions and the like, but also moods, enthusiasms, mistakes, likes and dislikes. At times the personal idiosyncrasies of the teacher help us to connect the subject matter to life. This is merely to make the point that we teach by manner as well as matter. Whitehead's "ignorant man thinking" or the Platonic Socrates may strike some as inefficient teachers, but to eliminate the waste in their approaches is to lose the vitality of the encounter. As Brumbaugh puts it, "Communication in a shared present is radically different from fixed messages beamed into the present from a completed past. . . . No film or written text [nor computer program, we might add] records the kind of jeopardy that present creative communication faces. And if periodic failures occur, so more frequently do successes."[28]

This is what Martin Buber has called the "dialogue principle" in education. For Buber, "Contact is the root and basis of education . . . a connection between personalities, so that one human entity confronts another . . . a truly reciprocal conversation in which both sides are full partners. The teacher leads and directs it, and he enters in without any restraint."[29] Computers have become more "user friendly," and their programs are more creative and do call for a kind of reciprocal conversation with the students; nonetheless, there is still something to be said for the intersubjective elements of traditional education, the human components of teaching and learning. In a high-technology society such as ours we should remember that in school we continue to have the opportunity for human interaction and conjoint experience. Many classrooms fall short of being Dewey's miniature community, and contact between teachers and students can be of a perfunctory or even a hostile sort; yet the potential is there to develop an exciting atmosphere for teaching and learning.

Perhaps the key is to assign the computer certain tutorial tasks rather than others. Mortimer Adler distinguishes three different teaching methods as appropriate for different goals and subject matters: 1) didactic instruction (lectures, textbooks, other aids) for the acquisition of organized knowledge (as found in literature, mathematics, science, history, for example); 2) coaching (exercises, supervised practice, drill) for the development of intellectual skills (i.e., skills of learning such as the three R's, problem solving, calculating); and 3) Socratic questioning (discussion, active participation, reciprocal conversation) for the enlarged understanding of ideas and values.[30] Adler's point is that we should vary the methods of teaching according to our different aims and content. The computer seems well suited for didactic instruction and coaching. This could free the human teacher for more questioning and discussion of ideas and values. Not all subjects, nor all teachers, for that matter, are clearly definable in terms of one method or the other; but this is simply to recognize the fact that teaching is an art, not a science. Some blending of resources is in order if we are to maximize the tutorial function of the computer while preserving the personal contributions of the human teacher.

A less controversial function of the computer is as a tool. Its amazing capacity for statistical analysis, the calculation and projection of probabilities, word processing, map making, and even musical notation has just barely been tapped. The computer as a tool makes it more feasible to fulfill Dewey's ideal of providing each student with the opportunity to test his or her ideas. By simulating experiments in chemistry or physics or making long-range economic forecasts, the comuputer can expedite problem solving and let us see the results of our hypothetical solutions quickly and painlessly. Tool and die makers, and their counterparts in technical schools, now use the computer to test various designs, thereby bringing about a nearly instantaneous trial-and-error procedure and obviating the need for costly, time-consuming efforts to construct working models. Whitehead's charge that we seek ways to connect head and handwork in our schools is well served by the use of the computer as a tool.

The most exciting possibility seems to be that of using the computer as a kind of tutee to be "taught" by the student, who learns how to talk to the machine, instruct it in the performance of certain tasks, and, where necessary, "debug" a program that does not produce the expected results. Teachers often claim they learn better, come to understand their material more thoroughly, and think about it more critically when they must explain it to their students. This experience of "learning by teaching" can now be made available to our students by allowing them to be directly involved in programming the computer to function as a tutor or tool. By instructing the computer, students can come to a greater comprehension of the subject matter and a more vital appreciation of the process of teaching and learning. This is a variant of Dewey's learning by doing that would probably have his full support.

There are other aspects of the computer and education that philosophers should reflect upon. We must avoid the assumption that all thinking can be modeled on the sequential, linear progression followed by the computer. Just as our students should not be regarded as having minds which are "blank tablets" to be filled in, so they should not be seen as machines to be programmed. Nor should we force every subject into a computerized mode. Grammar, mathematics, and logic all strike me as eminently programmable; poetry, fine arts, and metaphysics much less so. The humanities will undoubtedly come under increasing pressure to fit the technology that becomes available; we must take care lest the tail wag the dog. The greatest benefit of the computer revolution as it pertains to the philosophy of education is that it should provoke us into reexamining some of the larger issues as to the nature of the human mind and how we come to know, the role of the human element in schooling, and the kind of society we want to construct. This is a prime example of an area of education that could use more thinking things through.

Gender and Education

The reemergence of feminism in our day has roused a number of persons in academic disciplines from their dogmatic slumbers and caused them to reconsider their priorities and procedures. Traditional ways of speaking and thinking and dealing with the sexes in education have been severely challenged. There are demands for equal access to educational opportunities and affirmative action programs to redress previous imbalances along sexual lines. Textbooks are being scrutinized to detect evidence of sexual bias and avoid the promulgation of sexual stereotypes. Classes in nontraditional occupations are now available for both males and females. Female accomplishments are beginning to receive greater recognition from historians, art critics, social scientists, and the like.

Philosophers of education have not been immune to such controversies. Indeed, in the past there have been important philosophical theories that made a determined effort to come to grips with the question of education and gender. Plato certainly made it clear that he thought his ideal state could be ruled by a man or a woman and consequently that his educational proposals were applicable to either sex. It should be noted, however, that he saw fit to abolish the family for his potential guardians and stressed the development of traits that have usually been regarded as masculine, such as courage in battle, physical prowess, and facility in abstract speculation. Some critics claim that the sexes are indeed equal in Plato's eyes, so long as they both think and act like males.

Rousseau took another tack. He stressed the natural differences between the sexes and proposed a radically different education for Sophie from that to be given to Emile. Whereas his training sought to bring out political, vocational, and intellectual qualities, hers centered on social, domestic, and emotional characteristics. She was to be subservient to his needs and wishes; yet, she was also to take over from the tutor the rule of Emile. Rousseau saw the sexes as complementary factors making up a unit of ideal humanity. Each contributed a distinctive way of thinking and acting; together they constituted a totality of desirable human characteristics. Again, this has been criticized as an attempt to preserve male dominance, all the more objectionable because it is presented under the guise of following the dictates of nature.[31]

The whole question of gender and education might be seen as an offshoot of the old nature/nurture controversy. Do we educate the young to fulfill their natural potential, which is seen as a relatively fixed, God-given essence that with proper encouragement will simply unfold in a kind of preordained manner; or do we stress the impact of the environment on the organism, restraining certain tendencies and reviving others? Do we treat males and females differently in school in accordance with their "natural" differences, or do we seek to develop a certain kind of person regardless of sex or race or economic status? Ruth Jonathan has criticized the kind of ethical essentialism that holds that women must be educated to fulfill a predetermined nature. She points out that "we are not automatically committed to maximising the defining characteristics of things, unless those things are objects (like lawnmowers) for which prime function constitutes sole purpose."[32]

She goes on to reject the view that we can draw up a list of defining sexual characteristics that have major educational significance. It is one thing to distinguish biological differences between the sexes but quite another to claim that these determine the kind of education and thus the kind of person who should be developed. For Jonathan, "anatomical equipment and hormones do not *cause* behaviour; they make ranges of physical experience possible."[33] If we are to value autonomy as an educational goal, then we cannot say to the females in our classes that they, and they alone, must follow the dictates of biology. Just as we would not tell male students that reproduction was a necessary element in whatever they eventually chose to do with their lives, because, after all, their bodies were made to propagate; so too, we must beware of leading females to believe that they have no choice in the matter. The point of education would seem to be that we all, males and females, do have a choice and that our biological functions do not constitute our sole purpose.

Other differences between the sexes, such as size and shape, are of decreasing importance as our technological control of the environment increases. Even the distinctively female reproductive system, with its accompanying nurturant qualities of care, sensitivity, and support, need not lead us to different educational content or practices for the sexes; if such qualities are seen to be valuable, then it would be in society's interest to foster them in all human beings. To the claim that the development of such nurtural qualities in males violates well-established cultural norms, Jonathan replies that human beings develop in a cultural nexus not merely responsively but in a way that also produces and modifies the nexus.[34] This is a view of an organism interacting with its environment that is very close to Dewey's notion of growth.

Another aspect of the gender and education controversy centers on the notion of the educated person. Jane Roland Martin has criticized Richard Peters for advocating an ideal of the development of the educated mind rather than the educated person. Peters's educated person is noticeably lacking in empathy, intuition, sensitivity to others, and care and concern for interpersonal relationships. His ideal coincides with our cultural stereotype of the male: cool, objective, analytical, interested in things and ideas more than people. Little is said about nurture and supportiveness. Not unlike Plato, Peters has come up with a very masculine version of the educated person.[35]

Martin objects to the forms of knowledge theory of Paul Hirst for the same reason: "it conceives of liberal education as the development of mind, restricts the development of mind to the acquisition of knowledge and understanding, and restricts knowledge to true propositions."[36] She chides Peters and Hirst for defining education in terms of an initiation into forms of knowledge or modes of experience that incorporate an almost exclusively male cognitive perspective. The content of education reflects the productive processes of society (e.g., man's political, economic, scientific, and artistic activity), while the reproductive processes involved with the bearing and rearing of children are seen as peripheral. Martin argues that in order to give the reproductive processes their due, we must rethink the domain of the philosophy of education.[37] In addition, she criticizes Hirst for resurrecting the very sort of dualisms between reason and emotion, thought and action, education and life, that Dewey sought to lay to rest.[38] She calls upon philosophers to develop a gender-sensitive ideal of the educated person, "one which takes sex or gender into account when it makes a difference and ignores it when it does not."[39]

It is hard to object to such an ideal, since the alternative seems to be to adopt an avowedly sexist stance toward education.[40] There are some problems that would still have to be faced even if we all agreed to pursue Martin's ideal. For one thing, it is not obvious when gender does make a difference and therefore should be taken account of in education. To say the sexes are equal is not to say they are identical, or that they should necessarily receive identical treatment in school. Ruth Jonathan suggests that given the current cultural nexus within which we operate, we should take steps to provide a kind of compensatory education for boys and girls to rectify past wrongs in their upbringing or mistaken perceptions of socially approved attitudes and activities. She recommends that educators take special care to foster achievement motivation and independence of mind in girls and cooperation and sensitivity in boys.[41] Such deliberate singling out of what each sex lacks strikes me as promoting a stereotypical view as much as alleviating it. Can we assume that students need such compensatory treatment solely because of their sex? Does this not serve to highlight precisely those differences that we are claiming should no longer be part of nurture? This might indeed have the unintended result of fixing such differences in our minds and making the problem worse.

Others have argued that we should educate the young in a manner in which gender is simply ignored or not attended to. This seems to enforce the prejudice that sex could not possibly make a difference in education. To espouse an ideal of androgyny is, according to some, to open the door to a monolithic pattern of human development and to possible psychological and social tyranny.[42] We should also recognize the possibility that there may be hormonal differences between the sexes that call for different educational treatment. I do not think the issue of sexual differences has been settled and that instead of attributing them all to nature, we can now confidently assert they are all due to environment. We must, prodded one may hope by philosophers, continue to think the matter through and not close ouselves to evidence or alternative practices that go against the newly accepted common view.[43]

There is a growing body of analysis dealing with the alleged causes as well as the proposed remedies for sexism. Some want to place our sexual attitudes in the broader context of our political or economic systems. Very early in the debate, Simone de Beauvoir attempted to locate the relationship of men and women within the context of a Marxist critique of society. More recently, Ivan Illich has joined the fray by describing the advent of capitalism, industrialization, and scientific progress as the passage from gendered lifestyles to sexist role playing.[44] As usual, the practical educational problem of how we are to educate males and females forces us to consider more general, theoretical issues such as the nature of human beings, the role of the individual in society, the aim of life, and so on. Philosophers can make a definte contribution to such theoretical discussions. I urge them to do so.

Adult Education

One of the results of providing greater access to educational opportunities has been the rapid expansion of the area known as adult education. Adults seek education for various reasons: social or recreational, vocational, remedial, or simply personal development. They seek it through different media: classroom lectures, clubs, professional associations, television broadcasts, correspondence courses, or logging on to their home computers. They study different things, from wine making to calculus, and do so for differing periods of time. For all its apparent expansion, the area of adult education rarely intrudes upon philosophical considerations of what we mean by education and how we ought to go about it.

Most contemporary philosophers of education take their lead from Richard Peters and see education as a process by which the initiated pass on knowledge and skills to the uninitiated. Peters encapsulates this in his children-as-barbarians-outside-the-gate motif (see Chapter 2, p.00); the problem of the educator is "to get them inside the citadel of civilisation so that they will understand and love what they see when they get there."[45] There are two things I find bothersome about this view. First of all, it conveys a notion of the content of education as something fixed and solid, unassailable and fortresslike. This is not an apt description of much that is included in adult education. Secondly, the implication seems to be that learning is a one-way conveyance from the "haves" to the "have-nots". Instructional roles are clearly defined. One is either inside or outside the citadel; the teacher's job is to get students inside. Once again, this description falters when we try to apply it to mature students who may have more real-life experience, better vocational skills, more enthusiasm for the subject and even more knowledge of some of it than their teachers. By extending the term "education" to cover the manifold educational activities of adults, we can see that it has been too narrowly conceived by Peters and his followers. The content is more flexible and the process more reciprocal than they will admit. The whole issue of interpersonal relationships between teachers and students also comes to the fore. To my knowledge, Martin Buber is one of the few to attempt to spell out the elements involved in a teacher's encounter with mature students.[46]

The education of adults adds a dimension to the discussion of society's stake in education. Paulo Friere sees the education of poor adults as a key to the overthrow of their oppressors. His "pedagogy of the oppressed" spells out a theory whereby adults who learn to read and write can be brought to a new awareness of themselves and begin to look critically at their social situation.[47] Less revolutionary is the approach of R. W. K. Paterson who bases his philosophy of adult education on the notion of the making of persons. For Paterson, this is best accomplished through liberal education and is vitally important in a democracy because it is a form of government based on the meeting and interaction of persons. Paterson claims that "it is in the liberal education of its adult members, its citizens, that democracy can behold itself in its clearest and most appropriate mirror."[48] Many of the activities of Mortimer Adler on behalf of the study of the so-called "great books" can be seen as part of his commitment to adult education.[49]

The multifarious aims, content, and methods of adult education should make us more cognizant of the fact that teaching and learning should not be understood solely in the context of certain arbitrary constraints of time and place. Some psychologists now describe human life in terms of a series of stages or passages, each of which has its own special needs for resources or support. The idea of lifelong learning has been developed to take account of this. Ivan Illich's call to "de-school" society is based on the view that education is not limited to a legally specified time spent in an officially sanctioned place under the guidance of formally certified teachers, but rather should be seen as a continuous process drawing upon the resources of the entire community. Students should not be thought of as gaining entrance to a citadel but as being invited to join in a community activity or contributing to a common experience. Dewey's point about eliminating waste by overcoming the isolation of the component parts of the educational system from one another and from the community at large also seems apropos here. Taking adult education as our model, we can reconstruct all of education so that it is more flexible and makes better use of institutional and community resources.

Finally, I think that philosophical scrutiny of the means and ends of adult education will shed some light on the question of educating the young and help us to a better understanding of the dynamics of individual growth within a society. If we are indeed educating for life, we must realize that this cannot be done once and for all and that the child's needs and interests will change as he or she matures. Rather than try to do all things for all people in the school system, as we presently have it, we should begin to explore ways of making educational resources available and attractive throughout a lifetime: at home, on the job, in formal and informal settings. Some of the spirit of adult education should permeate all our pedagogical endeavors. This could well lead to new arguments for greater breadth in early education, less specializaton for a future that may see a variety of changes. Whitehead's notion of the value of generalization leading on to a new stage of romance may be helpful in this regard. Part of the task as philosophers of education should be to take a more thorough look at its later stages to get a better sense of what we should be doing at the earlier ones.

Peace Education

None of these issues can match the urgency that comes from the very real threat of nuclear devastation we all face today. As educators, we can argue about goals and methodologies, defend a theory of the ideal society or a view of what knowledge is most worth knowing, puzzle over the subtle interplay of freedom and discipline in the classroom; but all the while we are assuming that we, or at least our successors, will still be here to carry out our proposals. Many current writers are trying to shock us out of such a complacent assumption by warning of the danger posed to human survival by the huge arsenal of nuclear weapons in the East and the West. Father Theodore Hesburgh bluntly describes the kind of "future" that may be in store for mankind:

> all our institutions that we have labored to perfect, all learning, all science and technology, all art, all books, all music, all architecture, every human treasure, everything, but especially millions of men, women, and children, all their future and all futures, utter obliteration at worst, a return to the Stone Age at best.[50]

For those of us concerned with education, the nuclear threat cannot be ignored. It runs counter to the basic presuppositions of educating: a commitment to rational procedures and a belief in the perfectibility of man. To seek to pass on a cultural heritage or certain skills and dispositions is to presume that human beings can improve and grow and progress. To teach the young and old things they do not know, while respecting their own outlooks, is to encourage thinking and communication. To look for sound reasons for what we say and do is to stand on the side of rational argument and to eschew violence as an acceptable means of settling disputes. The attitudes that underlie education as a human enterprise are the opposite to the urge to annihilate one's enemies and the despair at the human condition that can be found in a more militaristic approach to life. Education by its nature should clearly be an education for peace.

What is not clear is exactly what we can do to bring this about. Too often we get graphic descriptions of the problem with meager accounts of how it might be solved. For example, in his influential book *The Fate of the Earth*, Jonathan Schell details the horrors of a nuclear holocaust and the desperate straits we are all in; but his answer is far too simple: We are to "lay down our arms, relinquish sovereignty, and found a political system for the peaceful settlement of international disputes."[51] Such advice is unexceptionable but impractical. How are we to get friend and foe to disarm and to trust one another to live up to such an agreement? Should we disavow all armaments, or only nuclear arms? Do we have the right to relinquish our sovereignty, and to whom should we relinquish it? What kind of political system will be able to peacefully resolve international disputes?

Schell's suggestions remind me of Russell's persistent pleas to promote international understanding by having all history textbooks written by foreigners. There are deeper factors at work than the spreading of false propaganda. Why do men fear and distrust one another and try to get the better of their fellow men? Can we reeducate humans so that they will be cooperative, not competitive, compassionate, not aggressive, helpful, not harmful? Russell devoted much of his life to the cause of peace and the advocacy of a world government. At times he made comments and criticisms of political leaders and whole countries that were strident, emotional, and unfair. He felt deeply about the issue of nuclear arms; and yet he recognized the complexity of the problem and managed to retain a sense of the need for careful thought that was not always manifested by his compatriots. For instance, when nearly ninety, he wrote a preface for a booklet entitled "Schools for Non-Violence" in which he chided some of his more ardent followers to remember that "all of us can work more strongly if we have thoroughly thought out our position and understood its implications."[52] A call for loyalty to reason that we could all take to heart.

This is not to say that all men are going to be reasonable in dealing with the nuclear threat and that international tensions will dissolve under the light of philosophical scrutiny. It is to challenge us to think about education in terms of man's awesome potential to destroy the entire world. One of Peters's more telling objections to Dewey was that life contains predicaments as well as problems, that not all of the difficulties men face can be treated as amenable to solution by testing hypotheses and acting upon them. Death, love, and perhaps even peace may be seen as aspects of the human situation that will not be "solved" but must be accommodated to as best we can. Peters also complained that Dewey virtually ignored man's irrational side.[53] This is relevant to the question of peace education. We must try to present our students a picture of man as he is. It is not just our nation's history that may be biased to reflect only our best accomplishments and feelings; the history of mankind often passes over our darker moments and thereby leads to an unrealistic approach to the world's problems. Philosophers should join with psychologists, sociologists, anthropologists, historians, and the like to develop a theory of human nature that incorporates all we know about ourselves. This is another occasion where interdisciplinary research is required.

We might try to do more through education to develop cooperative attitudes. Neither life nor education should be seen as a competitive struggle in which only the fittest deserve to survive. All our emphasis on grades and performance judged against that of one's peers runs against the obvious need to produce caring, sensitive, helping individuals. Russell said we need knowledge wielded through love, and he attempted, albeit unsuccessfully, to put this into practice in his school. He underestimated the latent hostility of the children and overestimated the effectiveness of preaching to the staff on his educational principles; but this does not mean his ideal was wrong. Dewey said that the school should be a miniature community wherein democratic procedures could be experienced at first hand. We must give more thought to the question of how to educate for peace in regard to the manner as well as the subject matter of schooling.

Russell was aware of the dangers inherent in a scientific society like our own where "habits of thought cannot change as quickly as techniques, with the result that, as skill increases, wisdom fails."[54] He wondered whether such a society must inevitably destroy itself. His hope resided in education as a means of liberating the human spirit. Whitehead shared this concern for vision and not just technique. He would want us to utilize our ideas about man and the world to create a peaceful society and a reverence for life. Dewey felt that personal interaction in the classroom should be the means to a fuller, more humane experience for all. Each man had specific goals in mind for the theory and practice of education; but none of these would supersede the need to avoid war and find the way to peace.

From the vantage point of the philosophy of education, the nuclear threat is an issue that calls for our most creative thinking. We must find ways to teach our students to appreciate the worth of every human being and to learn to cooperate and preserve, rather than attack and destroy. We must draw upon the findings of others to work out a theory of man which will guide us toward peace and the establishment of a just society. What greater challenge could there be for those who are dedicated to thinking things through about education? If we fail to meet the challenge, we may find ourselves, assuming that we survive at all, in a world where everyone is left in the state of the barbarian outside the gates.[55]

CONCLUSION

In yet another of the spate of retrospective studies now appearing on the recent past of the philosophy of education, D.C. Phillips claims that many in the field would like to make more of a contribution to educational policy and practice. According to Phillips, there has been a growing discontent with the sterility of analytical philosophy and its remoteness from practical affairs, together with an undiminished interest in metaphysical and normative questions. Phillips is not so sure that the philosophy of education can be revived, and so he titles his article in the form of a question: "Philosophy of Education: *In Extremis*?"[56]

My book has been an attempt to answer such a question. I have argued that we should look back to three of our predecessors, Dewey, Russell, and Whitehead, to regain a sense of the importance of applying philosophical insights to concrete educational situations. Their theories and practices provide us with a model for a more productive approach to the philosophy of education. I then suggested that we now look to the future and consider a new agenda consisting of such topics as the computer and education, the need for a gender-sensitive ideal in education, the ramifications of the aims, methods, and content of adult education, and the overarching need to contribute to an education for peace. Each of these offers us an opportunity to penetrate to what Dewey called the human significance of philosophical discussions.

In addition, I have urged philosophers to join with researchers in other fields to attempt to formulate a new theory of what man is and what he might become through education. All of this stems from my own conviction that philosophers of education have more to offer than they have displayed in the recent past. Our loyalty to reason and our determination to get to the root causes and goals of human endeavor are sorely needed in education today. We have more than enough to engage our critical attention. I hope to have reopened a conversation as to how this might come about. In doing so we will have produced an appropriate response to Phillip's query: "Philosophy of education: *semper vivens*."

Notes
Bibliography
Index

Notes

1. The Reconstruction of the Philosophy of Education

1. Sven Erik Nordenbo, "Philosophy of Education in the Western World: Developmental Trends During the Last 25 Years," *International Review of Education*, 25:2–3 (1979):435. Also of interest is R. F. Dearden, "Philosophy of Education, 1952–1982," *British Journal of Educational Studies*, 30 (February 1982):57–71.

2. These papers appeared in the *Journal of Philosophy*, 52 (27 October 1955):612–33.

3. Ibid., 632.

4. *Harvard Educational Review*, 26 (Spring 1956). Many of the important papers by philosophers on the philosophy of education from the fifties and sixties have been collected by Christopher Lucas in *What Is the Philosophy of Education?* (New York: Macmillan, 1969).

5. Nelson Henry, ed. *Modern Philosophies and Education* (Chicago: University of Chicago Press, 1955). The Eightieth Yearbook of the National Society for the Study of Education has recently been published and contains an interesting retrospective study by Harry Broudy, "Between the Yearbooks," *Philosophy and Education*, ed. Jonas Soltis (Chicago: University of Chicago Press, 1981), 13–35.

6. Israel Scheffler, ed., *Philosophy and Education* (Boston: Allyn & Bacon, 1958).

7. Cf. William Frankena, "Toward a Philosophy of the Philosophy of Education," *Harvard Educational Review*, 26 (Spring 1956):94–98, and his "Toward a Philosophy of Moral Education," *Harvard Educational Review*, 28 (Fall 1958):300–313; Israel Scheffler, *The Language of Education* (Springfield, Ill.: Charles Thomas, 1960), and *Conditions of Knowledge* (Fair Lawn, N.J.: Scott, Foresman, 1965).

8. Hardie's book has been reissued by Teachers College Press with a preface by James McClellan and Paul Komisar assessing its significance. O'Connor's book is still in print. For a thoughtful review of the development of the philosophy of education in England since World War II, see R. S. Peters, "The Philosophy of Education," in *The Study of Education*, ed. J. W. Tibble (London: Routledge & Kegan Paul, 1966), 59–89. Peters has also contributed to the special issue of the *Teachers College Record* (Winter 1979):463–82, which deals with "Philosophy of Education since Midcentury."

9. Nordenbo, "Philosophy of Education," 453.

10. A typical example of Peter's continuing influence is a recent collection of articles edited by Donald Cochrane and Martin Schiralli, *Philosophy of Education; Canadian*

Perspectives (Don Mills, Ontario: Collier Macmillan Canada, 1982). The editors admit that the main thrust of the articles follows the approach of the "London school" and add that this should not be surprising since "by far the largest number of active philosophers of education have their roots in the mode that Peters best exemplifies" (p. 4).

11. Reprinted as "Education as Initiation," in *Philosophical Analysis and Education*, ed. R. D. Archambault (London: Routledge & Kegan Paul, 1965), 87–111.

12. Ibid., 92.

13. R. S. Peters, *Ethics and Education* (London: George Allen & Unwin, 1966).

14. Ibid., 15.

15. Ibid., 16.

16. Ibid., 25.

17. A good recent translation of the *Meno* is that of G. M. A. Grube (Indianapolis: Hackett Publishing Co., 1976).

18. For a typical example of a view of values education that sees no need for further discussion or critical reflection on the matter, see Kathleen Gow, *Yes Virginia, There Is Right and Wrong* (Toronto: John Wiley and Sons, 1980). An effective antidote, which looks at some of the philosophical difficulties underlying moral education, is Robert Carter, *Dimensions of Moral Education* (Toronto: University of Toronto Press, 1984).

19. For a perceptive account of what Meno learns from his encounter with Socrates, see Robert S. Brumbaugh, "Plato's *Meno* as Form and Content of Secondary School Courses in Philosophy," *Teaching Philosophy*, 1 (Fall 1975):107–15.

20. P. H. Hirst and R. S. Peters, *The Logic of Education* (London: Routledge & Kegan Paul, 1970), 11.

21. Richard Robinson, "Socratic Definition," in *Plato's Meno: Text and Criticism*, ed. Alexander Sesonske and Noel Fleming (Belmont, Calif.: Wadsworth Publishing Co., 1965), 65–76. Also of interest is I. M. Crombie, "Socratic Definition," in *Paideia*, 5 (1976):80–102.

22. R. S. Peters, "Education and the Educated Man," in *Education and the Development of Reason*, Part 1, ed. R. F. Dearden, P. H. Hirst, and R. S. Peters (London: Routledge & Kegan Paul, 1972), 7.

23. Cf. William Dray's commentary on Peters's "Aims of Education—A Conceptual Inquiry," in *The Philosophy of Education*, ed. R. S. Peters (Oxford University Press, 1973), 34–39.

24. Cf. Abraham Edel, "Analytic Philosophy of Education at the Crossroads," in *Educational Judgments*, ed. James Doyle (London: Routledge & Kegan Paul, 1973), 232–57. Two other criticisms in a similar vein are R. J. Haack, "Philosophies of Education," *Philosophy*, 51 (1976):159–76, and Hugo Meynell, "What Is to Be Done about the Philosophy of Education?" *Education for Teaching*, 99 (Spring 1976):28–34. For Peters's reply to Haack's criticisms, see "Philosophies of Education," *Philosophy*, 52 (1977):477–81.

25. Jane Roland Martin, "The Ideal of the Educated Person," *Educational Theory*, 31 (Spring 1981):97–109.

26. Cf. I. A. Snook, *Indoctrination and Education* (London: Routledge & Kegan Paul, 1972), and Snook, ed., *Concepts of indoctrination* (London: Routledge & Kegan Paul, 1972). A thorough summary of much of the literature on the concept of "Indoctrination" can be found in Elmer Thiessen, "Intdoctrination, Education and Religion: A Philosophical Analysis," (Ph.D. diss., University of Waterloo, 1980). Walter Feinberg

has criticized the philosophical analysis of educational concepts for failing to capture the significance of those concepts in a total system of practice. He refers to the debate over the meaning of the concept of indoctrination as a specific instance of this failure in his *Understanding Education* (New York: Cambridge University Press, 1983), 96–114.

27. For example, the Hirst-O'Connor debate on educational theory in *New Essays in the Philosophy of Education,* ed. G. Langford and D. J. O'Connor (London: Routledge & Kegan Paul, 1973), 47–75.

28. For example, Paul Hirst's article, "Liberal Education and the Nature of Knowledge," which first appeared in Archambault (see note 11) and has been reprinted a number of times. This article has generated a large amount of critical commentary, which, in turn, has prompted several articles on the topic by Hirst. These have been collected in his book, *Knowledge and the Curriculum* (London: Routledge & Kegan Paul, 1974), which itself has been reviewed and subsequently defended by Hirst; see Jonas Soltis, "Knowledge and the Curriculum," *Teachers College Record,* 80 (May 1979):771–84, and Hirst's response, 785–88.

29. Richard Rorty, "Philosophy in American Today," in his *Consequences of Pragmatism* (Minneapolis: University of Minnesota Press, 1982), 227.

30. Ibid.

31. See my "Educational Fantasies and Philosophy," in *The Review of Education,* 7 (Spring 1981):167–73, and the reply by John Wilson, 246 (italics are Wilson's).

32. Ibid., 246.

33. See my "Wasted Resources: What Educational Philosophers Might Contribute to Educational Theory But Often Don't," *Journal of Educational Thought,* 16 (April 1982):15–22.

34. A noteworthy exception has been the work in "applied metaphysics" by Robert S. Brumbaugh. See his *Whitehead, Process Philosophy and Education* (Albany: State University of New York Press, 1982). Another promising venture is that of Anthony O'Hear, *Education, Society, and Human Nature* (London: Routledge & Kegan Paul, 1981).

35. Cf. R. S. Peters, *Education and the Education of Teachers* (London: Routledge & Kegan Paul, 1977), my review, "A New Phase in Educational Theory," *The Review of Education,* 4 (Spring 1978):91–94, and Peters's response, 179–80.

36. T. W. Moore, *Educational Theory: An Introduction* (London: Routledge & Kegan Paul, 1974), 7. That Moore is accurately recording the level on which conceptual analysts see themselves as operating can be seen from the strikingly similar three-tiered model proposed for the philosophy of religion by B. Mitchell in his *Morality: Religious and Secular* (New York: Oxford University Press, 1980), 98–99. I thank Jim Horne for pointing this out to me.

37. Ibid., 8.

38. T. W. Moore, "The Nature of Educational Theory," in *Theory and Practice of Curriculum Studies,* ed. Denis Lawton et al., (London: Routledge & Kegan Paul, 1978), 14.

39. Alfred North Whitehead, *The Aims of Education* (New York: Macmillan, 1929; reprint, New York: Free Press, 1967), 1.

40. John Dewey, *Democracy and Education* (New York: Macmillan, 1916; reprint, New York: Free Press, 1968), 328.

41. Ibid.

42. Israel Scheffler, preface to *Four Pragmatists* (New York: Humanities Press, 1974), x.

43. Richard Rorty, *Philosophy and the Mirror of Nature* (Princeton: Princeton University Press, 1979), 360.

44. John Smith, "The New Need for a Recovery of Philosophy," *Proceedings and Addresses of the American Philosophical Association*, 56 (September 1982):16–17.

45. See John Dewey, *Reconstruction in Philosophy* (New York: Henry Holt, 1920; 2d ed., Boston: Beacon Press, 1948).

2. *John Dewey and the Laboratory School*

1. This is from a copy of the Dewey School song found in the Katherine Camp Mayhew papers in the library of Teachers College, Columbia University.

2. George Dykhuizen, "John Dewey: The Chicago Years," *Journal of the History of Philosophy*, 2, (October 1964):240 n. 60. "Laboratory School" was shortened even further to the "Lab School."

3. John Dewey, "The University School," in *The Early Works of John Dewey,* ed. Jo Ann Boydston (Carbondale, Illinois: Southern Illinois University Press, 1972), 5:437. All subsequent references to either the Early Works or the Middle Works of Dewey will be made in the standard format, i.e., EW or MW.

4. "The Need for a Laboratory School," EW 5:434. As a graduate student at Johns Hopkins, Dewey had personal experience of the use of the laboratory for observation and experiment in his psychology course taught by G. Stanley Hall. See Dorothy Ross, *G. Stanley Hall* (Chicago: University of Chicago Press, 1972), 154. According to Ross, Hall opposed the renewal of Dewey's fellowship at Hopkins and later rejected a suggestion that Dewey be engaged to handle undergraduate instruction in philosophy (p. 146). Hall wrote a mildly critical review of Dewey's book, *Psychology* (New York: Harper and Bros., 1887), in the *American Journal of Psychology*, vol. 1, no. 1. (November 1887):146–59; and Hall referred to Dewey's work in "paidology" as having nothing new to offer in his autobiography, *Life and Confessions of a Psychologist* (New York: D. Appleton & Co., 1924), 500.

5. "Pedagogy as a University Discipline," EW 5:288.

6. "Report of the Committee on a Detailed Plan for a Report on Elementary Education," EW 5:454.

7. "The Relation of Theory to Practice in Education," MW 3:249–72.

8. Ibid., 249.

9. Ibid., 251 (italics are Dewey's).

10. This is from remarks of John Dewey recorded in a shorthand report of a departmental conference on "The Training of Teachers" held at the University of Chicago on 13 May, 1904 and found in the Anita McCormick Blaine Papers, The McCormick Collection, State Historical Society of Wisconsin in Madison.

11. "The Relation of Theory to Practice in Education." MW 3:252.

12. For some firsthand accounts on Dewey as a teacher, see George Dykhuizen, "John Dewey and the University of Michigan," *Journal of the History of Ideas*, 23 (1962):528; Sidney Hook, "Some Memories of John Dewey," in *Pragmatism and the Tragic Sense of Life* (New York: Basic Books, 1974), 101–14; Corliss Lamont, ed., *Dialogue on John*

Dewey (New York: Horizon Press, 1959); Harold Larrabee, "John Dewey as Teacher," in *John Dewey: Master Educator*, ed. William W. Brickman and Stanley Lehrer (New York: Society for the Advancement of Education, 1959), 50–57; Una Bernard Sait, "Studying Under John Dewey," *Claremont Quarterly*, vol. 11, no. 2 (Winter, 1964), pp. 15–22; and Herbert W. Schneider, "Recollections of John Dewey," *Claremont Quarterly*, vol. 11, no. 2 (Winter 1964):23–35.

13. "The Relation of Theory to Practice in Education," MW 3:263.

14. "The Relation of Theory to Practice in Education," MW 3:265.

15. *Democracy and Education* (New York: Macmillan, 1916); MW 9:177.

16. "A Pedagogical Experiment," EW 5:244.

17. Ibid.

18. "The University Elementary School," MW 1:319.

19. "Pedagogy as a University Discipline," EW 5:285–87.

20. "The Need for a Laboratory School," EW 5:434.

21. Robert L. McCaul, "Dewey and the University of Chicago," part 1: July 1894–March 1902, *School and Society* (25 March, 1961):153.

22. Alice Dewey in an unpublished sketch of the school, quoted by Lawrence A. Cremin, *The Transformation of the School* (New York: Knopf, 1961), 136 n. 8.

23. Cf. Robert L. McCaul, "Dewey's Chicago," *The School Review* (Summer 1959):266–67; Arthur Wirth, *John Dewey As Educator* (New York: John Wiley & Sons, 1966), 35; and Dykhuizen, "John Dewey: The Chicago Years," 231.

24. Katherine Camp Mayhew and Anna Camp Edwards, *The Dewey School* (New York: D. Appleton–Century Co., 1936; reprint, Atherton Press, 1966), 12.

25. Jane Dewey, ed. "Biography of John Dewey," in *The Philosophy of John Dewey*, ed. Paul Arthur Schlipp (New York: Tudor Publishing Co., 2d ed., 1951), 28. It should be noted that this biography was "written by the daughters of its subject from material which he furnished" (p. 3).

26. McCaul, "Dewey and the University of Chicago," Part 1, 153; this point was made by McCaul despite his own views on how supportive Harper was of the school.

27. "The University Elementary School," MW 1:317.

28. "The University Elementary School," MW 1:325. Smedley eventually became director of the Child Study Department of the Chicago Public Schools; cf. Wirth, *Dewey As Educator*, 195.

29. Mayhew and Edwards, *Dewey School*, 8.

30. Cremin, *Transformation*, 135.

31. Jane Dewey, "Biography of Dewey," 29. For a good recent biography of Mrs. Young, see Joan K. Smith, *Ella Flagg Young* (Ames: Iowa State University Press, 1979).

32. Max Eastman, *Great Companions* (New York: Farrar, Straus and Cudahy, 1959), 273.

33. McCaul, "Dewey and the University of Chicago," Part 1, 157.

34. Dykhuizen, "John Dewey and the University of Michigan," 534. He in turn is quoting from De Witt Parker and C. B. Vibbert, "The Department of Philosophy," in *The University of Michigan: An Encyclopaedic Survey*, vol. 2, ed. Wilfred B. Shaw (Ann Arbor: University of Michigan Press, 1951), 674.

35. B. A. Hinsdale, *Journal of Proceedings and Addresses of the Thirty-ninth Annual Meting of the National Educational Association* (Chicago: University of Chicago Press, 1900), 326–27. For Dewey's relationship to Hinsdale as a colleague at the University of

Michigan, see McCaul, "Dewey's Chicago," 260–61. There is also a reference to a debate between Dewey and Hinsdale at Michigan in John A. Axelson, "John Dewey 1884–1894: Decade of Ferment for Young Michigan Teacher," *Michigan Education Journal* (1 May, 1966), 14. The Hinsdale quote is incompletely given and incorrectly attributed to a meeting of the National Council of Education by Wirth, *Dewey As Educator,* 215–16. Wirth is quoting Hinsdale as presented in Ida B. DePencier, *The History of the Laboratory Schools: The University of Chicago,* 1896–1957 (Chicago: University of Chicago, 1960; 2d printing, Quadrangle Books, 1967), 16. The latter is a chatty but not very scholarly account of the Laboratory School.

36. Mayhew and Edwards, *Dewey School,* 57.

37. McCaul, "Dewey's Chicago," 275.

38. DePencier, *Laboratory Schools,* 23–24.

39. Richard J. Storr, *Harper's University, The Beginnings* (University of Chicago Press, 1966), 298.

40. Ella Flagg Young, "Democracy and Education," *Journal of Education,* vol. 84, no. 1 (6 July, 1916):5–6. This review of Dewey's *Democracy and Education* by his trusted follower and confidant is surprisingly missing from the list of reviews of the book listed in MW 9:379 n. 10.

41. Laura L. Runyon, "A Day with the New Education," *Chautauquan,* vol. 30, no. 6 (March 1900):589–92.

42. Harold Rugg, *Foundations for American Education* (New York: World Book, 1947), 555–56 (italics are Rugg's).

43. George Eastman, "John Dewey on Education: The Formative Years," D.Ed. diss., Harvard University, 1963,495; for a list of Dewey's Contributions to *The Elementary School Record,* see p. 646. Lawrence Cremin states that "The published records of the school are more voluminous and detailed than for any similar venture of the time," Cremin, *Transformation,* 139 n. 3.

44. Two excellent introductions to the Chicago of Dewey's times are: Ray Ginger, *Altgeld's America* (Chicago: Quadrangle, 1965), and Wayne Andrews, *Battle for Chicago* (New York: Harcourt, Brace, 1946). Also of interest is Bessie Louise Pierce, *A History of Chicago,* vol. 3, 1871–1893 (Chicago: University of Chicago Press, 1957). Good studies of the University of Chicago at the turn of the century are those of Storr, *Harper's University,* and McCaul "Dewey's Chicago." A lively portrait of the life of the immigrant in Chicago at that time is Jane Addams, *Twenty Years at Hull-House* (New York: Macmillan, 1910; reprint, New American Library, 1961).

45. McCaul, "Dewey and the University of Chicago," Part 1. A short summary of Parker's views and practices can be found in Cremin, *Transformation,* 128–35. Angela Fraley claims that Dewey simply adopted Parker's theories and used his methods. "At best," she says, "he can be said to have replicated Parker's less formally recorded experimental work"; *Schooling and Innovation* (New York: Tyler Gibson Publishers, 1981), 45. No one else, to my knowledge, sees the two men in this light. See, for example, Jack K. Campbell, *Colonel Francis W. Parker, The Children's Crusader* (New York: Teachers College Press, 1967). For Parker's own words, see his *Talks on Teaching* (New York: A. S. Barnes, 1883) and *Talks on Pedagogics* (New York: E. L. Kellogg & Co., 1984).

46. McCaul, "Dewey and the University of Chicago," Part 1.

47. J. M. Rice, *The Public-School System of the United States* (New York: The

Century Co., 1893), 19. For more background on Rice and his study see Wirth, *Dewey As Educator*, 31–33. Lawrence Cremin dates the beginning of the progressive movement in American education to the publication of Rice's study; Cremin, *Transformation*, 22.

48. Rice, *Public-School System*, 15.

49. Ibid., 210–11; McCaul, "Dewey and the University of Chicago," Part 1, 155.

50. *Interest and Effort in Education* (Boston: Houghton Mifflin, 1913).

51. "The Child and the Curriculum," MW 2:277–78.

52. Ibid., 278.

53. Ibid., p. 291 (italics are Dewey's).

54. "The Psychological Aspect of the School Curriculum," EW 5:166.

55. "The Child and the Curriculum," MW 2:285.

56. "The Psychological Aspect of the School Curriculum," EW 5:174.

57. "My Pedagogic Creed," EW 5:84.

58. "The Theory of the Chicago Experiment," in Mayhew & Edwards, *Dewey School*, 467. Dewey often took pains to dissociate his own view from the more extreme child-centered stance of many progressive educators. See, for example, his article, "How Much Freedom in New Schools," *New Republic* (9 July, 1930), 204–6, and his book, *Experience and Education* (New York, 1938). Despite his efforts, he continues to be described as a child-centered educational theorist. A recent example of this can be found in Christopher J. Lucas, *Foundations of Education* (Englewood Cliffs, N.J.: Prentice-Hall, 1984), 304–9.

59. "My Pedagogic Creed," EW 5:86–87.

60. Ibid., 90.

61. "Plan of Organization of the University Primary School," EW 5:230–31.

62. *The School and Society*, MW 1:15. Dewey showed such enthusiasm for the possibilities for learning to be derived from such simple social occupations that he might be criticized for the very thing that he found fault with in the Montessori method—i.e., being so eager to introduce children to the intellectual distinctions that adults have made that he ignores or reduces the amount of time devoted to the immediate crude handling of the familiar material of experience (*Democracy and Education*, MW 9:153–54). Margaret Naumberg makes this point when she claims that in the Dewey School "the making and doing of things was always subordinated to a social plan, not related to the individual capacities and tastes of the children," and that "neither individual nor group entities initiated much in the way of original planning, however much they may have expanded and adapted the social projects suggested by the teacher"; *The Child and the World* (New York: Harcourt, Brace, 1928), 111.

63. Dewey in Mayhew & Edwards, *Dewey School*, 47 n. 5. Walter Feinberg charges that Dewey's proposals for curriculum development differed significantly, depending upon the socioeconomic class of the children he was dealing with. After looking at *Schools of Tomorrow* (New York: E. P. Dutton, 1915), Feinberg asserts that we can see different assumptions in Dewey's treatment of all-black or working-class schools from middle- or upper-class schools, especially in Dewey's acceptance of the relative neglect of academic subjects in the former; Walter Feinberg, *Understanding Education* (New York: Cambridge University Press, 1983), 263 n. 17. A far-ranging rebuttal to this charge could be constructed from Dewey's writings and actual practices; suffice it to say that the book in question was written by Dewey in collaboration with his daughter Evelyn and that

she was responsible for the chapters that described specific schools of the type mentioned by Feinberg (see the preface to *Schools of Tomorrow*).

64. "Culture Epoch Theory," MW 6:408.

65. "Interpretation of the Culture-Epoch Theory," EW 5:250. A recent article claims that Dewey was closer to the Herbartian viewpoint than he cared to admit; Herbert M. Kliebard, "Dewey and the Herbartians: The Genesis of a Theory of Curriculum," *Journal of Curriculum Theorizing*, vol. 3, no. 1 (Winter 1981):154–61. For more on Herbart and the Herbartians see: Johann Friedrich Herbart, *Outlines of Educational Doctrine* (New York: Macmillan, 1901); Gabriel Compayre, *Herbert and Education by Instruction* (New York: Thomas Y. Crowell, 1907); Charles De Garmo, *Herbart and the Herbartians* (New York: Scribner, 1895); and Harold B. Dunkel, *Herbart and Herbartianism* (Chicago: University of Chicago Press, 1970). A good summary of Dewey's reactions to the Herbartians and to the other educational movements of his time can be found in Melvin C. Baker, *Foundations of John Dewey's Educational Theory* (New York: Atherton Press, 1966), 86–108.

66. *The School and Society*, MW 1:54–55.

67. "Science as Subject-Matter and as Method," MW 6:69–79.

68. *How We Think*, MW 6:236–37. Although this book was originally published in 1910, some years after he had left the school, Dewey acknowledged in the preface his indebtedness to his wife for inspiring the ideas of the book and "through whose work in connection with the Laboratory School . . . the ideas attained such concreteness as come from embodiment and testing in practice" (MW 6:179). Indeed, reviewers of the book praised its clear and simple style (MW 6:517–18).

69. *Democracy and Education*, MW 9.

70. "Democracy in Education," MW 3:239.

71. "Democracy in Education," MW 3:237.

72. MW 9:162.

73. *The School and Society*, MW L:21.

74. "Democracy in Education," MW 3:230.

75. "Creative Democracy," in *The Philosopher of the Common Man*, ed. Sidney Ratner (New York: Greenwood Press, 1968), 227.

76. Mayhew & Edwards, *Dewey School*, 64–66.

77. Ibid., chapter 5.

78. Ibid., 113.

79. Ibid., 126.

80. "The Primary Education Fetish," EW 5:268.

81. Mayhew & Edwards, *Dewey School*, 144.

82. Depencier, *Laboratory Schools*, 33–34.

83. Mayhew & Edwards, *Dewey School*, 155.

84. Ibid., 166.

85. Ibid., 175.

86. Baker, *Foundations*, 144.

87. Mayhew & Edwards, *Dewey School*, 183.

88. Ibid., 208.

89. Ibid., 200.

90. Ibid., 203.

91. Ibid., 213–14.

92. Ibid., 221.

93. Ibid., 248.

94. Ibid., 396.

95. Ibid., 240–48.

96. Young, "Democracy and Education," 6.

97. Mayhew & Edwards, *Dewey School*, 370–75.

98. Ibid., 382.

99. Letter from Dewey to Mrs. Emmons Blaine, 2 August, 1900, Anita McCormick Blaine Papers, The McCormick Collection, State Historical Society of Wisconsin in Madison.

100. McCaul, "Dewey's Chicago," 264.

101. Ibid.

102. Mayhew & Edwards, *Dewey School*, 438.

103. A recent appraisal credits Dewey with applying many innovations at his schools, such as "new methods of instruction, reduction in student conformity, students' evaluations of their own work, and the elimination of grading"; *Conflict and Continuity*, ed. John R. Snarey, Terrie Epstein, Carol Sienkiewicz, and Philip Zodhiates, *Harvard Educational Review*, Reprint Series No. 15, 1981, ix.

104. Robert McCaul, "Dewey and the University of Chicago," Part 2: April 1902–May 1903, *School and Society* (8 April, 1961):180.

105. Letter from Dewey to Mrs. Emmons Blaine, (4 August, 1902, Anita McCormick Blaine Papers, The McCormick Collection, State Historical Society of Wisconsin in Madison.

106. Letter from Alice Dewey to William Rainey Harper, 5 April 1904, President's Papers 1889–1925, Department of Special Collections, University of Chicago Library.

107. Letters from Dewey to Harper, ibid. McCaul attributes Dewey's peevishness in the matter to the tremendous strain caused by the intellectual and social stimuli of Chicago; McCaul, "Dewey's Chicago," 278–79. I think a simpler and more reasonable explanation is that Dewey became angered when his wife was told she was no longer wanted as principal.

108. Mayhew & Edwards, *Dewey School*, 18.

109. See, for example, Rugg, *Foundations*, 554–55.

110. Mayhew & Edwards, *Dewey School*, 366.

111. Ibid., 370.

112. An example of this approach is the experience of Miss Emily Rice (a staunch follower of Parker), whom Dewey consulted about the merger of the two schools and the question of his wife's assuming the principalship. She did not oppose the plan to Dewey's face but expressed reservations privately in a letter to Mrs. Blaine, claiming that she felt unable to speak frankly to him or to Mrs. Young on such a delicate, personal matter; McCaul, "Dewey and the University of Chicago," Part 2, 182 and George Dykhuizen, "John Dewey in Chicago: Some Biographical Notes," *Journal of the History of Philosophy*, 3 (April 1965):228 n. 67. Presumably, Mrs. Blaine communicated Miss Rice's reservations to Dewey: he strongly criticized Miss Rice for this in his own letter to Mrs. Blaine and sarcastically remarked that "Miss Rice has so completely and repeatedly misrepresented both Mrs. Young and my own statements that I attach no further impor-

tance to any statement she makes about other people, so far as that reflect upon them";
Dewey to Mrs. Blaine, 30 April 1903, Anita McCormick Blaine Papers, The McCormick
Collection State Historical Society of Wisconsin in Madison.

113. Mayhew & Edwards, *Dewey School*, 467–68.

114. Ibid., 35.

115. Ibid., 376.

116. "The Psychology of Elementary Education," MW 1:73. This statement is also
quoted with a slight change of wording in Mayhew & Edwards, *Dewey School*, 248.

117. Wirth, *Dewey As Educator*, 71.

118. See McCaul, "Dewey and the University of Chicago," Part 2, 182, and
Dykhuizen, "John Dewey in Chicago," 228.

119. Eastman, *Great Companions*, 277. Joan K. Smith reports that Wilbur Jackman
had been advised by the Board of Trustees to document any difficulties occurring
between Mrs. Dewey and the faculty of the school. He found the basic problem lay in her
nature: "so critical that it becomes destructive . . . making it impossible for her to direct
others . . . without continual combat"; Smith, *Ella Flagg Young*, 98.

120. R. S. Peters, among others, has noted the extremely favorable teacher-pupil ratio
in the Dewey School and suggests that this be kept in mind when we evaluate its apparent
success; "John Dewey's Philosophy of Education," in *John Dewey Reconsidered*, ed. R.
S. Peters (London: Routledge & Kegan Paul, 1977), 108.

121. Robert McCaul, "Dewey and the University of Chicago," Part 3: September
1903–June 1904," *School and Society* (22 April 1961):205.

122. Henry J. Perkinson, *Two Hundred Years of American Educational Thought* (New
York: McKay, 1976), 215.

123. Hinsdale, *Thirty-ninth Annual Meeting*, 237. Hinsdale's cautious sentiment was
echoed in a review of Dewey's *School and Society* that appeared in *Dial*, 29 (16 August
1900):98, coauthored by Hinsdale and A. S. Whitney: "While no one can tell what the
future of the University Elementary School may be, it does not require much foresight to
see that it can never become the type of the public elementary school; its cost and the
delicacy of the organization make this impossible." A more extreme reaction is that of
Maxine Greene, who claims that "a look at the *Addresses and Proceedings* of the NEA in
the years immediately following Dewey's Chicago experiments shows us that his work
impressed public-school teachers little, if at all"; "Dewey and American Education,
1894–1920," in Brickman and Lehrer, *John Dewey*, 40. I am not sure that such a
conclusion is warranted. From the evidence she cites, the most one could say is that those
who gave addresses to the NEA during that period did not seem to be talking much about
Dewey. A similar observation has been made on the apparent lack of influence of Dewey
on educational reformers in England who were at work in the period of 1914–24;
"Furthermore the textbooks of the period while respectful, show no signs that Dewey's
ideas had penetrated the minds of their writers." R. W. Selleck, *English Primary
Education and the Progressives*, 1914–1939 (London: Routledge and Kegan Paul,
1972), 113.

David Hawkins goes even further and asserts, "Dewey has so far had almost no
influence at all on the practical level except, for a time, in a few private schools for
children most of whom would have succeeded academically in any case." "Liberal
Education: A Modest Polemic," in *Content and Context*, ed. Carl Kaysen (New York:
McGraw-Hill, 1973), 156. Unfortunately, Hawkins provides no evidence whatsoever to

back up this assertion; William Boyd and Wyatt Rawson in their book, *The Story of the New Education* (London: Heinemann, 1965), make the same point: "The schools of Parker and Dewey at Chicago were day schools for city children; but they had their most interesting outcome in the later establishment of private-venture Country Day Schools, in which children could grow up in free conditions which afforded greater scope for individual initiative and effort than the ordinary public schools of America" (p. 3).

124. Mayhew & Edwards, *Dewey School*, 7.

125. *The Sources of a Science of Education* (New York: Liveright, 1929), 43.

126. Mayhew & Edwards, *Dewey School*, 361–62.

127. Paul Hirst, "Liberal Education and the Nature of Knowledge," in *The Philosophy of Education*, ed. R. S. Peters (New York: Oxford University Press, 1973), 87–111. Many of Hirst's writings on this topic have been collected in his book, *Knowledge and the Curriculum* (London: Routledge & Kegan Paul, 1974). A response to Hirst, somewhat in the spirit of Dewey, is that of Richard Pring, *Knowledge and Schooling* (London: Open Books, 1976).

128. Hirst, "Liberal Education," 96.

129. John White, *Towards a Compulsory Curriculum* (London: Routledge & Kegan Paul, 1973). Also of interest are Keith Thompson and John White, *Curriculum Development: A Dialogue* (London: Pitman Publishing Company, 1975), and Robin Barrow, *Common Sense and the Curriculum* (London: George Allen & Unwin Ltd., 1976).

130. Frederick Olafson, "The School and Society: Reflections on John Dewey's Philosophy of Education," in *New Studies in the Philosophy of John Dewey*, ed. Steven M. Cahn (Hanover, N.H.: University Press of New England, 1977), 195.

131. Ibid., 201.

132. This criticism is also made by Charles Frankel, who argues that a scientific community is a community of specialized competence whose opinions are checked against the evidence; whereas democracy is a procedure for melding and balancing human interests. "John Dewey's Social Philosophy," in Cahn, *New Studies*, 20.

133. Kathryn Morgan, "Children, Bonsai Trees, and Open Education," in *Philosophy of Education: Canadian Perspectives*, ed. Donald B. Cochrane and Martin Schiralli (Don Mills, Ontario: Collier Macmillan Canada, 1982), 314.

134. R. S. Peters, "Education as Initiation," in *Philosophical Analysis and Education*, ed. R. D. Archambault (London: Routledge & Kegan Paul, 1965), 107.

135. Peters, *Dewey Reconsidered*, 121. Some early critics saw Dewey's pragmatism as an inadequate philosophy of life in the face of the irrationality of war. Thus, Randolph Bourne wrote in 1917 that Dewey's philosophy assumes the existence of a society that is peaceful, prosperous, and has a strong desire for progress; *War and the Intellectuals, Essays by Randolph S. Bourne*, 1915–1919, ed. Carl Resek (New York: Harper & Row, 1964). John C. Farrell believes that the outcome of the World War I did not shake Dewey's faith in reason, progress, and the scientific method, because this was really in the nature of an a priori assumption on Dewey's part; "John Dewey and World War I: Armageddon Tests a Liberal's Faith," *Perspectives in American History*, 9 (1975):337. A good counter to such objections to pragmatism can be found in Hook, *Pragmatism and the Tragic Sense of Life*.

136. Richard Hofstadter, *Anti-intellectualism in American Life* (New York: Knopf, 1970), 385. Anthony Quinton (in Peters, *Dewey Reconsidered* has also characterized Dewey's approach as anti-intellectual but only in the sense that his theory of knowledge

disagrees with the Cartesian tradition. Quinton looks favorably upon Dewey's anti-Cartesian contentions that all our beliefs are fallible and corrigible, that the knower is an active experimenter, and that the pursuit of rational belief is an essentially social undertaking. Part of my objection to analytic philosophy of education may well be a response to its Cartesian elements—i.e., the view that we can have beliefs that are certain and definitions for which we can find necessary and sufficient conditions, and the assumption that the knower is some kind of contemplative theorist pursuing truth in isolation from his or her fellow investigators.

137. See, for example, *Democracy and Education* MW 9:24–26.

138. Thus, in a review of Dewey's Lectures in the *Philosophy of Education:* 1899, John Childs remarks that these lectures show that Dewey recognizes that "adult guidance is written into the very constitution of the school," and the regard for the individuality of the child and his interests "is no substitute for adult interpretation, evaluation and selection from among genuine social alternatives, each with its own pattern for the molding of the immature." *Studies in Philosophy and Education*, 5 (Winter 1966–67):69.

139. J. O. C. Phillips, "Dewey in Mid-Passage," *History of Education Quarterly*, vol. 20, no. 1 (Spring 1980):123. This view also finds support in a recent article on Dewey that concludes that he seems to have been "more of a social engineer than a pure scientist"; Merle Borrowman, "The School and Society: Vermont in 1860, Chicago in 1890, Idaho in 1950, California in 1980," *Educational Studies*, 11 (Winter 1981):381.

140. Cremin, *Transformation*, 140.

141. Joe R. Burnett, introduction to *The School and Society,* MW 1:xix–xx. Burnett's judgment is overly harsh. Dewey continued to write on practical pedagogy throughout the rest of his life. In 1924, for example, he went to Turkey to prepare a "Report and Recommendation upon Turkish Education." The report has been described as speaking directly "to the problems of school systems in all developing countries, today and for many coming decades"; MW 15:xx and 275–97. Even near the end of his life, Dewey was writing about practical pedagogical matters such as the "project method" developed by Professor Kilpatrick at Teachers College; Dewey's introduction to Samuel Tenebaum, *William Heard Kilpatrick* (New York: Harper & Brothers, 1951).

3. *Bertrand Russell and the Beacon Hill School*

1. E. Lyttelton (ex-headmaster of Eton), *The Evening Standard* (14 October 1925), quoted by Dora Russell, *The Right to be Happy* (New York: Harper & Brothers, 1927).

2. Robert Skidelsky, *English Progressive Schools* (Middlesex: Penguin Books, 1969), 153. Often repeated, this anecdote is presented in essentially the same form in Ronald Clark, *The Life of Bertrand Russell* (Middlesex: Penguin Books, 1978), 530; Joe Park, *Bertrand Russell on Education* (London: George Allen & Unwin, 1964), 119; Katherine Tait, *My Father Bertrand Russell* (New York: Harcourt, Brace, Jovanovich, 1975), 71; and Alan Wood, *Bertrand Russell: The Passionate Sceptic* (London: George Allen & Unwin, 1957), 157; among others. David Harley dismisses the story as apocryphal in his "Beacon Hill School," *Russell*, 35–36 (Autumn-Winter 1979–80):5. Ironically, the story may have originated as one of the jokes of W. B. Curry, longtime headmaster of Dartington Hall School, and would have been a more likely occurrence at that school

than at Beacon Hill; Michael Young, *The Elmhirsts of Dartington* (London: Routledge & Kegan Paul, 1982), 163, 177.

3. Bertrand and Dora Russell, *The Prospects of Industrial Civilization*, 2d ed. (London: George Allen & Unwin, 1959), 243.

4. Dora Russell, *The Tamarisk Tree* (London: Elek/Pemberton, 1975), 199. For the views of Margaret McMillan, see her *The Nursery School* (London: J. M. Dent & Sons, 1919) and E. Stevinson, "Margaret McMillan, Prophet and Pioneer," *Journal of Education* 79 (September 1947): 488–90

5 Dora Russell, *The Tamarisk Tree 2* (London: Virago, 1980), 56.

6. Dora Russell, "What Beacon Hill Stood For," *Anarchy* 71, vol. 7, no. 1 (January 1967):12.

7. Bertrand Russell, *The Autobiography of Bertrand Russell*, vol. 2, 1914–1944 (Boston: Little, Brown, 1968; Bantom, 1970), 267–68.

8. D. Russell, *Tamarisk Tree*, 199.

9. Bertrand Russell, *On Education* (London: Allen & Unwin, 1926, Unwin Paperbacks, 1976), 82.

10. B. Russell, *Autobiography*, 222–23, (italics are Russell's).

11. There seems to be some disagreement as to just how much land was involved. David Harley, in "Beacon Hill and the Constructive Uses of Freedom," Ph.D. diss., University of Toronto, 1980, says 230 acres, but in "Beacon Hill School" says 250. Russell himself says 240 acres in "Education without Sex Taboos," *New Republic* (16 November 1927):346, then 230 in *Autobiography*, 223. Park in *Russell on Education* says 240. I leave it to scholars even more pedantic than I to resolve this riddle.

12. Russell also spoke of what he hoped to accomplish in his school in "A Bold Experiment in Child Education," *New York Times Magazine* (2 October 1927):8–9, 22.

13. D. Russell, *Tamarisk Tree 2*, 9–12.

14. Ibid., 15.

15. Letter from Russell to Lady Ottoline Morell quoted in Clark, *Life of Russell*, 526.

16. Harley, "Beacon Hill School," 10.

17. Clark, *Life of Russell*, 532.

18. B. Russell, *Autobiography*, 278–79.

19. D. Russell, *Tamarisk Tree 2*, 27.

20. See Clark, *Life of Russell*, 641.

21. An excellent account of Russell's lecture tours to America can be found in Barry Feinberg and Ronald Kasrils, *Bertrand Russell's America*, vol. 1, 1896–1945 (London: George Allen & Unwin, 1973).

22. B. Russell, *Autobiography*, 225.

23. See D. Russell, *Tamarisk Tree*, 50, 242, and Clark, *Life of Russell*, 528.

24. Bertrand Russell, *Principles of Social Reconstruction* (London: Allen & Unwin, 1916, reprint, 1960). This book was to have a profound effect on W. B. Curry, headmaster at Dartington Hall School, who said that it radically altered his views on education; Victor Bonham-Carter, *Dartington Hall* (London: Phoenix House, 1958), 195. Russell favorably reviewed Curry's book, *The School and a Changing Civilisation* (London: John Lane, 1934) for the *New Era in Home and School* (August 1934):196. It is interesting to note that after the breakup of his marriage, Russell sent Kate and John to Dartington "where they were very happy"; B. Russell, *Autobiography*, 285. Some years later Russell and his third wife Peter sent their son Conrad there as well, but he apparently did

not like it and was taken away; Young, *Elmhirsts*, 173. For a fascinating account of the origins, past history, and present problems of English public schools, see Jonathan Gathorne-Hardy, *The Old School Tie* (New York: Viking Press, 1977).

25. Tait, *My Father*, 48.

26. B. Russell, *Principles*, 101.

27. B. Russell, *On Education*, 123; see also his *Autobiography*, 222.

28. B. Russell, *Principles*, 102-5.

29. He presents the same idea in modified form in *Education and the Social Order* (London: Allen & Unwin, 1932; Unwin Books, 1967), where he says "History ought to be taught in exactly the same way in all countries of the world, and history text-books ought to be drawn up by the League of Nations, with an assistant from the United States, and another from Soviet Russia" (p. 82).

30. B. Russell, *Principles*, 108-12.

31. Ibid., 114, 116.

32. B. Russell, *The Prospects of Industrial Civilization*, 242-48.

33. Ibid., 261-63.

34. "Freedom or Authority in Education," *The Century Magazine*, vol. 109, no. 2 (December 1924):172-80.

35. Ibid., 180.

36. Paul Arthur Schilpp, ed., *The Philosophy of Bertrand Russell*, 3rd ed. *The Philosophy of Bertrand Russell*, (New York: Tudor Publishing Co., 1951), 731.

37. Harley, "Beacon Hill and Freedom," 123-24.

38. See B. Russell, *Autobiography*, 221.

39. John Dewey, "A Key to the New World," *New Republic* (19 May 1926), 410-11.

40. Letter from Russell to Dewey, 15 June 1926, copy in Russell Archives, McMaster University, Hamilton, Ontario. There is only scanty evidence that Russell had a favorable impression of Dewey's own school. A public debate was held in New York City between Russell and Will Durant on the topic, "Is Modern Education a Failure?" at which Dewey introduced the speakers; *New York Times*, 7 October 1929. From Russell's notes for the debate, we can derive the following: not all modern education is a failure; for example, "Dewey: modern schools: my own" (Russell Archives, Recent Acquisitions, 19a). Whether this was said in deference to Dewey's presence, we have no way of knowing. Durant's position in the debate appears in his *Adventures in Genius* (New York: Simon & Schuster, 1931), 414-26. Russell never credits Dewey for having influenced his views on education. He told Joe Park that he read Dewey's educational works *after* he had formulated his own ideas and that he then found himself in substantial agreement; Park, *Russell on Education*, 59, n. 4. It strikes me as unlikely that Russell would launch his experimental venture at Beacon Hill while still totally unfamiliar with Dewey's educational thoughts and practices. One of my students recently wrote to Dora Russell, asking about her acquaintance with the works of Dewey at the time of setting up Beacon Hill School. She replied: "I did not read or discuss any of Professor Dewey's writings on education, and I am ashamed to say that I have never read them. Russell may have met and talked with him in the USA but was certainly not influenced by him in setting up Beacon Hill School"; letter from Dora Russell to Gerry Conroy, 5 March 1984. Russell and Dewey had originally met in 1914 (Clark, *Life of Russell*, 285–86) and began to react critically to one another's philosophical outlooks soon after; Elizabeth R. Eames, "A Discussion of the Issues in the Theory of Knowledge involved in the Controversy

between John Dewey and Bertrand Russell," Ph.D. diss., Bryn Mawr College, 1951. It is of interest to note that among the books that Russell lists as having read between February 1891 and March 1902 are the two volumes of William James's *Psychology* as well as his *Talks to Teachers*; *The Collected Papers of Bertrand Russell*, vol. 1 ed. Kenneth Blackwell, Andrew Brink, Nicholas Griffin, Richard A. Rempel, and John G. Slater (London: George Allen & Unwin, 1983), appendix 2: "What Shall I Read?"; also of interest is William James, *Talks to Teachers on Psychology* in *The Works of William James*, ed. Frederick Burkhardt, Fredson Bowers, and Ignas K. Skrupskelis (Cambridge, Mass.: Harvard University Press, 1983). Such an awareness of the very latest work emanating from America on psychological and educational topics makes me suspect that Russell may well have learned more from Dewey on education than he was willing to acknowledge.

41. In Schilpp, *Philosophy of Russell*, Russell responds favorably to the suggestion that there is no necessary relation between his epistemology and metaphysics and his social philosophy, including his views on education. As he puts it, "I have always maintained that there was no logical connection, pointing to the example of Hume, with whom I agree so largely in abstract matters and disagree so totally in politics. But other people, for the most part, have assured me that there was a connection, though I was not aware of it" (p. 727). There are times, in reading Russell's educational theory, when one wishes that he had made more of an effort to make a connection with his more technical views on knowledge and reality.

42. B. Russell, *On Education*, 15–30.

43. Ibid., 41.

44. Ibid., 158.

45. Ibid., 176. This is not as obvious a point as it may seem if one can judge from the trouble A. S. Neill encountered when he wanted to hire a Frenchman to teach French in his school. Government officials resisted and he wrote to Russell enlisting his help. The best that could be accomplished was permission for a one-year appointment. Russell eventually wrote to the Ministry of Labour suggesting that they extend the principle of confining employment as far as possible to the British by training English women to replace the many foreign wives of Englishmen; B. Russell, *Autobiography*, 270–78. No official reply to Russell's suggestion is extant.

46. B. Russell, *On Education*, 186.

47. Ibid., 195, 200, 202.

48. One of the clearest indications of this Platonic aspect of Russell's thought can be seen in his *The Problems of Philosophy* (London: Williams and Norgate, 1912). Surprising support for the elitist view of higher education can also be found in Dewey. Writing at the turn of the century, Dewey said "Hardly one per cent of the entire school population ever attains to what we call higher education: only five per cent to the grade of our high school; while much more than half leave on or before the completion of the fifth year of the elementary grade. The simple facts of the case are that in the great majority of human beings the distinctively intellectual interest is not dominant"; *The School and Society*, MW 1:18.

49. B. Russell, *On Education*, 203.

50. Dora Russell, "Beacon Hill," in *The Modern Schools Handbook*, ed. Trevor Blewitt (London: Victor Gollancz, 1934), 24–42.

51. B. Russell, Tait, *My Father*, 86.

52. B. Russell "Education Without Sex Taboos," 347. Cf. Dewey, *The School and Society*, MW 1:21.

53. James Wedgewood Drawbell, *A Gallery of Women* (London: Collins, 1933), 23–41.

54. D. Russell, *Tamarisk Tree 2*, 47.

55. Quoted in Feinberg and Kasrils, *Russell's America*, 153.

56. The whole sorry affair is summarized in "How Bertrand Russell was Prevented from Teaching at the College of the City of New York," which appears as an appendix to his book, *Why I am Not a Christian*, ed. Paul Edwards (London: Allen & Unwin, 1957; New York: Simon and Schuster, 1966), 207–59. Many American academics were outraged at this decision, and Dewey for one helped to edit and contributed to a volume of essays in Russell's defense; *The Bertrand Russell Case*, ed. Horace Kallen and John Dewey (New York: The Viking Press, 1941).

57. Wood, *Bertrand Russell*, 159.

58. D. Russell, "Beacon Hill," 33.

59. Cf. B. Russell, *On Education*, 172 and D. Russell, "What Beacon Hill Stood For," 15.

60. Tait, *My Father*, 84–85.

61. "Free Speech in Childhood," *New Statesman and Nation*, 1 (30 May 1931):486–88.

62. *New Statesman and Nation*, 1 (6 June 1931):539–40.

63. Ibid. (13 June 1931):575.

64. Ibid. (20 June 1931):606–7.

65. Ibid. (27 June 1931):643.

66. D. Russell, "Beacon Hill," 34.

67. Dora Russell, *Thinking in Front of Yourself and Other Plays* (London: James Press, 1934).

68. Tait, *My Father*, 87–91.

69. B. Russell, "Modern Tendencies in Education," *The Spectator* (13 June 1931); 926–27.

70. Susan Isaacs (1885–1948) ran an experimental school at Malting House, Cambridge. Although Russell was impressed with what she was doing, she bridled at his suggestion that her school represented an application of psychoanalytic theory to education. For her, "It was far more an application to the education of very young children of the educational philosophy of John Dewey"; *Social Development in Young Children* (London, 1933; reprint, New York: Schocken Books, 1972), 19, n. 1. A good summary of the Malting House School (1924–29) can be found in Willem van der Eyken and Barry Turner, *Adventures in Education* (London: Allen Lane, 1969), 15–67.

71. B. Russell, "Modern Tendencies," 927

72. D. Russell, "Beacon Hill," 36.

73. A. S. Neill, *Summerhill* (New York: Hart Publishing Co., 1960).

74. D. Russell, "What Beacon Hill Stood For," 13.

75. B. Russell, *Autobiography*, 296.

76. B. Russell, "In Our School," *New Republic* (9 September 1931):92–94. David Harley has discovered that the school did issue report cards. One, which dates from 1930, contains the following headings: "Height, Weight, Physical Report, Reading, Writing, Arithmetic, History, Geography, French, English Literature and Grammar, German,

Science, Hand and Craft Work, Eurythmics and Music, Music (again), and General Psychology," "Beacon Hill School," 14. In a letter to the editor of *Time and Tide* (8 January 1930), Russell reiterates his point about discipline: "It may possibly interest you to know that self-discipline, and more particularly intellectual discipline, is one of the main things taught in our school" (p. 6).

77. B. Russell, *Autobiography*, 225; Cf. D. Russell, *Tamarisk Tree 2*, 16.

78. Wood, *Bertrand Russell*, 161.

79. D. Russell, *Tamarisk Tree*, 198.

80. See Clark, *Life of Russell*, 552–53.

81. Tait, *My Father*, 79.

82. Wood, *Bertrand Russell*, 161.

83. H. W. Leggett, *Bertrand Russell, O.M.* (New York Philosophical Library, 1950).

84. Drawbell, *Gallery of Women*, 26. Dora herself gives us a vivid picture of the negative impression that the school often had on visitors, when she describes an unexpected visit to Beacon Hill from Beatrice Webb and George Bernard Shaw. Russell, not unexpectedly, was away; and it was just before tea, "when the children are at their wildest." When confronted by all those eager, but dirty faces, Shaw was heard to mutter, "Let's get out of here." As Dora hurriedly dispensed their tea, "Mrs. Webb and Shaw lectured the staff and myself on the care and education of children, and then went away." Dora somewhat acidly adds, "We could not help reflecting that both were childless." Dora Russell, "Shaw—A Personal Impression," *Civil Liberty*, 10 (Winter 1950):5. A. J. Ayer once visited the school and found it "anarchic." See his autobiography, *Part of My Life* (London: Collins, 1977), 111.

85. D. Russell, *Tamarisk Tree 2*, 51.

86. Letter from Russell to Joe Park, 1 February 1961, quoted in Clark, *Life of Russell*, 532.

87. Park, *Russell on Education*, 122–23. Though in another letter to Park, Russell expands upon this and says, "I do not feel inclined to say anything about Beacon Hill School. For various reasons, unconnected with educational theory, it was not a success"; letter from Russell to Joe Park, 17 March 1960, copy in Russell Archives, McMaster University, Hamilton, Ontario.

88. D. Russell, *Tamarisk Tree 2*, 50.

89. Park, *Russell on Education*, 23.

90. Wood, *Bertrand Russell*, 161.

91. D. Russell, *Tamarisk Tree 2*, 34.

92. Clark, *Life of Russell*, 531–32.

93. D. Russell, *Tamarisk Tree 2*, 26.

94. Russell quoted in conversation in 1927 by Dilip Kumar Roy, *Among the Great* (Bombay: Nalanda Publications, 1945), 115. Robert Marsh claims that Russell would have preferred to open a free school for poor children but could not afford it; "Bertrand Russell's Philosophy of Education," D. Ed. diss., Harvard University, 1951, 40. I think this a romantic speculation with little factual backing.

95. B. Russell, *Autobiography*, 225–27, and B. Russell, *On Education*, 167.

96. B. Russell, *Autobiography*, 227.

97. Leggett, *Bertrand Russell*, 35.

98. Tait, *My Father*, 81–82.

99. R. F. Dearden, *Problems in Primary Education* (London: Routledge & Kegan

Paul, 1976), 66. Also of interest is R. S. Peters, *Authority, Responsibility and Education* (New York: Atherton Press, 1967; 3rd ed., London: Allen & Unwin, 1973).

100. C. E. M. Joad, "The Virtue of Examinations," *New Statesman and Nation* (11 March 1944):176–77. Curry's reply is in the issue of 25, March p. 208; Joad's response to Curry, 1 April, p. 225. Dora's rebuttal, entitled "Progressive Education," appears in the issue of 22 April, p. 274. For more of Joad's views on education see his *About Education* (London: Faber and Faber, 1945).

101. For example, in a press interview on the occasion of his withdrawing from the school, Russell was quoted as saying, "It was an experiment on my part. I wrote a book on education and wanted to try out my own theories. To my surprise the theories have worked out well." *News Chronicle (11* March 1931), quoted by Ray Hemmings, *Children's Freedom, A. S. Neill and the Evolution of the Summerhill Idea* (New York: Schocken Books, 1973), 80.

102. Harley, "Beacon Hill School," 16.

103. Katherine Tait, in *Russell* (Spring-Summer 1976), 52.

104. D. Russell, *Tamarisk Tree 2*, 212.

105. Wood, *Bertrand Russell*, 157. Claire Bloom in her recent autobiography describes her impressions of being sent as a child to Beacon Hill as it was run under Dora's leadership: "No one, including the teachers, had to wear clothes unless he wanted to. No one had to attend class unless he wanted to. Everyone was free to do as he or she wished. As I remember it, no one did much of anything. After the initial shock of seeing male teachers nude, I got into the mood of the place and discovered how delightful it was to swim naked and to be at a school where I hadn't any schoolwork"; *Limelight and After* (New York: Harper & Row, 1982), 24.

106. Terry Philpot, "The Russells and Beacon Hill," *Humanist*, vol. 84, no. 6 (June 1969), 173 (italics are Philpot's).

107. Ronald Jager, *The Development of Bertrand Russell's Philosophy* (London: George Allen & Unwin, 1972), 452–58.

108. B. Russell, *Education and the Social Order*. This book, according to Clark, "incorporated the lessons learned at Beacon Hill School and qualified the over-idealistic recipes of *On Education*"; Clark, *Life of Russell*, 558).

109. B. Russell, *Education and the Social Order*, 22–26.

110. Ibid., 100.

111. Ibid., 146.

112. "Education and Discipline," in *In Praise of Idleness* (London: George Allen & Unwin, 1935), 208.

113. "The Functions of a Teacher," in *The Basic Writings of Bertrand Russell*, ed. R. Egner and L. Dennon (London: George Allen & Unwin, 1961), 435–42.

114. "Proposals for an International University," *The Fortnightly*, 158 (July 1942):13. Russell expands upon this flagrantly intolerant proposal in his article, "Education after the War," *American Mercury*, 57 (August 1943):199, where he says, "Every author of a textbook would have to seek the *imprimatur* of the international university before his book could be used in schools. Any state which persistently rejected the internationally authorized textbooks in its national education would thereby afford *prima facie* evidence of its disloyalty, and would be penalized by the international authority." This reminds me of Plato's proposals for censoring literature in his ideal state.

115. Tait, *My Father*, 94.

116. B. Russell, "Education Without Sex Taboos," 346–47.

117. "As School Opens—The Educators Examined," *New York Times Magazine* (7 September 1952):45.

118. "Education for a Difficult World," *Fact and Fiction* (London: George Allen & Unwin, 1961), 149, (italics are Russell's).

119. Noam Chomsky finds this attitude in Russell's writings on education quite attractive. He sees Russell advocating a humanistic conception of education in the line of Marx, Kropotkin, and others. See his "Toward a Humanistic Conception of Education," in *Work, Technology and Education*, ed. Walter Feinberg and Henry Rosemont, Jr. (Chicago: University of Illinois Press, 1975), 204–20.

120. Katherine Tait in a talk with David Harley on "Bertrand Russell as an Educator", presented at the University of Waterloo, 15 July 1982.

121. Bertrand Russell, *The Autobiography of Bertrand Russell*, vol. 1, 1872–1914 (Boston: Little, Brown, 1967; Bantam, 1968), 3–4.

4. *Alfred North Whitehead and the Rhythm of Education*

1. Whitehead quoted in William Ernest Hocking "Whitehead as I Knew Him," *Journal of Philosophy*, (14 September 1961):512, (Whitehead's emphases).

2. Alfred North Whitehead, "The Study of the Past—its Uses and its Dangers,"in *Essays in Science and Philosophy*, ed. Alfred North Whitehead (London: Rider and Co. 1948), 121.

3. Alfred North Whitehead, "Autobiographical Notes," in *The Philosophy of Alfred North Whitehead*, 2d ed., ed. P. A. Schilpp (New York: Tudor Publishing Co., 1951), 3.

4. Victor Lowe, "Alfred North Whitehead," *Encyclopedia of Education* (New York: Macmillan, 1969), 9:550.

5. Alfred North Whitehead, "The Education of an Englishman," in Whitehead, *Essays*, 32.

6. Letter from Whitehead to the Provost of University College, London, 16 March 1912, and quoted in Victor Lowe, "A. N. Whitehead and his Mathematical Goals: a Letter of 1912," *Annals of Science*, 32 (1975):85–101. A good account of the difficulties scholars face in obtaining biographical material of this sort on Whitehead is Victor Lowe, "A. N. W.: A Biographical Perspective," *Process Studies*, 12 (Fall 1982):137–47.

7. Whitehead, "Autobiographical Notes," 8.

8. Ibid.

9. Bertrand Russell, "Alfred North Whitehead," in B. Russell, *Portraits from Memory* (London: Allen & Unwin, 1956), 93.

10. Bertrand Russell, "Whitehead and Principia Mathematica," *Mind*, 57 (April 1948):138.

11. B. Russell, *Portraits from Memory*, 93.

12. Ronald Clark, *The Life of Bertrand Russell* (Middlesex: Penguin Books, 1978), 107.

13. Lowe, "Whitehead and his Mathematical Goals."

14. See *The Wit and Wisdom of Alfred North Whitehead*, ed. A. H. Johnson (Boston:

Beacon Press, 1947), 7, and F. H. Page, "A. N. Whitehead: A Pupil's Tribute," *Dalhousie Review*, 28 (1948):72.

15. Whitehead, "Autobiographical Notes," 11.

16. Harold B. Dunkel, *Whitehead on Education* (Columbus: Ohio State University Press, 1965),7.

17. Nothing, to my knowledge, has yet been written about Whitehead's membership on the Surrey Education Committee. I thank Professor Victor Lowe for bringing it to my attention, and the staff at the Surrey Record Office, Kingston upon Thames, for their help in finding this information.

18. S. J. Curtis, *History of Education in Great Britain* (London: University Tutorial Press, 1948), 316.

19. See the minutes of the meeting of the Surrey Education Committee for 16 July 1921 and 17 March 1922.

20. For the full terms of reference of this subcommittee, see the minutes of the Surrey Education Committee for 24 March 1903.

21. According to the minutes, from 10 June 1921 to 19 October 1921, he attended 4 of 9 possible meetings of the Education Committee and the various subcommittee of which he was a member; from 20 October 1921 to 25 October 1962, 4 of 27 possible meetings; from 26 October 1922 to 8 March 1924, he was present at none of the 36 possible meetings. All told, he attended 8 of 72 possible meetings, and of these 5 were meetings of the Standing Committee on Higher Education.

22. Report of the Committee for 12 June 1924.

23. Whitehead, "Autobiographical Notes," 11–12.

24. Lowe, "Whitehead and his Mathematical Goals," 100.

25. Nathaniel Lawrence, *Alfred North Whitehead: A Primer of his Philosophy* (New York: Twayne Publishers, 1974), 22.

26. Letter from Whitehead to Mark Barr, 13 January 1924, quoted in Hocking, "Whitehead as I Knew Him," 508.

27. B. Russell, *Portraits from Memory*, 93.

28. John Smith, *The Spirit of American Philosophy* (New York: Oxford University Press, 1966), 188.

29. Alfred North Whitehead, *An Introduction to Mathematics* (London: Home University Library, 1911; rev. ed., New York: Oxford University Press, 1958), 1.

30. Ibid., 144.

31. Ibid., 100.

32. Ibid., 128–29.

33. Ibid., 188.

34. Alfred North Whitehead, "Mathematics and Liberal Education," in Alfred North Whitehead, *A Philosopher Looks at Science* (New York: Philosophical Library, 1965), 27–29.

35. Ibid., 35. This is reminiscent of Dewey's enthusiasm for weaving; see *The School and Society*, MW 1:15.

36 Ibid., 39–40.

37. "The Principles of Mathematics in Relation to Elementary Teaching," in Alfred North Whitehead, *The Organisation of Thought: Educational and Scientific* (London: Williams & Norhgate, 1917; reprint, Westport, Conn.: Greenwood Press, 1974), 101–2.

38. Ibid., 101.

39. Ibid., 102. Cf. the more recent statement of R. S. Peters to the same effect; "Education as Initiation," in *Philosophical Analysis and Education*, ed. R. D. Archambault (London: Routledge & Kegan Paul, 1965), 107.

40. Alfred North Whitehead, "The Mathematical Curriculum," in *The Aims of Education and Other Essays* (New York: Macmillan, 1929; reprint, Free Press, 1967), 77–89.

41. Ibid., 182.

42. Lowe, "Whitehead and his Mathematical Goals," 96, (italics are Lowe's).

43. Whitehead, "The Mathematical Curriculum," 88.

44. Whitehead, "The Aims of Education," in Whitehead, *Aims of Education*, 1–3.

45. Ibid., 7.

46. Ibid., 8–9.

47. "Education and Self-Education," address delivered on Founders' Day at the Stanley Technical Trade School in South Norwood, London, 1 February 1919, in Whitehead, *Essays*, 127.

48. "Aims of Education," 11–12.

49. Alfred North Whitehead, "A Polytechnic in War-time," in Whitehead's *Organisation of Thought*, 58–68.

50. Alfred North Whitehead, "Technical Education and Its Relation to Science and Literature," in Whitehead, *Aims of Education*, 45.

51. Ibid., 53–54.

52. Ibid., 56.

53. As recorded in the *Report of the 87th Meeting of the British Association for the Advancement of Science* held in Bournemouth, 1919 (London: John Murray, 1920), 361. See also Robert S. Brumbaugh, "Discussion Upon Fundamental Principles of Education," *Process Studies*, 14 (Spring 1984):41-43.

54. I am grateful to the Public Record Office, Kew, Richmond, for allowing me to consult and for providing me with copies of this material. All references are to the Ministry of Education Private Office Papers, 1851–1935, hereafter ED 24/1188.

55. *Report of the Committee Appointed by the Prime Minister to Inquire into the Position of Classics in the Educational System of the United Kingdom* (London: His Majesty's Stationary Office, 1921), 1.

56. Ibid., 7–8.

57. Ibid., 13.

58. Ibid., 19.

59. Ibid., 159.

60. Robert S. Brumbaugh, "Whitehead's Educational Theory: Two Supplementary Notes to the Aims of Education," *Educational Theory*, 16 (July 1966):215.

61. Frederick Kenyon, ed., *Education, Scientific and Humane*, (London: John Murray, 1917), 10–11.

62. *Report*, 254–56.

63. This is gleaned from Circular 1294, *Circular to Local Education Authorities (PA II) and Secondary Schools in England*, 8 December 1922. The circular itself was reviewed in *Education* (15 December 1922). Also of interest are the *Report of the 11th Annual Conference of Educational Associations*, joint conference held on 30 December 1922 (London: His Majesty's Stationary Office, 1923) and the *Report of the Board of Education for the Year 1921–2* (London: His Majesty's Stationary Office, 1923).

64. In the Archives of the Committee on the Classics, ED 24/1188.

65. Personal correspondence from Victor Lowe, 6 September 1980. An address by Dame Dorothy Brock on "The Classics as the Foundation of the Humanities" has been summarized in *The Educational Times* (July 1922):301.

66. Lowe, "Alfred North Whitehead," 553.

67. Brumbaugh, "Whitehead's Educational Theory," 211.

68. Alfred North Whitehead, "The Place of the Classics in Education," in Whitehead, *Aims of Education*, 61–62.

69. Ibid., 74–75. A more conservative defense of the classics can be found in a British government report on "Reconstruction Problems" entitled *The Classics in British Education* (London: Ministry of Reconstruction, 1919).

70. Alfred North Whitehead, "Science in General Education," in Whitehead, *A Philosopher Looks at Science*, 50–51.

71. Alfred North Whitehead, "The Rhythm of Education," in Whitehead, *Aims of Education*, 15–28. Others from time to time have expressed a similar idea, notably Percy Nunn who spoke of "a rhythm of alternate phases" in knowledge in an address to the Aristotelian Society (1907–8). He later (1920) developed this into a "rhythm of teaching" with three stages—wonder, utility, and system—and pointed out that "It is of interest to observe that Professor A. N. Whitehead has formulated independently a similar rhythmic law"; Percy Nunn, "On the Concept of Epistemological Levels," *Proceedings of the Aristotelian Society*, n.s., vol 8 (London, 1907–8):139–59, and *Education: Its Data and First Principles*, rev. ed. (London: Edward Arnold, 1933). A good study of Nunn is that of J. W. Tibble, "Sir Percy Nunn: 1870–1944)," *British Journal of Educational Studies* 10 (1961):58–75.

72. Alfred North Whitehead, "The Rhythm of Education," 17.

73. Ibid., 18.

74. B. Hendley, "A Whiteheadian Model for Teaching Introductory Philosophy," *Metaphilosophy*, 7 (July/October 1976):307–15.

75. Whitehead, "Rhythm of Education," 22. Cf. Dora Russell, *The Tamarisk Tree* (London: Elek/Pemberton, 1975), 199 and Dewey, *Democracy and Education*, MW 9:160.

76. Whitehead, "Rhythm of Education," 26.

77. Alfred North Whitehead, "The Rhythmic Claims of Freedom and Discipline," in Whitehead, *Aims of Education*, 29–41.

78. Ibid., 36–37.

79. Alfred North Whitehead, "Historical Changes," in Whitehead, *Essays in Science and Philosophy*, 151. Cf. Dewey, MW 9:177.

80. Alfred North Whitehead, "Universities and Their Function," in Whitehead, *Aims of Education*, 92–93.

81. Ibid., 98. For Dewey on the scholar as teacher cf "The Relation of Theory to Practice in Education," MW 3:263. Also of interest are Russell's comments in *On Education* (London: George Allen & Unwin, 1926; reprint 1976), 200.

82. Alfred North Whitehead, "Harvard: The Future," *Atlantic Monthly*, 158 (September 1936):260–70, reprinted in A. H. Johnson, ed., *Whitehead's American Essays in Social Philosophy* (New York: Harper, 1959),156–76.

83. Ibid., 160–61.

84. Ibid., 164.

85. Ibid., 170–75. Not every educator agrees with Whitehead's assessment of prac-

tical studies at universities. See, for example, Robert M. Hutchins, "A Reply to Professor Whitehead," *Atlantic Monthly*, 158 (November 1936):582–88. Hutchins believed that "The danger of the American universities is not celibacy, but polygamy. They are mated to so many different kinds of action that nothing but a few divorces can save them from the consequences of their ardor" (p. 583).

86. B. Russell, *Portraits from Memory*, 97.

87. J. E. Littlewood, *A Mathematician's Miscellany* (London: Methuen, 1953, reprint, 1957), 70, 76–77.

88. Not all of Whitehead's students found him approachable on a personal level. See, for example, A. H. Johnson, "Whitehead as Teacher and Philosopher," *Philosophy and Phenomenological Research*, 29 (March 1969):351–76, and Joseph Gerard Brennan, "Alfred North Whitehead: Plato's Lost Dialogue," in *Masters, Portraits of Great Teachers*, ed. Joseph Epstein (New York: Basic Books, 1981), 47–68. The flavor of Whitehead's conversation has been recorded by Lucien Price, *Dialogues of Alfred North Whitehead* (New York: Mentor Books, 1956). A. H. Johnson has described his own experiences of Whitehead as a lecturer and a tutor at Harvard. Johnson seems fiercely protective of his memories of the great man, and he criticizes the published recollections of some of Whitehead's other students at Harvard, among them Paul Weiss, George Burch, Joseph Brennan, and F. Hilton Page; *Whitehead and His Philosophy* (Lanham, Md.: University Press of America, 1983).

89. A good study is Joe Burnett, "The Educational Philosophy of Alfred North Whitehead," Ph.D. diss., New York University, 1958. Also of interest are Henry Holmes, "The Educational Views of Alfred North Whitehead," Occasional Pamphlets, no. 5, April 1943 (Harvard University Graduate School of Education) and A. H. Johnson, "Whitehead's Discussion of Education," *Education* (June 1946):1–19. An excellent recent attempt to expand upon Whitehead's insights on education is Robert S. Brumbaugh, *Whitehead, Process Philosophy, and Education* (Albany: State University of New York Press, 1982. See also John B. Bennett, "Whitehead and a Framework for Liberal Education," *Teachers College Record*, 82 (Winter 1980):329–41.

5. The Philosopher as Educator Today

1. *The Ethics of Aristotle*, trans. J. A. K. Thomson (London: George Allen & Unwin, 1953), book 6, chapter 7.

2. John Dewey, *The Sources of a Science of Education* (New York: Liveright, 1929), 43–44

3 For a good account of Dora Russell's continuing involvement with educational reform movemets, cf. Jonathan Croall, *Neill of Summerhill, The Permanent Rebel* (London: Routledge & Kegan Paul, 1983).

4. George Eastman lists four instances during the Chicago years when Dewey generalizes from "empirical, experimental findings" but gives no instances where the experimental findings caused him to alter or modify his theories; "John Dewey on Education: The Formative Years" (D.Ed. diss., Harvard, 1963), 606–7 n. 36.

5. See chapter 2, note 112 for an example of Dewey's reaction to criticism from his staff.

6. B. F. Skinner, in his autobiography, credits Whitehead with being one of the moving forces behind the establishment of the Junior Fellows Program at Harvard. This was to be modeled on the Trinity Prize Fellows at Cambridge University; *The Shaping of a Behaviorist, Part Two of an Autobiography* (New York: Alfred A. Knopf, 1979), 121. Victor Lowe feels that Whitehead had "a real but diffuse influence on the Harvard Business School" but adds that "it would be almost impossible to document it" (personal letter, 17 October 1983). Some scant evidence of Whitehead's impact can be gathered from references to his *Aims of Education* in Elton Mayo's *Social Problems of an Industrial Civilization* (London: Routledge & Kegan Paul, 1949; reprint 1975). Mayo had been professor of industrial research at the Harvard Business School during Whitehead's tenure there. Wallace Brett Donham, dean of the Graduate School of Business Administration at Harvard at the same time, used Whitehead's address to the Harvard School, "On Foresight," as the introduction to his own book, *Business Adrift* (New York: Whittlesey House, 1931). Whitehead's address was reprinted as chapter 6 of his *Adventures of Ideas* (New York: Macmillan, 1933). Donham also wrote *Education for Responsible Living* (Cambridge, Mass.: Harvard University Press, 1944), in which he quotes from *The Aims of Education and Other Essays* (New York: Macmillan, 1929; reprint, Free Press, 1967) and several of Whitehead's other works. Another link is Whitehead's son, North, who was on the faculty of the Harvard Business School in the 1930s.

7. Whitehead, *Aims of Education*. 98, 5.

8. Cf. Robert S. Brumbaugh, *Whitehead, Process Philosophy, and Education* (Albany: State University of New York Press, 1982); Kieran Egan, *Educational Development* (New York: Oxford University Press, 1979); and B. Hendley, "A Whiteheadian Model for Teaching Introductory Philosophy," *Metaphilosophy*, 7 (July/October 1976):307–16. Also of interest is Bernard Meland, *Higher Education and the Human Spirit* (Chicago: University of Chicago Press, 1953).

9. Cf. *Democracy and Education*, MW 9:338 ff. (italics are Dewey's).

10. Israel Scheffler, *Four Pragmatists* (New York: Humanities Press, 1974), 251–52.

11. For a similar view of philosophy, cf. Brand Blanshard, "Autobiography," in *The Philosophy of Brand Blanshard*, ed. Paul Arthur Schilpp, Library of Living Philosophers, vol. 15 (La Salle, Ill.: Open Court, 1980), 96.

12. For some of the difficulties that Aquinas encountered from his fellow ecclesiastics because of his use of non-Christian authors, cf. Daniel Callus, "The Condemnation of St. Thomas at Oxford," Aquinas, paper no. 5 (London: Aquinas Society of London, 1946).

13. *The Metalogicon of John of Salisbury*, trans. Daniel D. McCarry (Berkeley: Unversity of California Press, 1955; reprint 1962), 167.

14. Cf. B. Hendley, "Wasted Resources: What Educational Philosophers Might Contribute to Educational Theory But Often Don't," *Journal of Educational Thought*, 16 (April 1982):15–22.

15. Robert S. Brumbaugh and Nathaniel M. Lawrence, *Philosophical Themes in Modern Education* (Boston: Houghton Mifflin, 1973). Also of interest is their *Philosophers on Education: Six Essays on the Foundation of Western Thought* (Boston: Houghton Mifflin, 1963).

16. R. S. Peters, *Psychology and Ethical Development* (London: George Allen & Unwin, 1974).

17. R. S. Peters, *Education and the Education of Teachers* (London: Routledge &

Kegan Paul, 1977). Cf. also my review of this book and Peter's reply in *The Review of Education*, 4 (Spring 1978):91–94, 179–80.

18. For an example of this hostility, see John Wilson's reply, pp.245–46, to B. Hendley, "Educational Fantasies and Philosophy," 7 (Spring 1981):167–73.

19. John Dewey, From Absolutism to Experimentalism," in *Contemporary American Philosophy: Personal Statements,* vol. 2, ed. George P. Adams and W. P. Montague (New York, 1930; reissued, Russell & Russell, 1962), 23. In a detailed comparison of the philosophies of Dewey, Russell, and Whitehead, Joseph Ratner criticizes the latter two for not recognizing the philosophical importance of experimentation. It should be noted that Ratner makes no references to their educational writings; cf. his "Introduction to John Dewey's Philosophy," in *Intelligence in the Modern World,* ed. Joseph Ratner (New York: Modern Library, 1939), 3–241. Also of interest is Howard Woodhouse, "The Concept of Growth in Bertrand Russell's Educational Thought," *Journal of Educational Thought,* 17 (April 1983):12–21. Woodhouse finds Russell's concept of growth to be inexact in comparison with Whitehead's and to be cast in a more romantic spirit than Dewey's. Surprisingly, he refers only to Russell's *Principles of Social Reconstruction* and makes no mention to *On Education* or *Education and the Social Order.*

20. Cf. Anthony O'Hear, *Education, Society, and Human Nature* (London: Routledge & Kegan Paul, 1981), and Walter Feinberg, *Understanding Education, Toward a Reconstruction of Education Inquiry* (New York: Cambridge University Press, 1983).

21. John White, *The Aims of Education Restated* (London: Routledge & Kegan Paul, 1982), x.

22. Mortimer J. Adler, *The Paideia Proposal* (New York: Macmillan, 1982). For a discussion of this book with a reply by Adler, see *Harvard Education Review,* 53 (November 1983).

23. For example, Carol Levine and Robert M. Veatch, eds., *Cases in Bioethics,* Hastings-on-Hudson, N.Y.: Hastings Center, 1982). I thank my colleague Michael McDonald for bringing this book to my attention.

24. Ibid., x.

25. Cf. B. Hendley, "Five Mistaken Approaches to Education," *McGill Journal of Education,* 9 (Spring 1974):25–33.

26. Robert P. Taylor, ed., *The Computer in the School: Tutor, Tool, Tutee* (New York: Teachers College Press, 1980). I thank William Goodman for bringing this book to my attention. Also of interest is Seymour Papert, *Mindstorms: Children, Computers and Powerful Ideas* (New York: Basic Books, 1980).

27. Eric Hoyle, "Computers and Education: A Solution in Search of a Problem?" *World Yearbook of Education* 1982/3 Computers and Education, ed. Jacquetta Megarry, David Walker, Stanley Nisbett, and Eric Hoyle (London: Kogan Page, 1983), 60. A look at the problem from the student's point of view is Harriet K. Cuffaro, "Microcomputers in Education: Why Is Earlier Better?" *Teachers College Record,* 85 (Summer, 1984):559–568.

28. Brumbaugh, *Whitehead,* 115.

29. Buber quoted in B. Hendley, "Martin Buber on the Teacher/Student Relationship: A Critical Appraisal," *Journal of Philosophy of Education,* 12 (1978):141–48. Cf. also my article, "Teaching and Personal Relationships: A Response to Joseph Abinun," *Educational Theory,* 29 (Winter 1979):73–75.

30. Adler, *Paideia Proposal*, 23.

31. Cf. Jane Roland Martin," Sophie and Emile: A Case Study of Sex Bias in the History of Educational Thought," *Harvard Educational Review*, 51 (August 1981):357–72.

32. Ruth Jonathan, "Education, Gender and the Nature/Culture Controversy," *Journal of Philosophy of Education*, 17 (1983):8–9. Of enduring interest is Simone de Beauvoir's *The Second Sex* (New York: Alfred A. Knopf, 1952).

33. Jonathan, "Education, Gender," 16 (italics are Jonathan's).

34. Ibid., 10.

35. Jane Roland Martin, "The Ideal of the Educated Person," *Educational Theory*, 31 (Spring 1981):108.

36. Jane Roland Martin, "Needed: A New Paradigm for Liberal Education," in *Philosophy and Education*, Eightieth Yearbook of the National Society for the Study of Education, part 1, ed. Jonas Soltis (Chicago: University of Chicago Press, 1981), 44.

37. Martin, "Ideal of Educated Person," 109.

38. Martin, "Needed," 51.

39. Martin, "Ideal of Educated Person," 109. For a critical response to Martin's view, see Harvey Siegel, "Genderized Cognitive Perspective and the Redefinition of Philosophy of Education," in *Philosophy of Education 1983, Proceedings of the Philosophy of Education Society*, ed. Robert E. Roemer (Normal, Ill.: Illinois State University, 1984), 35–51. Carol Gilligan extends Martin's feminist critique to the area of the psychology of moral development where she claims that researchers like Lawrence Kohlberg have ignored a feminine moral perspective, which stresses compassion and care in interpersonal relationships, in favor of a more masculine view of the value of autonomous judgment and action. Divergence from the masculine standard is then depicted as a failure of moral development; Carol Gilligan, "In a Different Voice: Women's Conceptions of Self and Morality," *Harvard Educational Review*, 47 (November 1977):481–517. Also of interest is her *In A Different Voice: Psychological Theories and Women's Development* (Cambridge, Mass.: Harvard University Press, 1982). For critical reactions to Gilligan, see Lorraine B. Code, "Responsibility and the Epistemic Community: Woman's Place," *Social Research*, 50 (Autumn 1983):537–55, and the review by Madhu Suri Prakash in *Educational Studies*, 15 (Summer 1984):190–200.

40. Maryann Ayim and Barbara Houston, "A Conceptual Analysis of Sexism and Sexist Education," in *Philosophy of Education: Canadian Perspectives*, ed. Donald B. Cochrane and Martin Schiralli (Don Mills, Ontario: Collier Macmillan Canada, 1982),145–70. Also of interest is Maxine Greene, "Sexism in the Schools," in her *Landscapes of Learning* (New York: Teachers College Press, 1978), 244–55.

41. Jonathan, "Education, Gender," 19.

42. Kathryn Morgan, "The Androgynous Classroom: Liberatian of Tyranny?" in Cochrane and Schiralli, *Philosophy of Education*, 171–81.

43. Some of these ideas were discussed at a session on the topic "Should Public Education be Gender-Free?" given by Maryann Ayim, Barbara Houston, and Kathryn Morgan at the thirty-ninth annual meeting of the Philosophy of Education Society, held in Cincinnati, Ohio, 10 April 1983.

44. Ivan Illich, *Gender*, (New York: Pantheon Books, 1982). Also of interest are the forthcoming World Yearbook of Education 1984 entitled *Women and Education*, ed. Sandra Acker, Jacquetta Megarry, Stanley Nisbet, and Eric Hoyle (London: Kogan Page),

and Nel Noddings, *Caring: A Feminist Approach to Ethics and Moral Education* (Berkeley: University of California Press, 1983).

45. R. S. Peters, "Education as Initiation," in *Philosophical Analysis and Education*, ed. R. D. Archambault (London: Routledge & Kegan Paul, 1965), 107.

46. See note 29, above.

47. Paulo Friere, *Pedagogy of the Oppressed* (New York: Seabury Press, 1970).

48. R. W. K. Paterson, *Values, Education and the Adult* (London: Routledge & Kegan Paul, 1979), 268. I thank Stephen Jones for bringing this book to my attention.

49. Cf. Mortimer J. Adler, *Philosopher At Large, An Intellectual Autobiography* (New York: Macmillan, 1977).

50. Excerpt from an address by Rev. Theodore M. Hesburgh at the first joint meeting of the Association of Universities and Colleges of Canada and the American Council on Education, reported in *University Affairs* (December 1983), 20.

51. Jonathan Schell, *The Fate of the Earth* (New York: Avon Books, 1982), 226.

52. Bertrand Russell, 12 October 1961 preface to a pamphlet on *Schools for Non-Violence* drafted by Anthony Weaver for the Committee of 100.

53. R. S. Peters, "John Dewey's Philosophy of Education," in *John Dewey Reconsidered*, ed. R. S. Peters (London: Routledge & Kegan Paul, 1977).

54. Bertrand Russell, *Has Man A Future?* (London: Allen & Unwin, 1961; Penguin, 1961), 9.

55. A recent step in the right direction is S. I. Benn, "Deterrence or Appeasement? or, On Trying to be Rational about Nuclear War," *Journal of Applied Philosophy*, 1 (March 1984):5–19. Also of note are the special issue of the *Harvard Educational Review*, 54 (August 1984) on "Education and the Threat of Nuclear War" and the special issue of *Ethics*, 95 (April 1985) on "The Ethics of Nuclear Deterrence and Disarmament."

56. D. C. Phillips, "Philosophy of Education: *In Extremis?*" *Educational Studies*, 14 (Spring 1983):1–30.

Bibliography

JOHN DEWEY

COLLECTED PRIMARY SOURCES

The Early Works of John Dewey, 1882–1898. Edited by Jo Ann Boydston. Vol.
I: 1882– 88 (pub. 1969); Vol. 2: 1887 (pub. 1967); Vol. 3: 1889–92 (pub.
1969); Vol. 4 1893–94 (pub. 1971); Vol. 5: 1895–98 (pub. 1972). Carbondale: Southern Illinois University Press.

The Middle Works of John Dewey, 1899–1924. Edited by Jo Ann Boydston. Vol.
I: 1899–1901 (pub. 1975); Vol. 2: 1902–03 (pub. 1976); Vol. 3: 1903–06
(pub. 1977); Vol. 4: 1907–09 (pub. 1977); Vol. 5: 1908 (pub. 1978); Vol. 6:
1910–11 (pub. 1978); Vol. 7: 1912–14 (pub. 1979); Vol. 8: 1915 (pub.
1979); Vol. 9: 1916 (pub. 1980); Vol. 10: 1916–17 (pub. 1980); Vol. 11:
1918–19 (pub. 1982); Vol. 12: 1920 (pub. 1982); Vol. 13: 1921–22 (pub.
1983; Vol. 14: 1922 (pub. 1983); Vol. 15: 1923–24 (pub. 1983). Carbondale:
Southern Illinois University Press.

The Later Works of John Dewey, 1925–1953. Edited by Jo Ann Boydston. Vol.
I: 1925 (pub. 1981); Vol. 2: 1925–27 (pub. 1984); Vol. 3: 1927–28 (pub.
1984); Vol. 4: 1929 (pub. 1984); Vol. 5: 1929–30 (pub. 1984); Vol. 6:
1931–32 (pub. 1985); Vol. 7: 1932 (pub. 1985); Vol. 8–16 (forthcoming).
Carbondale: Southern Illinois University Press.

Other Primary Sources

Lectures in the Philosophy of Education: 1899. Edited by Reginald D. Archambault. New York: Random House, 1966.

Educational Essays. Edited by J. J. Findlay. London: Blackie & Son, 1910.

Interest and Effort in Education. Boston: Houghton Mifflin, 1913.

Schools of Tomorrow. With Evelyn Dewey. New York: E. P. Dutton, 1915.

"The Changing Intellectual Climate." (Review of *Science and the Modern
World*, by A. N. Whitehead). *The New Republic* (17 February 1926): 360–61.

"Art in Education—and Education in Art." *The New Republic* (24 February
1926); 11–13.

"The Key to the New World." (Review of *Education and the Good Life,* by Bertrand Russell), *The New Republic* (19 May 1926): 410–11.

The Sources of a Science of Education. New York: Liveright, 1929.

"From Absolutism to Experimentalism." *Contemporary American Philosophy: Personal Statements.* Vol. 2, edited by George P. Adams and W. P. Montague. New York: Macmillan Co., 1930.

"How Much Freedom in New Schools?" *The New Republic* (9 July 1930): 204–6.

Philosophy and Civilization. New York: Minton, Balch & Co., 1931.

"Appreciation and Cultivation." *Harvard Teachers Record* 1 (April 1931): 75–76.

"The Adventure of Persuasion." (Review of *Adventures of Ideas,* by A. N. Whitehead), *The New Republic* (19 April 1933): 285–86.

A Common Faith. New Haven: Yale University Press, 1934.

Art as Experience. New York: Minton, Balch & Co., 1934.

Experience and Education. New York: Macmillan, 1938.

Intelligence in the Modern World. Edited by Joseph Ratner. New York: Random House, Modern Library, 1939.

"Creative Democracy—The Task Before Us." In *The Philosopher of the Common Man: Essays in Honor of John Dewey to Celebrate his Eightieth Birthday,* edited by Sidney Ratner, 220–28. 1940. Reprint. Westport, Conn.: Greenwood Press, 1968.

Education Today. Edited by Joseph Ratner. 1940. Reprint. Westport, Conn.: Greenwood Press, 1969.

"Modern Philosophy." In *The Cleavage in Our Culture,* edited by Frederick Burkhardt, 15–29. Boston: Beacon Press, 1952.

Dewey on Education, Selections. Edited by Martin S. Dworkin. New York: Teachers College Press, 1959.

John Dewey and Arthur Bentley, A Philosophical Correspondence, 1932–1951. Edited by Sidney Ratner and Jules Altman. New Bruswick, N. J.: Rutgers University Press, 1964.

John Dewey on Education, Selected Writings. Edited by Reginald D. Archambault. New York: Random House, Modern Library, 1964.

Secondary Sources

Addams, Jane. *Twenty Years at Hull-House.* New York: Macmillan, 1910.

Ames, Van Meter, ed. *Beyond Theology, The Autobiography of Edward Scribner Ames.* Chicago: University of Chicago Press, 1959.

Andrews, Wayne. *Battle for Chicago.* New York: Harcourt, Brace, 1946.

Archambault, Reginald D., ed. *Dewey on Education, Appraisals.* New York: Random House, 1966.

Armytage, W. H. G. *The American Influence on English Education.* London: Routledge & Kegan Paul, London: 1967.

Axelson, John A. "1884–1894: A Decade of Ferment for Young Michigan Teacher John Dewey." *Michigan Education Journal* 1 (May 1966): 13–14.

Axtelle, George E., and Joe R. Burnett. "Dewey on Education and Schooling." In *Guide to the Works of John Dewey,* edited by Jo Ann Boydston, 257–305. Carbondale: Southern Illinois University Press, 1970.

Baker, Melvin Charles. "A Critical Examination of the Theory of Schooling Underlying John Dewey's Laboratory School, 1896–1904." D. Ed. diss., University of Illinois, 1951.

———. *Foundations of John Dewey's Educational Theory.* New York: Atherton Press, 1966.

Barnes, Albert C. "The Educational Philosophy of John Dewey." *The Humanist* 5 (January 1946): 160–62.

Bayles, Ernest E. *Pragmatism in Education.* New York: Harper & Row, 1966.

Beck, Robert Holmes. "American Progressive Education, 1875–1930." Ph.D. diss., Yale University, 1942.

Bernstein, Richard J. *John Dewey.* New York: Washington Square Press, 1967.

———. "Philosophy in the Conversation of Mankind." *Review of Metaphysics* 33 (June 1980): 745–75.

Borrowman, Merle. "The School and Society: Vermont in 1860, Chicago in 1890, Idaho in 1950, California in 1980." *Educational Studies* 11 (Winter 1981): 377–92.

Boyd, William, and Wyatt Rawson. *The Story of the New Education.* London: Heinemann, 1965.

Boydston, Jo Ann. "John Dewey and the Journals." *History of Education Quarterly* (Spring 1970).

———. *John Dewey's Personal and Professional Library, A Checklist.* Carbondale: Southern Illinois University Press, 1982.

Boydston, Jo Ann, and Kathleen Paulos, eds. *Checklist of Writings About John Dewey, 1877–1977.* 2d ed. Carbondale: Southern Illinois University Press, 1978.

Brickman, William M., and Stanley Lehrer, eds. *John Dewey: Master Educator.* New York: Atherton Press, 1959.

Brodsky, Gary. "Rorty's Interpretation of Pragmatism." *Transactions of the Charles S. Peirce Society* 18 (Fall 1982): 311–37.

Brumbaugh, Robert S., and Nathaniel M. Lawrence. *Philosophers on Education: Six Essays on the Foundations of Western Thought.* Boston: Houghton Mifflin, 1963.

———. *Philosophical Themes in Modern Education.* Boston: Houghton Mifflin, 1973.

Burston, William H. "The Influence of John Dewey in English Official Reports." *International Review of Education* 7 (1961): 311–23.

Cahn, Steven M., ed. *New Studies in the Philosophy of John Dewey.* Hanover, N. H.: University Press of New England, 1977.

Campbell, Jack K. *Colonel Francis W. Parker, The Children's Crusader.* New York: Teachers College Press, 1967.

Clayton, Stafford A., ed. "John Dewey in Perspective: Three Papers in Honor of John Dewey." Bloomington: Indiana University, Division of Research and Field Services, 1960.

Cohen, Marshall J. "Dewey in Process." *Perspectives in American History* 3 (1969): 497–508.

Coughlan, Neil. *Young John Dewey.* Chicago: University of Chicago Press, 1975.

Cremin, Lawrence A. *The Transformation of the School.* New York: Knopf, 1961.

Cremin, Lawrence A., David A. Shannon, and Mary Evelyn Townsend. *A History of Teachers College Columbia University.* New York: Columbia University Press, 1954.

Curti, Merle. *The Social Ideas of American Educators.* Patterson, N. J.: Pageant Books, 1959.

Cushman, Lillian S. "Elementary Art Teaching in the Laboratory School." *Elementary School Teacher* 3 (June 1903): 680–85.

———. "Elementary Art Teaching in the Laboratory School." *Elementary School Teacher* 4 (September 1903): 9–15.

De Pencier, Ida B. *The History of the Laboratory Schools, The University of Chicago, 1896–1965.* Chicago: Quadrangle Books, 1967.

Dykhuizen, George. "An Early Chapter in the Life of John Dewey." *Journal of the History of Ideas.* 13 (1952): 563–72.

———. "John Dewey and the University of Michigan." *Journal of the History of Ideas* 23 (1962): 513–44.

———. "John Dewey at Johns Hopkins (1882–1884)." *Journal of the History of Ideas* 22 (1961): 103–16.

———. "John Dewey in Chicago: Some Bibliographical Notes." *Journal of the History of Philosophy* 3 (April 1965): 217–33.

———. "John Dewey: The Chicago Years." *Journal of the History of Philosophy* 2 (October 1964): 227–53.

———. "John Dewey: The Vermont Years." *Journal of the History of Ideas* 20 (1959): 515–44.

———. *The Life and Mind of John Dewey.* Carbondale: Southern Illinois University Press, 1973.

Eastman, George. "John Dewey on Education: The Formative Years." D. Ed. diss., Harvard University, 1963.

Eastman, Max. "John Dewey: My Teacher and Friend." In his *Great Companions,* 249–98. New York: Farrar, Straus & Cudahy, 1959.

Eby, Frederick. "The Function of the Practice School in Connection with Chicago University." In *Proceedings of the Thirty-Seventh Annual Conven-*

tion of the Ontario Educational Association, 287–93. Toronto: Rowsell & Hutchinson, Printers, 1898.

Edman, Irwin. "Columbia Galaxy: John Dewey and Others." In *Great Teachers,* edited by Houston Peterson, 185–201. New Brunswick, N.J.: Rutgers University Press, 1946.

———. *Philosopher's Holiday.* New York: Viking Press, 1938.

Emerson, Goldwin J., and Maryann Ayim. "Dewey and Peirce on Curriculum and the Three R's." *The Journal of Educational Thought* 14 (April 1980): 23–37.

Farrell, John C. "John Dewey and World War I: Armageddon Tests a Liberal's Faith." *Perspectives in American History* 9 (1975): 299–340.

Feuer, Lewis S. "John Dewey and the Back to the People Movement in American Thought." *Journal of the History of Ideas* 20 (1959): 545–68.

———. "John Dewey's Reading at College." *Journal of the History of Ideas* 19 (1958): 415–21.

Fraley, Angela. *Schooling and Innovation.* New York: Tyler Gibson Publishers, 1981.

Frankena, William K. *Philosophy of Education.* New York: Macmillan, 1965.

———. *Three Historical Philosophies of Education.* Glenview, Ill.: Scott, Foresman, 1965.

Ginger, Ray. *Altgeld's America.* Chicago: Quadrangle Paperbacks, 1965.

Gordon, Peter, and John White. *Philosophers as Educational Reformers.* London: Routledge & Kegan Paul, 1979.

Greene, Maxine. "Dewey and American Education, 1894–1920." In *John Dewey: Master Educator,* edited by W. W. Brickman and Stanley Lehrer, 32–49. New York: Atherton Press, 1959.

Hall, Stanley G. *Life and Confessions of a Psychologist.* New York: D. Appleton, 1924.

———. "Review of John Dewey's *Psychology.*" *American Journal of Psychology* 1 (November 1887): 146–59.

Handlin, Oscar. *John Dewey's Challenge to Education.* New York: Harper & Brothers, 1959.

Hardie, C. D. *Truth and Fallacy in Educational Theory.* Cambridge, England: Cambridge University Press, 1942; re-issued, New York: Teachers College Press, 1962.

Harding, Mrs. Charles F. "Annual Report of the Home Committee of the Parents Association of the School of Education of the University of Chicago." *Elementary School Teacher* 5 (October 1904): 65–71.

Harper, William R. "Ideals of Educational Work." *National Education Association of the United States Addresses and Proceedings,* 987–98, 1895.

Hawkins, David. "Liberal Education: A Modest Polemic." In *Content and Context,* edited by Carl Kaysen. New York: McGraw-Hill, 1973.

Hendel, Charles W., ed. *John Dewey and the Experimental Spirit in Philosophy.* New York: Liberal Arts Press, 1959.

Hines, Vynce A. "Progressivism in Practice." In *A New Look at Progressive Education* (1972 Yearbook of the Association for the Study of Curriculum Development), 118–64. Washington, D.C.: 1972.

Hinsdale, A. B., "Educational Progress During the Year 1899–1900." In *Journal of the Proceedings and Addresses of the Thirty-Ninth Annual Meeting of the National Educational Association,* 312–32. Chicago: University of Chicago Press, 1900.

Hinsdale, A. B., and A. S. Whitney. "Review of John Dewey's *The School and Society.*" *The Dial* (16 August 1900): 98–99.

Hofstadter, Richard. *Anti-intellectualism in American Life.* New York: Knopf, 1970.

Hook, Sidney. *John Dewey, An Intellectual Portrait.* New York: John Day Co., 1939.

———. "Portrait: John Dewey." *The American Scholar,* 17 (Winter 1947–48): 105–10.

———. *Pragmatism and the Tragic Sense of Life.* New York: Basic Books, 1974.

Jackman, Wilbur Samuel. "A Brief History of the School of Education." *University Report* (Chicago) 9 (May 1904): 2–7.

Kilpatrick, William H. "Philosophy of Education from the Experimentalist Outlook." Chapter 2 in *The National Society for the Study of Education.* Forty-first Yearbook, Part I: "Philosophies of Education," edited by Nelson B. Henry, 39–86. Chicago: University of Chicago Press, 1942.

Kliebard, Herbert M. "Dewey and the Herbartians: The Genesis of a Theory of Curriculum." *Journal of Curriculum Theorizing* 3 (Winter 1981): 154–61.

Lamont, Corliss, ed. *Dialogue on John Dewey.* New York: Horizon Press, 1959.

Lucas, Christopher J. *Foundations of Education,* Englewood Cliffs, N. J.: Prentice-Hall, 1984.

McCaul, Robert L. "Dewey and the University of Chicago, Part 1: July, 1894–March, 1902." *School and Society* (25 March 1961): 152–57.

———. "Dewey and the University of Chicago, Part 2: April, 1902–May, 1903." *School and Society,* (8 April 1961): 179–83.

———. "Dewey and the University of Chicago, Part 3: September, 1903–June, 1904." *School and Society* (22 April 1961): 202–6.

———. "Dewey's Chicago." *The School Review* (Summer 1959): 258–80.

MacClintock, Porter Lander. *Literature in the Elementary School.* Chicago: University of Chicago Press, 1907.

MacMillan, D. P. "The Elementary School of the University of Chicago." *The Educational Review,* (April 1899): 247–49.

Malone, Dumas, ed. "William Rainey Harper." *Dictionary of American Biography* 8: 281–92. New York: Charles Scribner's Sons, 1943.

Marcell, David W. *Progress and Pragmatism, James, Dewey, Beard and the American Idea of Progress*. Westport, Conn.: Greenwood Press, 1974.

Mayhew, Katherine Camp, and Anna Camp Edwards. *The Dewey School*. 1936. Reprint. New York: Atherton Press, 1966.

Nathanson, Jerome. *John Dewey: The Reconstruction of the Democratic Life*. New York: Charles Scribner's Sons, 1951.

Naumburg, Margaret. *The Child and the World*. New York: Harcourt, Brace, 1928.

O'Connor, D. J. *An Introduction to the Philosophy of Education*. London: Routledge & Kegan Paul, 1957.

O'Connor, Nellie Johnson. "The Educational Side of the Parents' Association of the Laboratory School." *Elementary School Teacher*, 4: 532–35.

Parker, DeWitt H., and Charles B. Vibbert. "The Department of Philosophy." In *The University of Michigan, An Encyclopedic Survey*. Vol. 2, edited by Wilfred B. Shaw, 668–79. Ann Arbor: University of Michigan Press, 1951.

Parker, Francis W. *Talks on Pedagogics,* New York: E. L. Kellogg and Co., 1894.

_____. *Talks on Teaching,* New York: A. S. Barnes, 1883.

Perkinson, Henry J. *Two Hundred Years of American Educational Thought*. New York: McKay, 1976.

Peters, R. S., ed. *John Dewey Reconsidered*. London: Routledge and Kegan Paul, 1977.

Phillips, J. O. C. "Dewey in Mid-Passage." *History of Education Quarterly* 20 (Spring 1980): 117–23.

Pierce, Bessie Louise. *A History of Chicago*. Vol. 3, 1871–93. Chicago: University of Chicago Press, 1957.

Pring, Richard. *Knowledge and Schooling*. London: Open Books, 1976.

Randall, John Herman, Jr. "The Department of Philosophy." *A History of the Faculty of Philosophy, Columbia University*. New York: Columbia University Press, 1957.

Resek, Carl, ed. *War and the Intellectuals*. New York: Harper & Row, 1964.

Rice, J. M. "The Public Schools of Chicago and St. Paul." *The Forum* 15(1893): 200–215.

_____. *The Public School System of the United States*. New York: The Century Co., 1893.

Rorty, Richard. *Consequences of Pragmatism*. Minneapolis: University of Minnesota Press, 1982.

_____. *Philosophy and the Mirror of Nature*. Princeton: Princeton University Press, 1979.

_____. "Pragmatism, Relativism and Irrationalism." In *Proceedings and Addresses of the American Philosophical Association* (August 1980): 719–38.

_____. "Pragmatism Without Method." In *Sidney Hook, Philosopher of*

Democracy and Humanism, edited by Paul Kurtz, 259–73. Buffalo: Prometheus Press, 1983.

Ross, Dorothy. *G. Stanley Hall, The Psychologist as Prophet.* Chicago; University of Chicago Press, 1972.

Rucker, Darnell. *The Chicago Pragmatists.* Minneapolis: University of Minnesota Press, 1969.

Rugg, Harold. *Foundations for American Education.* New York: World Book, 1947

Runyon, Laura L. "A Day With The New Education." *Chautauquan* 30 (March 1900): 589–92.

Sait, Una Bernard. "Studying Under John Dewey." *Claremont Quarterly* 11 (Winter 1964): 15–22.

Savage, Willinda. "John Dewey and 'Thought News' at the University of Michigan." In *Studies in the History of Higher Education in Michigan,* edited by Claude Eggersten. 12–17. Ann Arbor: Ann Arbor Publishers, 1950.

Schack, William. *Art and Argyrol: The Life and Career of Dr. Albert C. Barnes.* New York: Thomas Yoseloff, 1960.

Scheffler, Israel. "Educational Liberalism and Dewey's Philosophy." *Harvard Educational Review* 26 (1956): 190–98.

_____. *Four Pragmatists.* New York: Humanities Press, 1974.

Schilpp, Paul Arthur, ed. *The Philosophy of John Dewey.* 2d ed. New York: Tudor Press, 1951.

Schneider, Herbert. "Recollections of John Dewey." *Claremont Quarterly* 11 (Winter 1964): 23–35.

Selleck, R. J. W. *English Primary Education and the Progressives, 1914–1939.* London: Routledge and Kegan Paul, 1972.

Shapiro, Michael Steven. *Child's Garden: The Kindergarten Movement from Froebel to Dewey.* University Park: Pennsylvania State University Press, 1983.

Skilbeck, Malcolm, ed. *Dewey.* London: Collier-Macmillan Ltd., 1970.

Smith, Joan K. *Ella Flagg Young, Portrait of a Leader.* Ames: Iowa State University Press, 1979.

Smith, John E. *The Spirit of American Philosophy.* New York: Oxford University Press, 1963.

Storr. Richard J. *Harper's University: The Beginnings.* Chicago: University of Chicago Press, 1966.

Tenenbaum, Samuel. *William Heard Kilpatrick, Trail Blazer in Education.* New York: Harper & Brothers, 1951.

Thayer, V. T. "John Dewey and Experimentalism in Education." In *Formative Ideas in American Education,* 243–74. New York: Dodd, Mead, 1968.

Williams, Robert Bruce. "John Dewey and Oil City." *Peabody Journal of Education* (January 1969): 222–26.

_____. *John Dewey, Recollections.* Washington, D.C.: University Press of America, 1982.

Wirth, Arthur G. "The Deweyan Tradition Revisited: Any Relevance for Our Time?" *Teachers College Record* 69 (December 1967): 263–69.

_____. *John Dewey as Educator.* New York: John Wiley & Sons, 1966.

_____. "John Dewey's Design for American Education: An Analysis of Aspects of his Work at the University of Chicago, 1894–1904." *History of Education Quarterly* 4 (June 1964): 83–105.

_____. "John Dewey in Transition from Religious Idealism to the Social Ethic of Democracy." *History of Education Quarterly* 5 (December 1965): 264–68.

_____. "The Psychological Theory for Experimentation in Education at John Dewey's Laboratory School, the University of Chicago, 1896–1904." *Educational Theory* 16 (July 1966): 271–80.

Young, Ella Flagg. "Democracy and Education." *Journal of Education* 84 (6 July 1916): 5–6.

BERTRAND RUSSELL

PRIMARY SOURCES

Cambridge Essays, 1888–1899. Edited by Kenneth Blackwell, Andrew Brink, Nicholas Griffin, Richard A. Rempel, John G. Slater. *The Collected Papers of Bertrand Russell.* Vol. 1. London: George Allen & Unwin, 1983.

The Problems of Philosophy. London: Williams and Norgate, 1912.

Principles of Social Reconstruction. London: George Allen & Unwin, 1916; 2d ed., 1960.

Mysticism and Logic. London: Longmans, Green, 1918.

The Prospects of Industrial Civilization. In collaboration with Dora Russell. London: George Allen & Unwin, 1923; 2d ed., 1959.

"Freedom or Authority in Education." *The Century Magazine* 109 (December 1924): 172–80.

"Socialism and Education." *Harpers Magazine* 151 (September 1925): 413–17.

On Education. London: George Allen & Unwin, 1926: reprint, 1976.

"Relativity and Religion." (Review of Whitehead's *Science and the Modern World*). *The Nation and Athenaeum* 39 (29 May 1926): 206–7.

Selected Papers of Bertrand Russell. New York: Modern Library, 1927.

"The New Life that Is America's." *The New York Times Magazine* (22 May 1927).

"A Bold Experiment in Child Education." *The New York Times Magazine* (2 October 1927): 8–9, 22.

"Education without Sex Taboos." *New Republic* (16 November 1927): 346–48.

"Education in a Scientific Society." In his *The Scientific Outlook,* 243–50. New York: W. W. Norton, 1931.

"Free Speech in Childhood." *The New Statesman and Nation* 1 (30 May 1931): 486–88.

"Modern Tendencies in Education." *The Spectator* (13 June 1931): 926–27.

"In Our School." *The New Republic* (9 September 1931): 92–94.

Education and the Social Order. 1932. Reprint. London: Unwin Books, 1967.

In Praise of Idleness. London: George Allen & Unwin, 1935.

Sceptical Essays. London: George Allen & Unwin, 1935.

An Inquiry into Meaning and Truth. William James Lectures, Harvard, 1940. London: Pelican Books, 1965.

"Proposals for an International University." *The Fortnightly* 158 (July 1942): 8–16.

"Education after the War." *American Mercury* 57 (August 1943): 194–203.

A History of Western Philosophy. London: George Allen & Unwin, 1946.

Unpopular Essays. London: George Allen & Unwin, 1950.

"The Science to Save Us From Science." *The New York Times Magazine* (19 March 1950): 9, 31–33.

"Can We Afford to Keep Open Minds?" *The New York Times Magazine* (11 June 1950): 9, 37–39.

"If We Are to Survive This Dark Time." *The New York Times Magazine* (3 September 1950): 5, 17–18.

"The Kind of Fear We Sorely Need." *The New York Times Magazine* (29 October 1950): 9, 50–53.

"To Replace Our Fears With Hope." *The New York Times Magazine* (31 December 1950): 5, 23, 25.

"To Face Danger Without Hysteria." *The New York Times Magazine* (21 January 1951): 7, 42, 44.

"As School Opens—The Educators Examined." *The New York Times Magazine* (7 September 1952): 9, 44–45.

Portraits from Memory. London: George Allen & Unwin, 1956.

Why I am Not a Christian. London: George Allen & Unwin, 1957.

The Basic Writings of Bertrand Russell. Edited by Robert E. Egner and Lester E. Denonn. London: George Allen & Unwin, 1961.

"Education for a Difficult World." *Fact and Fiction,* 144–56. London: George Allen & Unwin, 1961.

Has Man a Future? London: George Allen & Uwin, 1961.

"Schools for Non-Violence." Drafted by Anthony Weaver; preface by Bertrand Russell. (12 October 1961).

The Autobiography of Bertrand Russell, 1914–1944. Vol. 2. Boston: Little, Brown, 1968.

Secondary Sources

Ayer, A. J. *Part of My Life*. London: Collins, 1977.

Barnes, Albert C. *The Case of Bertrand Russell vs. Democracy and Education*. Merion, Penn.: Albert C. Barnes, n.d.

Bloom, Clare. *Limelight and After, The Education of an Actress*. New York: Harper & Row, 1982.

Bode, Boyd H. "Russell's Educational Philosophy." In *The Philosophy of Bertrand Russell*, edited by Paul Arthur Schilpp. New York: Tudor Publishing Co., 1951.

Bonham-Carter, Victor. *Dartington Hall, The History of an Experiment*. London: Phoenix House, 1958.

Chomsky, Noam. "Toward a Humanistic Conception of Education." In *Work, Technology and Education*, edited by Walter Feinberg and Henry Rosemont, Jr. Urbana: University of Illinois Press, 1975.

Clark, Ronald W. *The Life of Bertrand Russell*. London: Penguin Books, 1978.

Crawshay-Williams, Rupert. *Russell Remembered*. London: Oxford University Press, 1970.

Croall, Jonathan. *Neill of Sommerhill, The Permanent Rebel*. London: Routledge & Kegan Paul, 1983.

Curry, W. B. *Education for Sanity*. London: Heinemann, 1947.

_____. *The School and a Changing Civilization*. London: John Lane, 1934.

Dearden, R. F. *Problems in Primary Education*. London: Routledge & Kegan Paul, 1976.

Dewey, John, and Horace M. Kallen, eds. *The Bertrand Russell Case.*. New York: Viking Press, 1941.

Dickson, Lovat. *H. G. Wells: His Turbulent Life and Times*. Toronto: Macmillan, 1969.

Drawbell, James Wedgwood. *A Gallery of Women*. London: Collins, 1933.

Durant, Will. *Adventures in Genius*. New York: Simon & Schuster, 1931.

Eames, Elizabeth Ramsden. "A Discussion of the Issues in the Theory of Knowledge Involved in the Controversy between John Dewey and Bertrand Russell." Ph.D. diss., Bryn Mawr College, 1951.

Feinberg, Barry, and Ronald Kasrils. *Bertrand Russell's America*. Vol. 1, 1896–1945. London: George Allen & Unwin, 1973.

Feinberg, Walter. *Understanding Education, Toward a Reconstruction of Educational Inquiry*. London: Cambridge University Press, 1983.

Gathorne-Hardy, Jonathan. *The Old School Tie*. New York: Viking Press, 1977.

Gotesky, Rubin. "Three Books and Three Perspectives." *Educational Theory* 15 (October 1965): 341–48.

Green, Joe L. "Dewey, Russell, and the Integration of the Social." *Educational Theory* 29 (Fall 1979): 285–96.

Harley, David. "Beacon Hill and the Constructive Uses of Freedom." Ph.D. diss., University of Toronto, 1980.

―――. "Beacon Hill School." *Russell* 35–36 (Autumn–Winter 1979–1980): 5–16.

Hemmings, Roy. *Children's Freedom, A. S. Neill and the Evolution of the Summerhill Idea.* New York: Schocken Books, 1973.

Isaacs, Susan. *Intellectual Growth in Children.* New York: Schocken Books, Young 1930; reprint 1966.

―――. *Social Development in Young Children.* New York: Schocken Books, 1933; reprint 1972.

Jager, Ronald. *The Development of Bertrand Russell's Philosophy.* London: George Allen & Unwin, 1972.

Joad, G. E. M. *About Education.* London: Faber and Faber, 1945.

―――. "The Virtues of Examination." *The New Stateman and Nation* (11 March 1944): 176–77.

Leggett, H. W. *Bertrand Russell, O.M.* New York: Philosophical Library, 1950.

McKenney, John. L. "Dewey and Russell: Fraternal Twins in Philosophy." *Educational Theory* 9 (January 1959): 24–30.

McMillan, Margaret. *The Nursery School.* London: J. M. Dent & Sons, 1919.

Marsh, Robert. "Bertrand Russell's Philosophy of Education." D. Ed. diss., Harvard University, 1951.

Meyer, Adolph E. *Modern European Educators.* Freeport, N. Y.: Books for Libraries Press, 1934; reprint 1971.

Neill, A. S. *"Neill! Neill! Orange Peel!".* New York: Hart Publishing Co., 1972.

―――. *Summerhill.* New York: Hart Publishing Co., 1960.

O'Hear, Anthony. *Education, Society, and Human Nature.* London: Routledge & Kegan Paul, 1981.

Park, Joe. *Bertrand Russell on Education.* London: George Allen & Unwin Ltd., 1964.

Peters. R. S. *Authority, Responsibility and Education.* New York: Atherton, 1967.

Philpot, Terry. "The Russells and Beacon Hill." *The Humanist* 84 (June 1969): 173–75.

Ready, William. *Necessary Russell.* Toronto: Copp Clark, 1969.

Roy, Dilip Kamur. *Among the Great.* Bombay: Nalanda Publications, 1945.

Russell, Dora. "Art and Education." In *The Practice and Theory of Bolshevism,* by Bertrand Russell, 45–71. London: George Allen & Unwin, 1920.

―――. "Beacon Hill." In *The Modern Schools Handbook,* edited by Trevor Blewit, 29–42. London: Victor Gollancz, 1934.

―――. *Children: Why Do We Have Them?* New York: Harper & Brothers, 1933.

―――. *In Defense of Children.* London: Hamish Hamilton, 1932.

_____. *The Dora Russell Reader.* London: Routledge & Kegan Paul, 1983.

_____. *Hypatia, Or Woman and Knowledge.* London: Kegan Paul, Trench, Trubner & Co., 1925.

_____. *The Prospects of Industrial Civilization.* In collaboration with Bertrand Russell. 1923. 2d. ed. London: Allen & Unwin, 1959.

_____. *The Religion of the Machine Age.* London: Routledge & Kegan Paul, 1983.

_____. *The Right to be Happy.* New York: Harper & Brothers, 1927.

_____. "Shaw—A Personal Impression." *Civil Liberty* 10 (Winter 1950).

_____. *The Tamarisk Tree, My Quest For Liberty and Love.* London: Elek/Pemberton, 1975.

_____. *The Tamarisk Tree 2.* London: Virago, 1980.

_____. *Thinking in Front of Yourself and Other Plays.* London: Janus Press, 1934.

_____. "What Beacon Hill School Stood For." *Anarchy* 7 (January 1967): 11–16.

Schilpp, Paul Arthur. "Some Recollections of Bertrand Russell, 1872–1970." *Journal of Thought* 6 (April 1971): 68–79.

_____, ed., *The Philosophy of Bertrand Russell.* New York: Tudor Publishing Co., 1951.

Shouse, J. B. "Contemporary Realism and Education." *Peabody Journal of Education* 13 (November 1935): 107–20.

Siskin, Sidney Sheffield. "The Skeptical Educator: Bertrand Russell's Educational Views in light of his Intellectual Development." Ph.D. Diss., Cornell University, 1974.

Skidelsky, Robert. *English Progressive Schools.* London: Penguin Books, 1969.

Stander, Philip. "Bertrand Russell on the Aims of Education." *Educational Forum* 38 (May 1974): 447–56.

Stevinson, E. "Margaret McMillan—Prophet and Pioneer." *Journal of Education* 79 (September 1947): 488–90.

Stewart, W. A. C. *The Educational Innovators. Vol. 2, Progressive Schools, 1881–1967.* London: Macmillan, 1968.

Tait, Katherine. *My Father Bertrand Russell.* New York: Harcourt Brace Jovanovich, 1975.

Taylor, Albert J. "Dewey and Russell as Educational Theorists: A Comparative Analysis." D.Ed. diss., Rutgers University, 1964.

Thomas, J. E., and Kenneth Blackwell, eds. *Russell in Review.* Toronto: Samuel Stevens, Hakkert & Co., 1976.

Van der Eyken, Willem, and Barry Turner. *Adventures in Education.* London: Allan Lane, 1969.

Wood, Alan. *Bertrand Russell The Passionate Sceptic.* London: George Allen & Unwin, 1957.

Woodhouse, Howard. "On a Suggested Contradiction in Russell's Educational Philosophy." *Russell* 15 (Autumn 1974): 3–14.

———. "The Concept of Growth in Bertrand Russell's Educational Thought." *Journal of Educational Thought.* 17 (April 1983): 12–21.

Young, Michael. *The Elmhirsts of Dartington.* London: Routledge & Kegan Paul, 1982.

ALFRED NORTH WHITEHEAD

PRIMARY SOURCES

An Introduction to Mathematics. London: Home University Library of Modern Knowledge, 1911. Rev. ed., New York: Oxford University Press, 1958.

The Organization of Thought, Educational and Scientific. London: Williams & Northgate, 1917. Reprint, Westport, Conn.: Greenwood Press, 1974.

Report of the 87th Meeting of the British Association for the Advancement of Science, 361. London: John Murray, 1920.

Science and the Modern World. New York: Macmillan, 1925.

Religion in the Making. New York: Macmillan, 1926.

The Aims of Education and Other Essays. New York: Macmillan, 1929. Reprint, Free Press, 1967.

The Function of Reason. Princeton: Princeton University Press, 1929.

Adventures of Ideas. New York: Macmillan, 1933.

Modes of Thought. New York: Macmillan, 1938.

Essays in Science and Philosophy. London: Rider & Co., 1948.

Whitehead's American Essays in Social Philosophy. Edited by A. H. Johnson. New York: Harper, 1959.

A Philosopher Looks at Science. New York: Philosophical Library, 1965.

Secondary Sources

Adler, Mortimer. *The Paideia Proposal.* New York: Macmillan, 1982.

Ashby, Eric, and Mary Anderson. *Portrait of Haldane at Work on Education.* London: Macmillan, 1974.

Bellot, H. Hale, *University College London, 1826–1926.* London: 1929.

Belth, Marc. "Education in the Universe of Whitehead." *Teachers College Record* 58 (1975): 323–28.

Bennett, John B. "Whitehead and the Framework for Liberal Eduation." *Teachers College Record* 82 (Winter 1980): 329–41.

Brennan, Joseph Gerard. "Alfred North Whitehead: Plato's Lost Dialogue." In *Masters: Portraits of Great Teachers,* edited by Joseph Epstein. New York: Basic Books, 1981.

———. *The Education of a Prejudiced Man.* New York: Charles Scribner's Sons, 1977.

Broad, C. D. "Alfred North Whitehead (1861–1947)." *Mind* 57(April 1948): 139–45.

Brock, Dorothy, "The Classics as the Foundation of the Humanities." *The Educational Times* (July 1922): 301.

Brumbaugh, Robert S. *Whitehead, Process Philosophy and Education.* Albany: State University of New York Press, 1982.

_____. "Whitehead's Educational Theory: Two Supplementary Notes to the Aims of Education." *Educational Theory* 16 (July 1966): 215.

Burnett, Joe. "The Educational Philosophy of Alfred North Whitehead." Ph.D. diss., New York University, 1958.

Curtis, S. J. *History of Education in Great Britain.* London: University Tutorial Press, 1948, Second Edition, revised and enlarged, 1950.

Dewey, John. "Whitehead's Philosophy." *Philosophical Review* 46 (March 1937): 170–77. Reprinted in John Dewey, *Problems of Men.* New York: Philosophical Library, 1946.

Donham, Wallace Brett. *Business Adrift.* New York: McGraw-Hill, 1931.

_____. *Education for Responsible Living.* Cambridge, Mass.: Harvard University Press, 1944.

Drennen, D. A. "Whitehead and the Idea of Education." *Proceedings of the American Catholic Philosophical Association* 41 (1967) 100–109.

Dunkel, Harold B. "Free Romance!" *Elementary School Journal* 68 (1967): 53–60.

_____. *Whitehead on Education.* Columbus: Ohio State University Press, 1965.

Egan, Kieran. *Educational Development.* New York: Oxford University Press, 1979.

Emmet, Dorothy. "Alfred North Whitehead 1861–1947." In *Proceedings of the British Academy,* 292–306. London: Oxford University Press, 1947.

_____. "Alfred North Whitehead: The Last Phase." *Mind* 57 (July 1948): 265–74.

Fisher, H. A. L. "Professor Whitehead and Education." (Review of *Aims of Education*), *The Nation and Athenaeum,* (22 June 1929): 401.

Gauss, Christian. "Vitalism in Education." (Review of *Aims of Education*), *The New Republic* 59 (1929): 157–58.

Haldane, Richard Burdon. *An Autobiography.* New York: Doubleday, Doran and Co., 1929.

Hendley, Brian. "A New Phase in Educational Theory." *Review of Education* 4 (Spring 1978): 91–94.

_____. "A Whiteheadian Model for Teaching Introductory Philosophy." *Metaphilosophy* 7 (July/October, 1976): 307–15.

_____. "Educational Fantasies and Philosophy." *Review of Education* 7 (Spring 1981): 167–73.

————. "Five Mistaken Approaches to Education." *McGill Journal of Education* 9 (Spring 1974): 25–33.

————. "Martin Buber on the Teacher/Student Relationship: A Critical Appraisal." *Journal of Philosophy of Education* 12 (1978): 141–48.

————. "Teaching and Personal Relationships: A Response to Joseph Abinun." *Educational Theory* 29 (Winter 1979): 73–75.

————. "Wasted Resources: What Educational Philosophers Might Contribute to Educational Theory But Often Don't." *Journal of Educational Thought* 16 (April 1982): 15–22.

————. "Whitehead, Process Philosophy and Education." (Review of *Whitehead, Process Philosophy and Education*, by Robert S. Brumbaugh), *Teaching Philsophy* 6 (April 1983): 162–64.

Hocking, William Ernest. "Whitehead as I Knew Him." *Journal of Philosophy* 58 (14 September 1961): 505–16.

————. "The Educational Views of Alfred North Whitehead." *Harvard University Graduate School of Education, Occasional Pamphlets* (April 1943): 1–21.

Holmes, Henry W. "Whitehead's Views on Education." In *The Philosophy of Alfred North Whitehead*, edited by P. A. Schilpp, 621–40. New York: Tudor Publishing, 1941; 2d. ed., 1951.

Hook, Sidney. "Whitehead's Final Views." *Nation* (1942): 401–3.

Hutchins, Robert M. "A Reply to Professor Whitehead." *Atlantic Monthly* 158 (November 1936): 582–88.

Joad, C. E. M. "Whitehead." *New Statesman and Nation* 35 (1948): 26.

Johnson, A. H. "Alfred North Whitehead." *The University of Toronto Quarterly* 15 (1946): 373–83.

————. *The Wit and Wisdom of Alfred North Whitehead*. Boston: Beacon Press, 1947.

————. *Whitehead and His Philosophy*. Lanham, Md.: University Press of America, 1983.

————. "Whitehead as Teacher and Philosopher." *Philosophy and Phenomenological Research* 29 (March 1969): 351–76.

————. "Whitehead's Discussion of Education." *Education* (June 1946): 1–19.

Jourdain, Philip E. B. "Review of *The Organization of Thought, Educational and Scientific*." *Mind* 27 (1918): 244–47.

Kenyon, Frederic C., ed. *Education, Scientific and Humane, A Report of the Proceedings of the Council for Humanistic Studies*. London: John Murray, 1917.

Langeveld, M. J. "Some Consideration on Whitehead's 'Aims of Education'." *Algeheen Nederlands Tijdschrift voor Wijsbegeerte en Psychologie* 58 (1966): 95–105.

Lawrence, Nathaniel. *Alfred North Whitehead: A Primer of His Philosophy*. New York: Twayne Publishers, 1974.

_____. "Nature and the Educable Self in Whitehead." *Educational Theory* 15 (July 1965): 205–16.

_____. "Whitehead's Educational Philosophy and Mechanized Teaching." *Philosophy of Education, 1967: Proceedings of the 23rd Annual Meeting of the Philosophy of Education Society,* 199–215. Carbondale: Southern Illinois University Press, 1967.

Levi, Albert William. "The Problem of Higher Education: Whitehead or Hutchins?" *Harvard Educational Review* 7 (1937): 451–65.

Levy, Paul. *G. E. Moore and the Cambridge Apostles.* London: Weidenfeld and Nicolson, 1979.

Littlewood, J. E. *A Mathematician's Miscellany.* London: Methuen, 1953.

Lowe, Victor. "Alfred North Whitehead." In *Classic American Philosophers,* edited by Max H. Fisch, 395–417. New York: Appleton-Century-Crofts, 1951.

_____. "Alfred North Whitehead." *Collier's Encyclopedia* 23 (1969): 467–69.

_____. "Alfred North Whitehead." *Encyclopedia Britannica* 19 (1974): 816–18.

_____. *Alfred North Whitehead: The Man and His Work.* Vol. 1, 1861–1910. Baltimore: Johns Hopkins Press, 1985.

_____. "A. N. W.: A Bibliographical Perspective." *Process Studies* 12 (Fall 1982): 137–47.

_____. "A. N. Whitehead on his Mathematical Goals: a Letter of 1912." *Annals of Science* 32 (1975): 85–101.

_____. *Understanding Whitehead.* Baltimore: Johns Hopkins Press, 1962.

_____. "Whitehead, Alfred North." *Encyclopedia of Education.* 9: 549–57. New York: Macmillan, 1969.

Mayo, Elton. *Social Problems of an Industrial Civilization.* London: Routledge & Kegan Paul, 1949.

Meland, Bernard. *Higher Education and the Human Spirit.* Chicago: University of Chicago Press, 1953.

Moore, G. E. "Professor Whitehead on Religion." (Review of *Religion in the Making), The Nation and Athenaeum,* (12 February 1927): 664.

Nagel, E. "Alfred North Whitehead." *Nation* 166 (1948): 187–88.

Nunn, Percy. *Education: Its Data and First Principles.* Rev. ed. London: Edward Arnold, 1933.

_____. "On the Concept of Epistemological Levels." *Proceedings of the Aristotelian Society.* London, n.s. 8 (1907–8): 139–59.

Page, F. A. "A. N. Whitehead: A Pupil's Tribute." *Dalhousie Review* 28 (1948): 71–80.

Peters, R. S. *Education and the Education of Teachers.* London: Routledge & Kegan Paul, 1977.

_____. "Education as Initiation." In *Philosophical Analysis and Education,* edited by R. D. Archambault. London: Routledge & Kegan Paul, 1965.

————. *Psychology and Ethical Development.* London: George Allen & Unwin. 1974.

Price, Lucien. *Dialogues of Alfred North Whitehead.* New York: Mentor Books, 1956.

Reconstruction Problems: The Classics in British Education. London: Ministry of Reconstruction, 1919.

Report of the Board of Education for the Year 1921–22. London: His Majesty's Stationery Office, 1923.

Report of the Committee Appointed by Prime Minister to Inquire into the Position of Classics in the Educational System of the United Kingdom. London: His Majesty's Stationery Office, 1921.

Report of the 11th Annual Conference of Educational Associations. Joint Conference held on December 30, 1922. London: 1923.

Rhinelander, Philip H. "Alfred North Whitehead." *American Scholar* 48 (Autumn 1979): 573–76.

Russell, Bertrand. "Alfred North Whitehead." In *Portraits from Memory.* London: Allen & Unwin, 1956.

————. "Science Relativity and Religion." (Review of *Science and the Modern World), Nation and Athenaeum* (29 May 1926): 206–7.

————. "Whitehead and Principia Mathematica." *Mind* 57 (April 1948): 137–38.

Schilpp, P. A., ed. *The Philosophy of Alfred North Whitehead.* 2d ed. New York: Tudor Publishing Co., 1951.

Shouse, J. B. "Some Modern Philosophers on Education." *The Educational Forum* 16 (1951): 55–63.

Skinner, B. F. *The Shaping of a Behaviorist,* New York: Knopf, 1979.

Stone, Ronald H. "The Essence of Education: Alfred North Whitehead." *Union Seminary Quarterly Review* 19 (November 1963): 35–47.

Tibble, J. W. "Sir Percy Nunn: 1870–1944. *British Journal of Educational Studies* 10 (1961): 58–75.

Wagner, Hilmar. "A Comparison of Bertrand Russell and Alfred North Whitehead on Education." *Journal of Thought* 2 (July 1967): 65–74.

Ward, Leo R. "Whitehead on Joy in Learning." *The Review of Politics* 32 (1970): 490–502.

Weiss, Paul. "Alfred North Whitehead, 1861–1947." *Atlantic Monthly* 18 (1948): 105–7.

————. *Philosophy in Process.* Vol. 7. Carbondale: Southern Illinois University Press, 1978.

White, John. *The Aims of Education Restated.* London: Routledge & Kegan Paul, 1982.

Wilson, Edmund. "A. N. Whitehead and Bertrand Russell." *The New Republic* 45 (1925): 161–62.

Index

Brian Hendley was born in Milwaukee, Wisconsin, where he received his B.A. from Marquette University. Following a year as a Fulbright Fellow in Germany, he attended Yale University and received the M.A. and Ph.D. in philosophy. He began teaching philosophy at the University of Waterloo in Canada in 1966 and he has been there ever since. In 1975 Hendley spent a year as a Visiting Scholar in England at the University of London Institute of Education. In May of 1985 he became Chairman of the Department of Philosophy at the University of Waterloo.